Schools Council
Research Studies

The Aims of Primary Education: a Study of Teachers' Opinions

Patricia Ashton
Pat Kneen
Frances Davies
B. J. Holley

M

Macmillan Education

First published 1975

SBN 333 17246 9 Boards
SBN 333 17207 8 Limp

Published by
MACMILLAN EDUCATION LTD
London and Basingstoke

Associated companies and representatives
throughout the world

Printed in Great Britain by
Hazell Watson & Viney Ltd
Aylesbury, Bucks

Contents

APPENDICES

The primary school study

Opinions of tutors in colleges of education

Opinions of secondary teachers

Aims and approaches of primary head teachers

Tables

A.P.E.—I*

Opinions of tutors in colleges of education

Opinions of secondary teachers

Aims and approaches of primary head teachers

Appendices

Preface

In October 1966, Professor P. H. Taylor, Head of the Curriculum and Method Division of the School of Education at Birmingham University, launched a new organization which came to be known as the Primary Schools Research and Development Group (PSRDG). Open to primary school teachers, college of education tutors and university staff, its object was to heighten the professional awareness and competence of teachers by promoting their involvement, in co-operation with the colleges and the School of Education, in educational research and development. Professor Taylor's perception of teachers' interest was amply justified. Initial meetings attracted as many as 400 teachers in one area of the West Midlands alone.

The Central Committee of the PSRDG, chaired by a junior school head master, H. W. J. Green, early conceived the idea of setting up a major research project. Professor Taylor was asked to suggest subjects for such a venture. Of those he put forward, the Central Committee chose a study of the aims of primary education. On the Committee's behalf Professor Taylor put the proposal to the Schools Council. The proposal was accepted and a grant made for a three-year project. An additional grant was made later for a six months' extension.

A full-time staff was appointed but very many members of the PSRDG have given endless time throughout the $3\frac{1}{2}$-year life of the project. It has been of immense value to the project team to start with a large existing group of interested teachers. Following the formal ending of the project, they plan to continue the work through the medium of study groups, each concerned with an issue which has arisen directly from the project.

Acknowledgements

The first immense debt of gratitude must go to the more than 300 primary school teachers who worked on the project, many of them for almost three years. It is a fact that, without this sustained co-operation, this study would not have been possible. The teachers spent very many hours in searching discussion in order to contribute their decisions about aims to the project. Thanks go, too, to the college of education tutors and local inspectors who joined in the discussions. A special debt of gratitude is owed to the group leaders who took responsibility for sending in a report of every meeting.

More than 2000 teachers in primary, middle, secondary modern, grammar and comprehensive schools and tutors in colleges of education completed questionnaires, and the time and thought thus given to the study is greatly appreciated.

Professor Philip Taylor, Head of the Curriculum and Method Division of the University of Birmingham School of Education, has been a constant source of encouragement and advice, and the study owes much to him.

Finally, considerable appreciation is owed to Mr Gilbert Peaker for his invaluable advice on the design and techniques of the sampling.

1 The scope of the project

The Aims of Primary Education Project was begun in January 1969 and continued for three and a half years. The main work of the project is reported in the following pages. It was generally agreed by representatives of the three bodies responsible for the project, the Schools Council, the Primary Schools Research and Development Group, and the University of Birmingham School of Education, that the project should be concerned predominantly with studying the opinions of primary school teachers about the aims of primary education.

Rather more than four million children go daily to the primary schools of England and Wales, and yet hitherto little has been known about how their teachers perceive the purposes to be served by the children's time there. Until the end of the Second World War, schools catering for the 5–11 age group had a well-established tradition of widely shared practices. Although innovation and change have never been wholly absent from the early years of schooling and many individual schools had a distinctiveness, generally schools tended to be much more alike than is the case now. The purpose of the activities which went on there was readily recognizable and, probably, generally approved. It was clear that teachers were concerned with competence in a relatively narrow range of skills related to reading, writing and arithmetic, with some formal knowledge of the culture, with proficiency in a few fringe activities in the fields of physical education, art, craft and music, and with the development of particular moral values. The whole of this was conducted within a rather formal framework, reflecting the moral values with which teachers were generally thought to be rightly concerned. Now, not only has there been a general change in the content and style of primary education, but a wide variety of practices exists within different schools. The purposes of these new practices are much more difficult to infer and there is certainly less agreement about their value. Whatever the origins of these changes, obviously it has been teachers who have put them into operation. Thus one vital element in the debate and sometimes near-controversy about primary education must be surely an understanding of the aims of the teachers themselves.

At the time the policy of the Aims of Primary Education Project was formulated, the Plowden Report* had been recently published. The Report pointed to the difficulties of stating aims. It referred, further, to the lack of coincidence between what observers judged to be good practice on the part of teachers and those teachers' own ability to state clear aims. The Plowden committee seemed therefore to be unconvinced about the value of teachers stating aims, although it should be remarked that in their own discussions of practice in primary schools they inevitably implied numerous aims. Indeed, since any practice has outcomes, the advocacy of any particular practices must, unless the choices are random, imply aims, whether consciously recognized or not. Teachers adopt particular practices and change them from time to time. It is a reasonable hypothesis that these decisions are based upon aims and the problem lies not in teachers deciding what the aims should be, but in stating them. As Dearden† has said, '. . . the refusal to reflect upon aims does not allow one to escape from actually having them, but simply begs a whole lot of questions by leaving them implicit and unexamined'. In the present climate of change and innovation in primary schools, and indeed, the changing societal context of education, it seems essential that teachers should 'reflect upon aims', in order to examine them and thus use them consciously as a means to rational choice of actual practices.

The task of the project was thus first to involve teachers in stating aims and then to study differences of opinion between teachers. The whole exercise was worked as a co-operative venture between teachers and the project team. Many discussion groups of primary teachers worked closely with the project throughout its existence. The whole problem of stating aims was worked out with them. The objective was, stage by stage, to increase the clarity and focus of the teachers' statements of aims while retaining the characteristics of their thinking. The product, a set of seventy-two aims for primary education, may be thought inadequate and amenable to all kinds of criticisms. As described in the following pages, the project had to find its way and work through successive experiences in this peculiarly difficult and certainly uncharted area of teachers' thinking about aims. But the result is a statement about how teachers themselves see the aims of their work. It is presented as a contribution to a debate. It is recognized to be an initial exploration and one which has thrown up many problems and conflicts, and points to numerous areas which need much further examination.

As the discussion with teachers progressed, it became clear that conceptions of aims were related to other important issues. These were explored in a preliminary way by means of a questionnaire which was developed and used

---

* Central Advisory Council for Education (England). *Children and their Primary Schools* [Plowden Report]. 2 vols. HMSO, 1967.
† R. F. Dearden. 'The aims of primary education', in *Perspectives on Plowden*, ed. R. S. Peters. Routledge, 1969, p. 24.

eventually in a national survey of teachers' aims. It was clear that the aims to which individual teachers subscribed might well have their roots in their fundamental beliefs about the whole purpose of education—in whether they perceived it as something primarily concerned with developing individual talents and interest or primarily as concerned with equipping children with skills and attitudes appropriate to the society in which they will live. It was certainly clear that views on this issue differed.

It also became clear that different views abounded about the aspects of children's development with which primary schools should most concern themselves. It was apparent that, for some teachers, moral development was the area of pre-eminent concern; for others, intellectual development was the major province of the primary school, and others had still different views. The range of opinions about this, and the relationship of these opinions to choice of aims, were again explored through the medium of the national survey.

Not surprisingly, the teachers' varying perceptions of their role seemed to relate to what they had to say about aims. If, for example (as they did), some teachers stress the value of obedience as a characteristic of children's behaviour and others stress assurance and initiative, then it is a reasonable hypothesis that these different teachers choose to teach in different ways. This issue too was, with the help of teachers, developed into a question and included in the survey.

Perhaps the most striking aspect of the results of the national survey was the widespread consistency of teachers' opinions on these various issues. Teachers' views about the fundamental purpose of primary education, the aspects of development they thought primary schools should most concern themselves with, the aims they stressed and the teacher's role they thought best, all fitted together in intuitively logical patterns. This would seem to lend strong support to the idea that, while teachers may have difficulties in stating aims, they undoubtedly have them. If they did not have such aims, it would seem unlikely that the completion of a long questionnaire dealing with various issues, and including a request to rate for importance no less than seventy-two statements of aims in random order, would have shown up these coherent patterns of opinion.

The ensuing pages contain a full account of the development of the set of aims, the national survey and its results. Following this account of the major work of the project are reports of three related but much smaller scale studies undertaken by different members and associates of the project team. The first study is of the opinions of tutors from a sample of one in ten colleges of education about the aims of primary education. They completed the same questionnaire as the primary teachers, and comparisons are made between the opinions of tutors and teachers. The second study (by Frances Davies, Patricia Ashton and Brian Holley) describes the responses of 459 teachers in secondary modern, grammar, comprehensive and middle schools to the same questionnaire. Once again, comparisons are made with the primary teachers' opinions. The last account (by Patricia Ashton and Pat Kneen) describes an investigation in which head teachers of the sample primary schools were asked to indicate what kinds of teaching methods they advocated in their schools. The particular concern of this study was to identify any possible relationship between the aims to which head teachers subscribe and the methods they prefer to see operating in their schools. All three studies raise issues of considerable current interest and importance. It is only to be hoped that this whole work will give rise to debate and much extended examination of the questions which have emerged from it.

Part one

The primary
school study

2 The preparatory work

Purposes of the study

The study had two purposes. First, to discover what practising primary school teachers think are the aims of primary education, and to examine the areas of consensus and divergence between them in their opinions about aims. Second, in developing material for this survey, to devise techniques for thinking about aims which teachers could readily employ for themselves.

Choice of strategy

In order to survey teachers' opinions on any acceptable scale, it was necessary to devise a questionnaire. This could have taken either of two forms; respondents could have been asked to write statements of aims, or they could have been asked to indicate their opinions of given statements. The first option was used experimentally and discarded for reasons which are given below. Thus it was decided that a set of statements of aims must be constructed.

Since the whole survey was concerned specifically with teachers' aims, it was decided that they themselves should be asked to supply the statements. Intensive work would be carried out with volunteer teachers in order to produce a set of aims for primary education; these aims would then be submitted to a national sample of teachers for rating. The particular value of this strategy was that teachers' own perception of aims, their ordering of their daily work in terms of its purposes, expressed in their own kinds of language, would be most likely to be meaningful to other teachers confronted with the statements. At the same time, the task of eliciting statements of aims from teachers would directly serve the second purpose of the project, that of developing techniques for thinking about aims which teachers could readily use for themselves.

The major problem and the solution employed

The major problem in eliciting statements of aims from teachers was ignorance about how teachers think about aims. There was no means of knowing whether teachers do in fact see their work in terms of its contribution to particular aims. Nor, if they do, how general or how specific those aims are. Given these two areas of uncertainty—whether teachers do think operationally about aims and, if so, how precisely—it was thought necessary to begin work with a minimum of constraints upon what they might say. The requirement was seen to be that of formulating aims as teachers saw them and not fitted to some predetermined theoretical framework, certainly until it might become clear that such a framework would be appropriate.

The solution employed to this problem was to begin by asking teachers to state aims without any suggestions about how this should be done; then the way in which teachers were asked to state aims was progressively structured but always on the basis of the kind of structuring seen to be appropriate, given the nature of what had been said spontaneously. In the event, it was found that three successive stages were needed before the teachers stated aims which were clear operational goals for primary education and which, collectively, covered the whole spectrum of primary school activity. The three stages are reviewed below.

Stage 1: writing and talking about aims spontaneously

WRITING ABOUT AIMS

Seventy Midland teachers volunteered to take part in this stage. These men and women teachers varied in respect of age, length of experience, position in school, age group taught and type of school. They had in common only that they were all teaching children within the 5–11 age range. The teachers were asked to complete a questionnaire which dealt with various aspects of their background and career history and concluded with the question 'What, in your opinion, are the aims of primary education ? Please express these as a list of statements numbered 1, 2, 3, etc.'

Fifty-four teachers completed and returned the questionnaire. Between them they wrote a total of 225 statements, an average of 4·17 statements each. A selection of the statements is given below:

the development of the full character and personality of the child;
variety of stimulating experience;
development of good social and moral standards and attitudes;
acquisition of basic skills;
to develop the child's natural potential;
to give the child security which in no way inhibits his development;
to foster happiness in children;
to allow the child to discover his environment.

The statements were not subjected to rigorous analysis but were examined for general characteristics which would inform subsequent work on eliciting statements of aims from teachers. Four characteristics were considered clearly apparent and relevant.

(a) Very wide scope and a high level of generality were found in the majority of the statements. That, on average, the respondents found it possible to describe the aims of primary education in marginally over four statements underlines this. Such aims are no doubt valid indications of very broad general intentions but are of limited value as direction indicators for daily work in school and classroom. It is noteworthy that the meaning of 'aim' for this group of respondents was 'indication of very broad general intention'.

(b) The statements were categorized on a simple basis of similarity of content. The distribution of the statements between categories was very irregular. It must be borne in mind that the teachers were free to write as many statements as they wished. Yet 73% of the statements fell into only three categories and the remaining 27% were distributed over another twenty-one categories. Specifically, the majority of teachers made one statement in each of the categories of moral education, all-round development and intellectual development, and their fourth statements were extremely varied. This would suggest that these are the three areas of high consensus and after these there is a considerable variety of opinion. Apart from the three categories mentioned above, no other was subscribed to by more than 29% of the sample and nine categories, more than one-third, were subscribed to by 12% or less. One of the three major categories, 'all-round development', is of course all-inclusive. Nevertheless, not one respondent confined himself to this statement alone. All made additional statements. Of these additional statements only eight referred to aesthetic development, for example, and only three to physical development. It seems unlikely that the great majority of the teachers would deliberately omit any reference to aesthetic and physical development when writing down their aims for primary education. A reasonable explanation might well be that these and other areas were simply overlooked by individual teachers because the stating of aims was an unfamiliar exercise and comprehensive sets of aims were not readily available in their minds.

(c) Statements were open-ended. Common phrases were 'as far as possible', 'to the utmost', 'to his full potential', 'in as many ways as possible'. Neither desired end-points nor desired processes were clearly defined. It may well be that such phrases were not masks for uncertainty or lack of clarity but accurately reflected the kinds of aims the teachers thought appropriate for primary education. Nevertheless, such aims cannot constitute meaningful goals for work in school and classroom. They afford little, if any, criteria for evaluation.

(d) Aims were mixed with method. The majority of statements were prefaced by 'to develop', 'to foster', 'to provide an environment in which', 'to stimulate interests which'. These and the many other similar prefaces imply a particular method of working in regard to the aim. Aims and methods are two different areas of debate. Furthermore, a method often implies another kind of aim which is not made explicit. For example, 'foster', 'teach', 'encourage' and 'stimulate' each imply a different aim for the child's personal approach to learning.

TALKING ABOUT AIMS

The same seventy teachers were asked to divide themselves into seven groups with a view to holding discussions about aims; two members of each group were asked to act as joint leaders. The object of these open discussions was to provide evidence on how teachers would handle discussions of aims, to look for any particular characteristics of the discussions and, with the view to developing a discussion brief, to identify any particular problems. No prior notice was given of the topics, in order that the discussions might approximate as nearly as possible to ordinary spontaneous discussions which teachers might hold. In short, no preconceptions about how teachers might talk about aims were built into the situation. In this way, the sort of guidance which could be useful for organizing such discussions might be more readily perceived.

The topics were found by re-sorting the written statements from the questionnaires, referred to above, into much broader groupings. Four major areas were discernible:

(a) to develop the basic skills and build up knowledge;
(b) to develop the child's capacity to think;
(c) to foster the child's moral and social development;
(d) to develop the full potential of the individual child in all aspects.

These discussions were crucial in the development of the project, and all were tape-recorded, although this proved to be very unpopular among the teacher groups.

A full account is given elsewhere[1]* of the analyses of these taped discussions. However, the major findings will be summarized below, since they informed the construction of the discussion brief which was subsequently worked out. These findings arose from the analysis of all seven groups' discussion of topic (a), 'to develop the basic skills and build up knowledge'. This was the first to be discussed and also the most straightforward topic. It was thus thought to be a useful basis on which to assess characteristics and difficulties related to discussing aims. All the findings are taken from the mean performance of the groups; each group discussion was also analysed separately

* For reference see end of chapter.

but in no detail did any individual group discussion differ significantly from the mean.

Nature of the contributions

The discussions were overwhelmingly taken up by the giving of opinions. Of all contributions, a mean of 71·8% represented expressions of opinion. Questions accounted for only 15% of contributions. Thus the process of discussion appeared to be one of statement and counter-statement rather than one of alternating question and answer. Reasons for this situation can only be speculated upon; it may indicate a high level of assurance in dealing with the discussion; it may indicate that the discussion was taking place in a shared area of knowledge where questioning was actually unnecessary; it may indicate something of the social climate of the discussion, in which people might have been reluctant to question one another. More important, however, is the fact that these 72% of contributions were expressions of 'pure' opinion, unsupported by reference either to academic sources or to experience.

Only 2% of contributions contained reference to academic sources and 2% to experience. Thus any sort of factual base to these discussions of aims, in terms either of reading or of personal experience, was negligible. This could reflect an assumption of shared knowledge and experience, to which it was thought unnecessary to refer; it could also reflect a lack of such knowledge, although certainly not of experience. Whatever the reason, the analysis indicates quite clearly that aims were seen as matters of personal opinion rather than matters of opinion requiring substantiation in some way.

Content of the contributions

Nineteen per cent of contributions were concerned with the procedure for the discussion. These contributions included suggestions of how to tackle the discussion, of what to discuss next, and so on. The high incidence of such contributions, one statement in five, would suggest unfamiliarity with holding a discussion about aims.

Definitions of the topic under discussion, the basic skills, accounted for 11% of contributions. A further 7% of statements were concerned with the definitions of other words which arose in the discussion. This would certainly seem to imply lack of a common background.

Statements of aims accounted for 11% of contributions. The addition of statements of aims which were involved with statements of method brought the total of references to aims to only 19%. This seems low in a discussion directly concerned with considering aims.

A further 10% of contributions were concerned with comparing the importance of different aims and the order in which teachers should approach them chronologically. In discussions where the content was rather widely dispersed, a somewhat high proportion of time seems to have been spent on this particular aspect. The proportion is nearly as high as that spent on stating aims and suggests as great a concern with discussing their relative order and importance as with what they should actually be.

Only 4% of contributions were direct justifications for aims stated. A further 7% dealt with influences upon aims such as 'parents expect this', 'the secondary schools want this'; these may have been disguised justifications for aims.

Six per cent of contributions, representing quite an appreciable amount of discussion time, were concerned with the teacher's role and function. Again this suggests a concern with the practicalities and is of a similar order to the discussion of the teaching order appropriate to aims.

The remaining contributions were spread thinly over a number of different categories, none of them representing an appreciable part of the discussion.

The major elements of the discussions are summarized in Table 2.1.

Table 2.1   Teacher group discussion contributions
distributed between content categories

Content category	%
Discussion procedure	19
Definitions	18
Statements of aims and of aims+methods	19
Relative importance and order of aims	10
Justifications for and influences upon aims	11
Teacher's role and function	6
Other (no category over 4%)	17
TOTAL	100

DISCUSSION OF THE IMPLICATIONS OF THE EVIDENCE TO
DATE AND OF THE STRATEGY DERIVED FROM THEM

The preliminary work was now completed. Material had been obtained on how teachers wrote about aims and how they discussed aims. This was examined and certain problems and implications became clear.

There seemed to be two areas of problems. First was the apparent unfamiliarity of teachers with thinking about aims. This was shown by the lack of comprehensiveness in the written statements; the amount of attention devoted to discussion procedure; possibly the discursiveness of the discussions, indicated by the range of categories in which contributions were made, and the relatively small amount of time actually given to formulating aims. Second was the breadth, generality and open-endedness of the aims stated. This was evidenced by the written statements.

That these were seen as problems needs some explanation. It could have been thought appropriate to accept the rather 'off the cuff' statements of general intentions as fair indications of primary school teachers' aims. However, the general impression to be gained from watching primary teachers in school is that they are usually purposeful, and often in quite precise ways. That the teachers had tended not to produce sets of clear goals did not necessarily imply that they did not have them. Rather, it seemed likely that such goals are somehow an implicit and possibly almost unconscious part of the individual's approach to teaching. The project team believed that, given time and some guidance, based on attempts to perceive the nature of this problem, the information about aims could be made explicit.

Furthermore, it was thought necessary to press for the identification of much more precise goals than had been stated spontaneously, in order that a meaningful sampling of teachers' opinions could be achieved. The greater the generality of an aim, the less likely it is to provoke disagreement. But that an aim is highly agreed in itself provides little information. For instance, to know that most teachers agree with 'developing the whole child' adds a negligible amount to understanding what goes on in primary schools. Greater precision in this area of aims should also help to clarify and make more productive current discussions about primary education.

The route to greater precision of statements of aims could have been to ask for definitions of statements like 'all-round development', 'full potential' and 'developing the child's capabilities as far as possible'. However, it was thought that such phrases probably do not conceal uncertainty but accurately reflect the current climate of teachers' opinions. Rather than trying to persuade teachers to be more precise about the definitions of their aims, it would be more useful to ask them to define minimum achievement levels within each aim area, leaving an unspecified margin for additional progress towards the more global aims. Thus, instead of defining the precise aspects and desired end points of 'all-round development', minimum end-points of minimum aspects of development should be established. 'Bonuses', in the shape of progress beyond these minimum end-points or aims, would probably depend on the teacher's and children's abilities and interests; the minimum aims, however, would be desirable in any circumstances. This involved a recognition of the possibly genuine open-endedness of teachers' aims, but made possible a set of goals in the shape of operational reference points which teachers would have declared to be essential.

On the basis of these considerations the following strategy was devised to elicit statements of aims from teachers of a type and on a scale appropriate to the ultimate intention of the project.

To meet the problem of unfamiliarity with formulating aims
(a) The mode of operation would be the discussion group. This would provide for the interaction of different individual teachers. This was

thought, in itself, to be helpful in clarifying ideas, but also to be the means of pooling more information. Decisions would be reached collectively by teachers of different levels of experience and working in different kinds of primary school. This seemed to be the best available means of increasing familiarity with this area of thought.

(b) For the same reason, and because the aims of primary education obviously constitute a very large topic, ample time would be allowed for the discussions. Twelve months were allotted for this phase of the work.

To meet the problem of the high level of generality of the aims stated

(a) Each discussion session would be provided with a more defined topic than hitherto. These narrower topics were found by recourse to the questionnaires; the twenty-four categories of aims identified in the written statements were taken to represent the range of teachers' concerns and used as the discussion topics.

(b) A precise question about the topic to be answered by means of a set of statements would be posed:

(i) 'What are the minimum desired end-points or processes within each category?'

The following note was appended.

Note of explanation: It is clear from the discussions that teachers' aims are generally open-ended. They aim for children to develop in as many ways as possible, and as far as possible. We think that this kind of statement should be left as it is. However, we think it would be helpful if some kind of agreed minimum could be established while leaving a margin in which it could be indicated that further progress towards the particular aim would be entirely a matter for the particular teacher's and children's interests and abilities. We think that these kinds of reference points might be very helpful, particularly to young teachers.

(c) Four additional questions would be posed, in order to encourage the relating of aims to the practical situation and to encourage justification for aims. These were as follows:

(ii) 'What major factors, if any, do you think might affect whether or not a teacher might hold that particular aim (e.g. area in which school is situated, length of teaching experience, etc.)?'

(iii) 'What justification (in any terms of your choice) would you offer for holding that particular aim?'

(iv) 'Are you clearly aware of what you can actually do in school or classroom to further that particular aim? Please give a few examples.'

(v) 'Have you clear ideas of how you would evaluate the progress towards that particular aim? Please give a few examples.'

(d) The discussion groups would be asked to confine their attention to children at the end of their primary education, in the middle range of ability and without special problems or difficulties. Desirable as it might have been to formulate aims for different ages, ability levels and circumstances, it was deemed to be an impossible task in the time available. Better, it was thought, to develop a single set of aims of specified scope constituting a set of clear reference points.

A meeting was called of the fourteen Midland group leaders and the strategy for this next phase of discussions was explained to them. Thorough discussion ensued. No problems emerged and the discussion design was accepted by the leaders as clear, useful and possible. All opted to continue with their groups into these structured discussions.

Stage 2: focused discussions

At this stage, teacher involvement in the project was expanded considerably. The original seven groups opted to continue and a further thirty-one were set up. Thirteen of these were located in Devon and Dorset and eighteen in Northumberland, Durham and north Yorkshire. Each of the additional thirty-one groups was asked to appoint a leader from among its number. The average membership of the groups was eleven or twelve teachers. Each group was well mixed in respect of age, sex, length of experience, age groups taught, position in school and type of school.

All groups were sent the same discussion brief and held discussion meetings until they considered that they had formulated a set of aims for primary education to their own satisfaction. An average of ten or eleven meetings were held by each group, although the range was from six to thirty-three. Liaison with the project headquarters was effected through each group's leader or leaders.

At the conclusion of the meetings, the leaders were asked to comment upon the exercise. On the whole, members were assessed by their leaders as being interested in the aims discussions and enthusiastic about discussion as a means of formulating aims. There seemed to be a core of regular attenders of at least three-quarters of the group in most cases; the members were prepared to meet for an hour and often longer over an average of ten or eleven meetings. In practical terms, this is sustained co-operation. On the whole, all members contributed to the discussion.

There seemed to be relatively few extraneous difficulties to contend with. There was some variation in the ease of discussing various topics which was partly peculiar to the individual group; the same topics were found easy by some groups and difficult by others. Broadly, however, as might be expected, it was found easier to discuss and formulate aims closely related to curricular areas and more difficult to specify aims for concerns which were not directly curricular, such as social and moral development.

Answers to question (i) on the first fifty reports received were studied critically with a view to confirming or amending the discussion task now that the groups had some experience of it. The reports reflected a general move to greater precision. The statements in answer to question (i) had become, on the whole, recognizable goals for action. The request for the specification of minimum aims or end-points within narrower topic areas for eleven-year-olds seemed to have closed the previous gap between aims and practice. The teachers appeared now to be using their knowledge and experience to specify meaningful, realistic aims rather than, as previously, formulating broad intentions which seemed peculiarly detached from their daily work. It was decided that the mode of operation, this question, and the way in which it was formulated, should stand.

By interacting with one another in a group, often of varying opinions, with the purpose of specifying precise aims, members appeared to feel they were being challenged to justify their opinions to one another. The justification question (iii) was dropped.

Progress was slow, and answering all five questions was clearly absorbing more time than could be afforded. The desired change in the character of the aims stated had taken place, it seemed, as a result of the formulation of question (i). The other questions, designed to maintain a sense of realism and practicality in the aims stated, were probably redundant, and in any case too time-consuming. Questions (ii), (iv) and (v) were dropped.

Even so, it seemed clear that more time was needed. One group, for example, spent sixteen hours discussing and formulating aims in the basic skills area alone. The discussion phase was extended by another term to the summer of 1970.

Stage 3: structured discussions

The groups moved from stage 2 to stage 3 without interruption. Stage 3 consisted of working to a more structured discussion brief, which was developed in the following way.

The statements formulated in response to question (i) were detached from each group's reports and listed together under the topics which had given rise to them. The topics had been drawn from the teachers' original written state-ments; they had been taken to represent the range of teachers' concerns and thus to constitute suitable 'triggers' for discussion. They were topics which were recognizably distinct from one another but by no means mutually exclusive. The list had been headed 'Provisional categories of aims: to be altered if and as group members see fit'. A number of groups had begun by sorting and grouping the list into related areas. The majority, who worked straight down the list, began to comment as they went on that new topics had been sometimes largely covered by discussion of an earlier topic. In short, the topics themselves, although initially useful in distinguishing areas of aims, were an inadequate basis for classification.

On the basis of the first fifty reports a classification was deemed necessary. Aims were now being formulated in very large numbers. A single long list of aims for primary education in almost indiscriminate sequence would have limited use. In order both to formulate aims comprehensively and to use the aims statements practically, some means of grouping them was necessary.

The aims were scrutinized for patterns of similarity and difference which could give rise to a categorization. Two kinds of patterns seemed to be fairly readily discernible. The first related to aspects of development. Numerous aims were clearly related to intellectual development; these were distinguishable from others related to physical development; others were distinguishable in the same way as relating to aesthetic development and others to spiritual/ religious development. Two other categories were discernible. To make clear the distinction they were labelled 'the child as an individual' and 'the child as a member of a group'. They were later re-named emotional/personal and social/moral, in conformity with more familiar practice.

Such development categories are not, of course, mutually exclusive. Nevertheless, this kind of difference between aims was apparent, and it was thought better to take this clue from the teachers' statements rather than to search for some more obscure, though perhaps more rigorous, distinction which might have created definition difficulties and thus obstructed rather than helped the discussions of aims.

The second apparent pattern of difference and similarity between aims was clearly a behavioural one: whether aims related to what a child was required to know, what he should be able to do, or what he should be. This was summarized as whether the aims concerned knowledge, skills or qualities. Knowledge was deemed to include definite pieces of information which the child was required to possess and to understand. Skills, although usually having a knowledge element, were distinguished by their focus on the child's actually being able to perform certain specified tasks or processes. Qualities, besides covering straightforward qualities of character, were taken to cover groups of skills which, when added together, were taken to include a disposition to behave in particular ways. Thus judgement, criticism, precise and economic body control and a personal appreciation of beauty were among the items subsumed by qualities. This twofold categorization is reproduced diagrammatically in Table 2.2.

A.P.E.—2

Table 2.2   Categorization of aims used in structured discussions

Aspect of development	Desired behavioural change		
	Knowledge	Skills	Qualities
Intellectual	1A	1B	1C
Physical	2A	2B	2C
Aesthetic	3A	3B	3C
Spiritual/religious	4A	4B	4C
Emotional/personal	5A	5B	5C
Social/moral	6A	6B	6C

The aims received to that date from each of the discussion groups were assigned to the eighteen cells of the framework in Table 2.2. The categorization was then sent or taken to each group leader. In both cases it was explained, and in the latter case also discussed; the groups were asked to scrutinize and comment upon it. Without exception the groups accepted the categorization and pronounced it useful. In a few instances, groups requested the removal of an aim from one cell to another. Thereafter the groups assigned the aims as they formulated them direct to the categories, and reports were remitted by group leaders in this form. In the few cases where reports had been sent in in the form of long verbatim accounts, all recognizable aims were abstracted, assigned to the categories and returned to the groups for comment in the same way. Each successive report from then on was brought up to date and circulated so that each group had copies of the cell framework showing a steadily accumulating set of aims. One of the greatest immediate uses of the categorization appeared to be in showing up omissions. The groups worked from the topics, formulated aims, distributed them among the cells and then checked whether any other cells should have relevance for the topic under discussion. The final check was to ignore the original topics and to look at each cell and consider whether it was adequately covered.

The final set of seventy-two aims

When the thirty-eight groups had completed their discussions, 2045 statements of aims had been accumulated. The task was then to reduce these to a single set of manageable size. The reduction was achieved very largely by deleting duplications or near-duplications, of which there were obviously very many. Any statements which were ambiguous or otherwise unclear were deleted, as were those which, besides indicating an aim, referred to or contained by implication the methods by which the aim was to be achieved.

The teachers' statements were of varying levels of generality, and those relating to small details of behaviour were associated in super-ordinate groupings; this was effected as far as was compatible with the important principle of not omitting any single idea submitted by the teachers.

In order to achieve consistency in the operational relevance of the statements, each one was prefaced by 'The child should . . .'. The grammatical structure of the aims was adjusted when necessary to conform to this formulation. Otherwise, the language in which the teachers had expressed the aims was retained in its original form. (The full list appears on pp. 239-44.)

Reference

1   F. Davies and P. M. E. Ashton. 'Statement and structure in teachers' discussion: an analysis of verbatim interaction in teachers' discussion groups', a draft report to the Schools Council of an exploratory study from the Aims of Primary Education Project (1972).

3 The questionnaires and the sample

The questionnaires

INTRODUCTION

The object of the questionnaires was to discover teachers' opinions of the seventy-two aims of primary education derived from the work of the discussion groups. Certain questions had been recognized initially and these gave the overall shape to the questionnaire. Further questions had emerged as the work progressed and relevant items were built into the questionnaires; these will be referred to below. The major initial questions which the survey was designed to investigate were:

(a) What relative importance would teachers generally give to different aims?

(b) What relationships might exist between aims considered important and such teacher variables as sex, age, type of training, position in school, age group taught, etc.?

(c) What relationships might exist between aims considered important and variables related to the environment and organization of the schools within which the teachers worked?

The sampling unit chosen, with a view to a possible examination of consensus about aims among fellow staff members, was the school. In order to avoid asking questions of teachers where the answers would be the same for each member of staff, a questionnaire was first constructed for head teachers.

THE HEAD TEACHERS' QUESTIONNAIRE (see Appendix A)

Local education authority lists of schools supply varying amounts of information. In order to check the nature of sample schools, heads were asked whether their school was infant, junior or primary/JMI (junior mixed and infants) and whether Church of England, Roman Catholic, other denomination or non-denominational. They were also asked whether they had a nursery class or classes within the school. The remaining questions covered the following points:

geographical area;
socio-economic class of pupils;
attitude of parents to the school;
quality of school buildings and facilities;
number of children on roll;
number of full-time and part-time staff;
head's responsibility or otherwise for a class;
class size;
type of grouping of pupils;
basis for assigning children to parallel year classes;
existence and nature of team teaching;
head's responsibility for planning the work of classes;
nature and amount of head's consultation with staff;
any special characteristics of the school.

The object was to establish a clear picture of the salient features of the school's environment and organization, to achieve some indication of the school's involvement in recent educational innovation by questioning about vertical grouping, non-streaming and team teaching, and to gauge the head's practical control of the work of the school by asking him to estimate how much planning he did for individual classes and to what extent and how he consulted with his staff.

THE TEACHERS' QUESTIONNAIRE (see Appendix B)

The teachers' questionnaire consisted of four sections:

Section I: biographical
Questions covered the following points:

sex;
age group;
marital status;
employment other than teaching;
qualifications;
length of teaching experience;
length of service in the present school;
full-time or part-time;
position in the school;
areas of special responsibility;
age group taught;
age groups taught in the past.

Section II
The construction of this section owed much to a similar section in the questionnaire designed and found effective by Taylor, Reid, Holley and

Exon for their study of influences upon the primary school.[1] They constructed a set of short descriptions of different broad purposes of education, each combining reference to a particular aspect of development and to either the social or the individual functions of education. For the purposes of the present questionnaire it was decided to separate these issues into two parts, as described below.

Part II.A : A recurrent theme in the teachers' discussions, although rarely actually made explicit, was a tension between emphasis on education for society, by equipping children with suitable skills and attitudes, and emphasis on education for the individual, as a means of exploiting his own particular capabilities and interests. Two short paragraphs were formulated to characterize (1) the former, socially oriented purpose of primary education and (2) the latter, individually oriented purpose. It was clear from the teachers' discussions that these two views tend not to be mutually exclusive; teachers appeared to hold both to some extent but to emphasize one more than the other. To bring this out, respondents were asked to share five points between the two paragraphs.

Part II.B : This section was intended to approach the issue of the emphasis that teachers might give to different aspects of primary education at the level of the child at the primary stage rather than in the long term. Elements of primary education were distinguished in a way already found to be familiar to teachers. Seven aspects of development were listed: aesthetic, emotional/personal, intellectual, moral, physical, social and spiritual/religious. This was the same list as had been used by the discussion groups in formulating aims (p. 17) with the exception that the social/moral category was split into two. While the combining of social and moral aspects of development into one category had posed no problem in formulating aims it was recognized that, although closely related, these two aspects of development have clearly different connotations and that teachers should be enabled to distinguish between them in the importance they give each one. The respondents were asked to indicate which they thought were the two most important aspects in primary education and which were the two least important.

Section III : aims
This section consisted of the seventy-two aims statements. Possible rating scales were thoroughly discussed and tried out by teachers. Of the different formulations tried, the most consistently meaningful to teachers was found to be that of assigning a level of importance to each aim. Various ways of distinguishing levels of importance were discussed and tried out, and the following five-point scale was accepted:

5   of the *utmost importance*;
4   of *major importance*;
3   *important*;

2   of *minor importance*;
1   of *no importance*.

The rating 'of no importance' was included in recognition of the possibility that there might be some aims which teachers would accept but would not stress. To fill out the respondents' options, a zero rating was added to the scale with the interpretation 'this should not be an aim of primary education'.

Section IV : the teacher's role
Implicit throughout the teachers' discussions had been different conceptions of the teacher's role. Discussion of this had never been invited, but the aims statements themselves hinted at marked variations in opinion about the process of teaching and the parts to be played by children and teachers respectively in the learning process. Intuitively, it seemed highly likely that relationships existed between a teacher's concept of his role and the kinds of aims to which he subscribed. It was decided to investigate this relationship.

A panel of thirteen teachers was meeting in Birmingham to work on a later phase of the project. The problem was put to them and their help sought in devising a suitable question. The dimension was characterized to the teachers' panel as 'traditional–progressive'. Although these are terms used commonly and loosely, they proved to be useful tool phrases in that the teachers appeared to be clear about their meaning and to share a common understanding of them.

The teachers identified three major elements in this dimension: the nature of the content of the curriculum, the style of the child's participation in learning, and the teacher's task. In view of the interrelated nature of these three elements, the teachers suggested that the sense of different approaches could best be conveyed by short descriptions. It was suggested that five paragraphs should be written, representing each end of the dimension, a middle approach, and an approach between the middle and each extreme. Several teachers wrote a variety of descriptions and a small group of them identified the recurrent ideas and combined these in five paragraphs. These were then sent in random order to the seventy Midland participants, who were asked to rate them from most traditional to most progressive. Twenty teachers returned them and, of these, eighteen had ordered them identically with the order intended by the teachers who had written them. The remaining two teachers had reversed two paragraphs at one end of the dimension. Minor alterations were made to these two to clarify the distinctions between them and the paragraphs were put into the questionnaire. Respondents were asked to rate each one on a five-point scale from 'strongly agree' (A) to 'strongly disagree' (E). They were also asked, finally, to indicate which paragraph was the description closest to their own approach to primary education.

The sample

The population from which the sample was drawn consisted of every primary school in England and Wales with the exception of those in four authorities in which the Chief Education Officers withheld permission for the survey; those in six authorities which were wholly or largely reorganized so that there were few, if any, schools terminating at age eleven—the target age for the aims; and all minority schools, that is, single sex or of denominations other than Church of England or Roman Catholic.

The local education authorities were listed in geographical order, beginning with Northumberland and working successively west and east to end with the Scilly Isles. From these lists, a random sample of one in seventy-five primary schools was drawn. A target number of 200 schools had initially been decided upon; the 1:75 sample, which yielded 288 schools, was an oversampling to allow for non-response and refusals.

The sample of 288 schools, in its proportion of infant, junior and primary/JMI schools, schools of different denominations and schools in different population size areas, was found to conform very closely to the national picture as discerned from current Department of Education and Science (DES) figures. The head teachers of all 288 schools were approached with a request for permission to send questionnaires for themselves and for each member of their staffs.

HEAD TEACHERS' RESPONSE

Of the head teachers 64·9% gave their consent and 26·4% refused. No reply was received from the remaining 8·7%. One substitution was made for each refusal; 50% of the head teachers of substitute schools agreed to accept questionnaires. The final sample consisted of 224 schools, 77·8% of the target 288.

The pattern of refusals and non-reply from schools was examined according to the sub-groups of type of school, denomination, area and region. The rate of refusal and non-reply in various sub-groups varied from one in thirteen or fourteen schools to one in three. However, only the very low refusal and non-response rate from the Southwest region was significantly (0·05) below what might have been expected by chance.

RESPONSE TO THE TEACHERS' QUESTIONNAIRE

The 224 accepting schools were collectively staffed by 2003 teachers and this number of questionnaires was distributed. A total of 1586 were completed and returned. Of these, 34 were unaccompanied by a head teacher's questionnaire and unusable without that information; 6 came from single sex schools and were deleted; and 33 were returned too late for inclusion. Thus 1513 were included in the final sample of teachers. These 1513 came from 201 schools, so that the final school sample was 69·8% and the final teacher sample was 75·5% of those approached.

Reference

1   P. H. Taylor, W. A. Reid, B. J. Holley and G. Exon. *Purpose, Power and Constraint in the Primary School Curriculum* (Schools Council Research Studies.) Macmillan Education, 1974.

4 The schools

THE THREE SAMPLE VARIABLES

The 201 schools which made up the completed sample were distributed among the three variables of type, denomination and local authority area, as shown in Table 4.1.

Table 4.1 Composition of the final sample of schools according to type, denomination and local authority area (national proportions shown)

	% of sample*	% of population†
Type		
Infant	26	25
Junior	23	20
Primary/JMI	51	55
Denomination		
County (i.e. non-denominational)	72	63
Church of England	21	29
Roman Catholic	6	8
Other	1	–
Local authority area		
Counties	69	67
Large county boroughs	17	17
Medium county boroughs	12	12
Small county boroughs	2	4

* Full data appear in Appendix C, Tables C.3, C.5 and C.2.
† Data for type and denomination are derived from DES, *Statistics of Education, 1968*, vol. 1, *Schools* (HMSO, 1969), Table I (type), p. ix and Table 15 (denomination). Data on local authority areas are from the *Education Committees Year Book, 1969–70* (Councils and Education Press, 1969).

In respect of both school type and local authority area the sample proportions were only marginally different from the population proportions. Primary schools were slightly under-represented in favour of infant and junior schools, and counties were over-represented by 2% at the cost of small county boroughs. The schools were more divergent from the national proportions in respect of their denominational or non-denominational character. County schools were markedly over-represented, by 9%, and the church schools, particularly the Church of England schools, correspondingly under-represented. The percentage rate of refusal or non-reply from church schools of both denominations was, in fact, double that of the county schools.

OTHER ECOLOGICAL VARIABLES

The DES regional grouping was used to classify the schools by geographical area (Appendix C, Table C.1). On this basis England was divided into nine regions and Wales as a whole constituted the tenth. The nine English regions were North, Northeast, Northwest, East Anglia, East Midlands, West Midlands, London, Southeast and Southwest. Seven of the English regions contributed between 10% and 11% of the sample schools. Wales was a little lower with 8%. Of the two remaining regions, East Anglia contributed only 4% of the schools, as might be expected from a low density population area, and correspondingly the Southeast, a high density area, contributed nearly 16% of the schools.

Two-thirds of the schools (65·6%) were situated in urban areas; of these, almost twice as many were in suburban as opposed to inner urban areas. The remaining third were divided almost equally between traditional and commuter rural areas.

The socio-economic background of the pupils in the sample schools was predominantly working class (Appendix C, Table C.7). Head teachers of a quarter of the schools described their pupils as wholly working class and a further 40% designated their pupils as mixed but mainly working class. Only 4% described their intake as wholly middle class and 9% as mixed but mainly middle class. Twenty-three per cent considered their pupils to be about equally mixed in respect of their socio-economic backgrounds. In view of the difficulty of making such subjective judgements, and the possible variety in criteria used by different people to make the judgements, these findings must be regarded as a very approximate indication of the socio-economic composition of the sample. However, it should be noted that in its broad proportions it conforms fairly closely to population estimates based on the Registrar General's Classification.

SIZES AND NUMBERS

The number of children on the rolls of the sample schools ranged between under 25 and over 600 (Appendix C, Table C.10). Three schools were in the former bracket and four in the latter. The modal size of school was 201–300; 31% of the schools fell into this size group. Twenty-nine per cent were larger than this, and a full 19% were small schools with 100 children or fewer on roll.

The distribution of staff numbers obviously followed a similar pattern (Appendix C, Table C.12). Staff numbers ranged from the head plus one (21 schools) to the head plus 32 (one school). The mean number of full-time teachers per school was 7·22 with a standard deviation of 4·72.

Over half (56%) of the schools had the services of one or two part-time teachers (Appendix C, Table C.11). Seven per cent had three or four such teachers. However, no definition of a part-time teacher was given in the questionnaire, and those included by their head teachers as such probably range from peripatetic teachers to those who, jointly, are equivalent to full-time teachers.

The head teachers were asked to indicate the size of the majority of their classes (Appendix C, Table C.14). Over two-thirds (69%) had the majority of their classes in the 30–39 range. Only 3% had larger classes with 40–49. Seven per cent had classes of under 20, and 21% were in the 20–29 range.

Nursery classes existed in only 8% of the schools (Appendix C, Table C.4).

ORGANIZATION

Half (51%) of the schools had some vertical grouping (Appendix C, Table C.15); of these, approaching half (22% of the sample) were fully vertically grouped in two-year, three-year or four-year ranges. The remaining 49% of the schools were organized wholly in year groups. It must be remembered that 9% of the schools would have been obliged to employ vertical grouping on the grounds of size (not more than 50 on roll) rather than policy, and that this could have obtained in anything up to a further 30%.

Of those schools (Appendix C, Table C.16) having two or more parallel classes to an age group, whether or not vertical grouping was also used in the school, children were assigned to classes on the basis of ability in 21% of them, on the basis of age in 52%, and on other criteria in 34% of cases. These percentages total more than 100 since eleven head teachers employed more than one grouping criterion. However, of the 155 schools in which children were year-grouped, one-fifth were at least partly ability streamed.

On the whole there was very little team teaching in the sample schools (Appendix C, Table C.17). Team teaching was defined as 'large groups of children in the joint charge of two or more teachers'. Fifty-eight per cent of the head teachers indicated that, on this definition, they had no team teaching in operation at all. In only one school was team teaching the mode of operation 'all the time for all children'. In 4·5% of the schools there was team teaching 'all the time for some children'. In 74 schools (37·2%) there was team teaching 'part of the time for all or some of the children'. Apparently, if team teaching is used at all, it is generally only for part of the time.

THE HEAD TEACHER'S ROLE

Some 30% of the head teachers had full-time or nearly full-time responsibility for a class (Appendix C, Table C.13). The remaining 70%, while no doubt undertaking varying amounts of teaching, were not actually in charge of a class.

The heads were asked how far they were responsible for the planning of work for most individual classes (Appendix C, Table C.18). One-fifth (19%) claimed that they were responsible for this 'to a very large extent'. Only five head teachers said that they were 'not at all' responsible for class planning. Over half (54%) said that they were responsible 'to some extent' and about a quarter (24·5%) 'to a very limited extent'. Questions of interpretation arise here in respect of how the heads would understand 'planning of work for most individual classes', and how they would interpret the rating scale. However, even bearing these reservations in mind, there seems to be a clear indication that the major part of work planning tends to be in the hands of class teachers rather than head teachers.

Following on from this, head teachers were asked what form most of their consultations with their staff took (Appendix C, Table C.19). Of the 184 heads who answered this question, only six held 'regular formal meetings' and a further two had 'occasional formal meetings'. Almost three-quarters (73%) of the heads consulted their staff mostly by means of 'frequent informal contact'. Although only one reply was asked for, a further 40 heads (22%) indicated that they consulted their staff by means of both frequent informal contact and occasional formal meetings. It would seem that even an occasional staff meeting was a feature of the organization of only one-quarter of the sample schools.

Two further questions were asked of the head teachers. They were asked which of three adjectives best suited their school building and facilities as an environment for primary education (Appendix C, Table C.9). The replies were almost equally divided; 34% assessed their buildings and facilities as 'good', 29% as 'adequate' and 37% as 'limited'. In short, only one-third of the heads considered their buildings and facilities as better than merely adequate. Finally, the heads were asked which of three adjectives best described the attitudes to school of the majority of their pupils' parents (Appendix C, Table C.8). Approaching two-thirds judged the parents to be 'interested' and a quarter (26%) 'highly interested'. Only 13% judged the parents to be 'indifferent'. This would indicate a higher level of interest than that found by other investigations such as that by Douglas.[1]

Assessment of the parents' attitudes as 'highly interested' was found to be significantly related (chi squared $> 0·05$) to the type of school and to the judged socio-economic background of the pupils ($G > 0·001$, see Appendix F). Head teachers of infant schools judged the parents to be highly interested significantly more often than head teachers of junior schools; primary heads fell exactly midway between the two. Similarly, there was a steady decline in the proportion of head teachers judging parents to be highly interested as their school intake became less middle class and more working class. At the extremes, 87·5% of head teachers of schools with a wholly middle class intake assessed the parents as highly interested and only 6·3% of heads with a wholly working class intake. Furthermore, no head teachers of schools with a wholly or largely middle class composition judged the parents to be 'indifferent' while one-third of heads of working class schools did so. In this respect, the heads' assessments of parents' interest are closely in line with the well-documented higher level of interest among middle class parents and parents of younger children.[2]

Of considerable interest was the just significant relationship $(G>0·05)$ found to exist between assessment of the parents' attitude and the extent to which head teachers planned work for individual classes. The more head teachers were involved in planning work for individual classes, the more interested were parents' attitudes judged to be. Numerous interpretations could be made of this finding. It could be a direct causal relationship, in that the head teacher who experiences a high level of parent interest finds it necessary to control work within the school to a greater extent in order to conform to parental expectations. Equally, the causal factor could be a third element in the situation, namely the kinds of school in which there tends to be a high level of parental interest. These seem to be infant and middle class schools. Infant schools are generally smaller; they are concerned with the vitally important early acquisition of basic skills and in many cases have engaged in substantial organizational changes. For any or all of these reasons, infant head teachers could be more likely to engage in extensive planning of work for individual classes. Alternatively, the link might be the social class of the catchment area. The stronger pressures to academic achievement probably existing in middle class areas may be the reason for the heads' greater involvement in planning.

Although the relationship between planning and parents' attitude was only just significant, it is a finding of sufficient interest to merit further exploration and verification.

SUMMARY

The schools conformed closely to the national proportions of type, population size and socio-economic areas. They were located in the full range of geographical and urban/rural type regions. County schools were over-represented at the expense of church schools.

The most commonly occurring school in the sample had between 201 and 300 children on roll, seven or eight staff and class sizes of between 30 and 39 children. One-third of the heads were responsible for a class.

The heads were about equally divided in describing their buildings and facilities as good, adequate and limited. The majority described parents as 'interested' or 'highly interested'. Even so, this assessment was more common among the heads of infant and middle class schools.

About half the schools were at least partly vertically grouped; team teaching was much less common. Only one in five schools was ability streamed.

Generally most planning of work was done by class teachers; where head teachers did a major share of planning, they tended to assess parents' interest as high. Staff meetings, regular or occasional, existed in only a minority of schools.

References

1   J. W. B. Douglas. *The Home and the School: a Study of Ability and Attainment in the Primary School.* McGibbon & Kee, 1964 (Panther, new imp. 1969), Chapter 7.
2   Ibid. Also Central Advisory Council for Education (England). *Children and their Primary Schools* [Plowden Report], vol. 2, *Research and Surveys.* HMSO, 1967, Appendix 3.

5 The teachers

Of the sample teachers 76·2% were women (Appendix D, Table D.1); this proportion is very close to the national proportion of 75% estimated by the DES for February 1970.[1]

AGE

The age distribution of the sample is given in Table 5.1. The available (1968) DES figures of age distribution, given in the table, combine both primary

Table 5.1 Ages of sample teachers (national proportions shown)

Age group	% of sample*	% of population (combined primary+secondary)†
21–29	33·0	32·1
30–39	24·2	23·1
40–49	23·1	20·5
50–59	15·6	19·9
60 and over	4·1	4·4
TOTALS	100·0	100·0

* From Appendix D, Table D.2
† Derived from DES, *Statistics of Education, 1968*, vol. 4, *Teachers* (HMSO, 1970), Table 20.

and secondary school teachers. The only difference for primary teachers would reflect the different sex composition of the two teaching forces. Figures for primary school teachers might be expected to show a greater recession in the numbers in the 30–49 age groups, the period at which women teachers tend to leave the profession to resume it later. The secondary teaching force, having at 59% a much higher proportion of men,[2] might be expected to show this recession to a rather lesser degree. However, the sample figures in fact show a slight reversal of this expected trend, having just larger proportions in the 30–49 age groups than the combined national figures. In compensation, the older age groups of 50 and over are marginally under-represented in the sample. There was some self-selection among the sample teachers, in that not every member of staff in some sample schools completed the questionnaire; there may have been a higher tendency among older teachers not to return the questionnaire.

MARITAL STATUS, AND EMPLOYMENT OTHER THAN TEACHING

Married teachers formed 71·7% of the sample (Appendix D, Table D.3). Some 28·7% of the sample had spent 'at least two years, or more, in continuous paid employment other than teaching' (Appendix D, Table D.4). This proportion of over a quarter may seem rather high but it should be remembered that those in their late forties and older may well have been involved in some form of war service.

QUALIFICATIONS (FIRST AND HIGHER)

In respect of qualifications, 93·2% of the sample teachers had a Teacher's Certificate, 5·6% were trained graduates and 1·2% were untrained graduates (Appendix D, Table D.5). This total percentage of 6·8% graduates is rather above the national proportion of 4·5%.[3] Fifty-four individuals (3·6%) held higher degrees, advanced diplomas, etc. in education (Appendix D, Table D.6).

LENGTH OF TEACHING EXPERIENCE

Table 5·2 shows the distribution among the sample of length of teaching experience (Appendix D, Table D.7). While long-established teachers of more than twenty years' experience constituted one-quarter of the sample and

Table 5.2 Length of teaching experience among teachers in the sample

Length of experience	No.	%
Under 1 year	142	9·4
1–5 years	418	27·7
6–10 years	248	16·5
11–20 years	336	22·3
Over 20 years	363	24·1
TOTALS	1507	100·0

almost as many had completed ten years' service, as high a proportion as one-third of the sample were, with less than five years' service, relatively inexperienced. In particular, 9·4% were actually in their probationary year at the time of completing the questionnaire.

LENGTH OF SERVICE IN PRESENT SCHOOL

The question relating to the length of service in the present school gave rise to a picture of a somewhat mobile profession (Appendix D, Table D.8). Although only 9·4% of the sample were in their first year of teaching, nearly three times as many, a quarter of the sample, were in their first year in their present school. Almost another third of the sample (32·4%) had served in their present school for more than one but less than three completed years. A further quarter (26·3%) had spent between four and ten years in their present school and only 15·4% (232 individuals) had served for longer than ten completed years in the same school.

PART-TIME TEACHING

In the case of each school questionnaires were supplied for the whole complement of both full-time and part-time staff. No definition was supplied of 'part-time' and it is possible that head teachers exercised their discrimination in whether to give a questionnaire to part-time members of their staff, probably on a basis of the amount of time spent by such teachers in the school. Overall, 112 questionnaires were received from part-time teachers, representing 7·4% of the total sample (Appendix D, Table D.9).

POSITION IN SCHOOL

As Table 5.3 shows, the distribution of the sample teachers among school positions conformed quite closely to the national distribution. Head teachers were a little under-represented; thirty-two heads of the 201 schools in the sample omitted to return a teachers' questionnaire on their own behalf.

Table 5.3   School positions of sample teachers (national distribution shown)

Position	% of sample*	% of population†
Head teacher	11·5	15·9
Deputy head	9·4	9·9
Head of department	4·1	2·3
Post of responsibility	13·7	9·3
Assistant teacher	61·3	62·6
Totals	100·0	100·0

* From Appendix D, Table D.10.
† Derived from DES, *Statistics of Education, 1968*, vol. 4, Table 21.

SUBJECT RESPONSIBILITY

Two-thirds of the sample (66·3%) had 'particular responsibility for teaching [a subject] to more than one class of children' (Appendix D, Table D.11). This seems a surprisingly high proportion and indicates a very widespread use of specialist interests and capacities in primary schools. Table 5.4 shows the frequency of these specialist responsibilities in descending order of number of instances.

Table 5.4 Incidence of specialist responsibilities among sample teachers

Subject	No.	%
Physical education/games/dance	274	*18·1*
Music	211	*14·0*
Art/craft	146	*9·7*
Mathematics	66	*4·4*
Religious education	53	*3·5*
Second language	51	*3·4*

The six areas in the table were the ones named in the questionnaire; respondents were asked to indicate if they were responsible for any other area and to state what it was. A further 200 teachers so indicated. Their special responsibilities covered every conceivable aspect of the primary school curriculum. The most frequently mentioned items were needlework (46), remedial work, especially reading (27), reading (19), English (19), geography and environmental studies (13), drama (11), swimming (10) and science (9). Other subjects mentioned in this connection were literature, nature study, history, writing, humanities, sex education and commercial subjects. The more traditional specialisms have tended to be those, such as music and physical education, which are associated with special abilities or aptitudes on the part of the teacher; the rest of the curriculum has been thought to be within the compass of every trained teacher. Later specialisms, like mathematics and science, have reflected changed conceptions of the subject matter appropriate for primary children and the consequent value of a special interest, if not a particular aptitude as well. The wide range of specialisms engaged in by the sample teachers, however, suggests both that interest is becoming an important factor in determining the composition of the teacher's job and that there is no longer any area which is considered to be inalienably the province of the class teacher. The picture emerges of primary school staffs working in quite a flexible and integrated way with one another.

AGE RANGES TAUGHT (YEAR AND VERTICAL GROUPS)

Two-thirds of the sample teachers (68·6%) taught year groups as opposed to vertical groups (Appendix D, Table D.12). The three infant and four junior year groups were fairly evenly represented, as Table 5.5 shows. Overall, 42·7% of the sample were teachers of infants and 57·3% teachers of juniors. As might be expected, vertical grouping was more common in infant than in

Table 5.5   Year groups taught by
sample teachers

Year group	No.	%
Age 4–5	4	0·3
Reception	111	8·3
Middle infants	97	7·2
Top infants	137	10·2
First year juniors	162	12·1
Second year juniors	136	10·1
Third year juniors	127	9·5
Fourth year juniors	147	10·9

junior schools. Of the sample infant teachers, 39% were working with vertical groups compared with 26% of the junior teachers. In the infant schools or departments a grouping of five- to seven-year-olds was rather more common than a grouping of five to six-plus. Table 5.6 shows the incidence of vertical grouping.

Table 5.6   Vertical groups taught
by sample teachers

Vertical group	No.	%
5–6+ years	86	6·4
5–7 years	138	10·3
7–9 years	68	5·0
9–11 years	87	6·3
7–11 years	43	3·2

AGE RANGES TAUGHT PREVIOUSLY

The last question in the biographical section dealt with the age ranges the teachers had previously taught (Appendix D, Table D.13). The results indicate a large amount of movement within the primary age ranges. The numbers of those with previous experience of a particular age group were substantially in excess of those actually teaching that age group at the time of the survey. Those with previous junior experience appeared to be more mobile than those with previous infant experience. Bearing in mind the 142 probationer teachers (9·4% of the sample) who obviously had not had any previous experience, and that those teaching each age group may have been teaching it for the first time, the indications have an element of approximation. However, something of the order of one-quarter of those with previous infant experience were teaching juniors at the time of the survey; approximately one-third of those with previous lower junior experience and half of those with upper junior experience were teaching either infants or the other half of the junior range. Table 5.7 shows the numbers and percentages of the sample with previous experience of the primary age ranges.

Table 5.7 Sample teachers'
experience of different
primary age ranges

Age range	No.	%
Infants	791	52·3
Lower juniors	987	65·2
Upper juniors	809	53·5

Particularly surprising were the 121 individuals (8% of the sample) who had previously taught nursery children, especially in the light of the fact that only four were still doing so at the time of the survey. Since obviously the remaining 117 teachers had at some time held a post in a nursery school or class, there does seem to be some indication of a voluntary movement out of nursery teaching.

The answers to this question indicated a fairly substantial movement not only within the primary range but across the education system. No less than one-quarter of the sample (427 teachers) had previously taught in secondary schools. Furthermore, 10·8% (164 teachers) had previously taught adults. This suggests a rather greater movement of primary school teachers than might well have been expected.

SUMMARY

The particular characteristic of these data is the remarkably even spread of the sample on most variables. Except, obviously, in respect of sex (76% of the sample were women), qualifications (93% were certificated as opposed to graduate) and position (61% were class teachers without posts of responsibility) all of which is as expected, the sample shows no biases in any particular direction. Variations on variables conform very closely to the national picture as discerned from the DES figures. Nevertheless, it may be useful to bear in mind that the 'typical' respondent was a married woman certificated class teacher, upwards of thirty and with at least five years' teaching experience.

References

1 Department of Education and Science. *Statistics of Education, 1968*, vol. 4, *Teachers*. HMSO, 1970, Table 13.
2 Ibid., Table 13.
3 Ibid., Table 22.

6 Broad purposes of primary education

INTRODUCTION

The respondents were asked in section II.A of the questionnaire to indicate the relative weight they would give to each of the two following statements by sharing five points between them:

The purpose of primary education is to begin to equip the child with skills and attitudes which will enable him to take his place effectively and competently in society, fitting him to make a choice of an occupational role and to live harmoniously in his community.

This will be referred to throughout as the *societal* purpose.

The purpose of primary education is to foster the development of the child's individuality and independence enabling him to discover his own talents and interests, find a full enjoyment of life in his own way and arrive at his own attitudes towards society.

This will be referred to throughout as the *individual* purpose.

The question was posed because differences of opinion along such a dimension clearly seemed to underlie differences among the aims formulated by the teachers. It was decided to test this assumption by examining associations between responses to such a question and preferred aims.

It is useful to remember that this issue has been a matter of long-standing debate. Indeed, as Curtis[1] remarks, 'The antithesis of the individual and society has always existed in philosophical and educational thought . . .' The opposition between the two ideas can be epitomized in the words of Nunn:[2] '. . . the primary aim of all educational effort should be to help boys and girls to achieve the highest degree of individual development of which they are capable', and of Sir Fred Clarke:[3] '[an educative society is] one which accepts as its overmastering purpose the production of a given type of citizen'.

Apart from any philosophical approach to the question, recently trained teachers are almost certain to have encountered support for both ideas in other ways. Most are likely to have made some study of the sociology of education. Such studies obviously draw particular attention to the social functions of education. In the words of Halsey,[4] for example, the universal functions of education are 'cultural transmission and the formation of social personalities'. At the same time, most teachers will have encountered much advocacy of child-centred practice. Plowden,[5] for instance, characterizes much current thought about educational practice in the now well-known words: 'At the heart of the educational process lies the child. No advances in policy, no acquisitions of new equipment have their desired effect unless they are in harmony with the nature of the child, unless they are fundamentally accept-able to him.' Statements of this kind imply, although they rarely make explicit, an individually oriented concept of the whole purpose of education.

Thus teachers are likely to have met a number of different approaches to, and points of view on, the purpose of education. It is fairly likely that in their own practice they compromise between the two views. Certainly, recent philosophical writers have eschewed taking either point of view entirely.

Hirst and Peters[6] conveniently summarize these two approaches as 'shaping' and 'growth'. They launch a compelling attack on the growth theory, seeing it as a peculiar confusion between aims and approaches stemming from the revolt of the progressives against the authoritarianism of the 'shapers'. While subscribing to the mode of teaching implicit in the growth theory, their central point is that the growth theorists have escaped moral responsibility for deciding what the ends of education should be, 'under the cover of a biological metaphor', and that this is an escape which, by definition of the situation, no teacher can make. 'Whether teachers like it or not a teaching situation is a directive one in which decisions about what is desirable are being made all the time.' Hirst and Peters go on to argue for a 'much needed' synthesis between these two approaches to education.

Dearden[7] argues that both approaches are valid and, indeed, to some extent overlap. He too asserts that the teacher cannot escape making judge-ments about what is valuable in the educational process. He argues that with-in our pluralist society there are both 'a quite substantial and acceptable consensus on what is basically valuable for personal and social competence in our form of life',[8] and 'various differing but morally acceptable ways and ideals of life, differing choices of how to live'.[9] Respecting the latter, he puts forward the view that state schools ought not to be partisan. The logical conclusion for schools is that 'children should choose for themselves what suits them best and where their loyalties are to lie'.[10] For Dearden, this argument gives rise to a set of aims which embrace social competence and personal autonomy. The curriculum will consist of elements which enable the child to function effectively in our society and of elements which will enable him to choose between its alternative values and ways of life.

FINDINGS

The question contained two characterizations, one of the societally oriented view of the broad purposes of primary education and one of the individually oriented view. The scoring was designed in recognition of the likelihood that at least some, and probably many, teachers would hold both views to some extent. Thus the teachers were asked not to opt wholly for one or the other view, although this was possible if they wished to do so, but to indicate the relative weight they would give to each. Indication of an emphasis on one rather than the other was forced by asking the respondents to share five points between the two statements and to use only whole numbers (Appendix D, Table D.14). In the event, only 2·6% (39 individuals) failed to complete this question, or answered it without following the instruction. The answers were distributed as shown in Table 6.1.

Table 6.1   Distribution of scores between 2 broad purposes of primary education

Score	Societal purpose		Individual purpose	
	No.	%	No.	%
0	31	2·1	49	3·3
1	149	10·1	180	12·2
2	440	29·9	625	42·4
3	625	42·4	440	29·9
4	180	12·2	149	10·1
5	49	3·3	31	2·1
TOTALS	1474	100·0	1474	100·0

Only eighty individuals (5·4% of the respondents) opted to subscribe to one purpose entirely. Almost three-quarters of the respondents (72·3%) balanced between the two views as nearly equally as the instruction allowed by giving a score of 3 to one and 2 to the other. Less than one-quarter (22·3%), while holding both views to some extent, clearly discriminated by assigning a score of 1 to one purpose and 4 to the other. The mean score assigned to the societal purpose was 2·62 and that to the individual was 2·38. Thus, overall, there was a very small marginal emphasis on the societal purpose as opposed to the individual one.

BROAD PURPOSES AND BIOGRAPHICAL VARIABLES

The question became more meaningful when responses to it were related to other variables; it proved to be a powerful discriminator between teachers sub-grouped on biographical variables and answers to other questions.

Emphasis on the societal as opposed to the individual purpose of primary education was significantly related to five biographical variables. Four of these were broadly related to one another. Older teachers tended markedly to give more weight to the societal purpose; the relationship between age and this preference was significant beyond the 0·001 level.* Obviously closely associated with age is length of teaching experience. The relationship between longer experience and emphasis on the societal purpose was again significant beyond the 0·001 level. Similarly, the longer the service in the present school, the greater was the emphasis on the societal purpose (0·001). Position in school was also significantly related to favouring the societal purpose of education, although to a lesser extent (0·05). A particularly interesting feature of these data was that while emphasis on the societal purpose regularly increased from class teachers to teachers with posts of responsibility, to heads of department through to deputy heads, head teachers reversed the process and were more like class teachers in their views than like any other status group. This may possibly illuminate something of the criteria for the selection of head teachers. Lastly, the societal purpose of education was significantly (0·01) more often preferred by non-graduate than by graduate teachers. Some of the implications of the preference for this view will be explored later (pp. 49, 84).

References

1 S. J. Curtis. *Introduction to the Philosophy of Education*. University Tutorial Press, 1958, p. 181.
2 P. Nunn. *Education: its Data and First Principles*. 3rd ed. Edward Arnold, 1945, Preface.
3 F. Clarke. *Freedom in the Educative Society*. University of London Press, 1948, p. 13.
4 A. H. Halsey. 'The sociology of education', in *Sociology: an Introduction*, ed. N. J. Smelser. New York: Wiley, 1967, p. 385.
5 Central Advisory Council for Education (England). *Children and their Primary Schools* [Plowden Report], vol. 1, *Report*. HMSO, 1967, para. 9.
6 P. H. Hirst and R. S. Peters. *The Logic of Education*. Routledge, 1970, Chapter 2 (particularly p. 31).
7 R. F. Dearden. 'The aims of primary education', in R. S. Peters, *Perspectives on Plowden*. Routledge, 1969.
8 Ibid., p. 29.
9 Ibid., p. 31.
10 Ibid., p. 31.

* The measure of difference used on these data and throughout the remainder of the analyses is *G* (see Appendix F).

7 Aspects of development

INTRODUCTION

Seven aspects of development were listed in section II.B of the questionnaire, and the respondents asked to indicate which they thought were the two most important and which the two least important in primary education. Hirst and Peters[1] argue that this kind of classification is 'indefensible', primarily on the grounds that the categories are not logically distinct; feeling, for example, is inseparable from cognition, and thus to distinguish emotional development from intellectual is absurd. However, as they themselves remark in opening their discussion, 'In most of the standard works on child development, studies are classified under the headings of physical, intellectual, social and emotional development.' It was primarily for this reason that the aspects of development were chosen as a means of determining something of teachers' emphases; the classification could reasonably be assumed to be a familiar one to teachers, in that they could be assumed to be accustomed to thinking about their work from these several points of view. On the basis of the earlier work with teachers (see p. 17), aesthetic, moral and spiritual/religious development were added to the list in the interests of comprehensiveness. Furthermore, the looseness of the classification was matched by latitude in the scoring requested. Teachers were asked only to pick out the two they considered most important (M) and the two they considered least important (L).

FINDINGS

Table 7.1 shows the overall results for the sample. Bearing in mind that the teachers were asked to select *two* most important and *two* least important aspects of development, it is noteworthy that barely half the sample agreed on any one aspect of development as being one of the two most important. The highest consensus (61·9% of the sample) was on rating spiritual/religious development as one of the two least important aspects. Roughly half the sample were agreed that emotional/personal, intellectual and social aspects were each one of the two most important. That only half of this sample of primary school teachers considered intellectual development as one of the two most important aspects of development within the context of a questionnaire about primary education is startling at first sight. However, evidence will be adduced (Chapter 9, pp. 65–8) to show that there were apparently three differ-

Table 7.1   Percentages of the sample judging each of 7 aspects of development as one of the two most important, one of the two least important, or neither*

Aspect of development	Most important	Neither	Least important	TOTALS
Aesthetic	6·2	43·2	50·6	100·0
Emotional/personal	53·6	38·6	7·8	100·0
Intellectual	52·9	34·4	12·7	100·0
Moral	22·7	67·0	10·3	100·0
Physical	3·6	45·4	51·0	100·0
Social	53·6	40·6	5·8	100·0
Spiritual/religious	7·5	30·6	61·9	100·0

* From Appendix D, Table D.15.

ent views of intellectual development, which may in part account for the large numbers opting against it as a major aspect of development.

Next to spiritual/religious development, aesthetic and physical aspects were thought to be the two least important by almost equal proportions of the sample (50·6% and 51·0% respectively). Moral development was an intermediate case; while less than a quarter (22·7%) of the sample rated it as most important, only 10·3% rated it as actually of least importance.

No aspect of development gave rise to a marked polarization, in that anything approaching equal numbers thought it respectively most and least important. In each case the trend was broadly the same and the teachers seemed to choose between rating each aspect as most important or neither, or least important or neither.

Overall, but remembering that only about half of the sample agreed about any one aspect, emotional/personal, intellectual and social development emerged as generally the most important and aesthetic, physical and spiritual/religious development as generally least important, with moral development between the two.

ASPECTS OF DEVELOPMENT AND BIOGRAPHICAL VARIABLES

Biographical sub-groups of the sample were markedly different in their views. Table 7.2 shows the sub-groups that rated each aspect as more important significantly more often. In calculating these relationships, all three options of rating each aspect as most important, least important or neither were taken into account. Thus, each of the sub-groups named in Table 7.2 significantly

Table 7.2 Sub-groups of the sample rating each of 7 aspects of
development as more important significantly more often

Aspect of development	Sub-group	Significance level
Aesthetic	Younger	0·05
	Less experienced	0·05
	Shorter time in present school	0·05
	Graduates	0·05
Emotional/ personal	Younger	0·001
	Less experienced	0·001
	Shorter time in present school	0·001
	Single	0·01
	Heads and class teachers	0·05
	Higher qualifications*	0·05
Intellectual	Married	0·01
	Part-time	0·05
Moral	Older	0·001
	More experienced	0·001
	Longer in present school	0·001
	Men	0·01
	Higher positions	0·05
Physical	Those without higher qualifications	0·01
Social	Younger	0·001
	Less experienced	0·001
	Shorter time in present school	0·05
	Lower positions	0·05
	Full-time	0·05
Spiritual/ religious	Older	0·001
	More experienced	0·001
	Longer in present school	0·001
	Higher positions	0·001

* Those with higher degrees, advanced diplomas, etc. in education.

differed from its counterpart in rating each aspect both more often as most important and less often as least important. These significant relationships, then, imply more than a difference of emphasis between sub-groups but something approaching an actual polarization.

It will be noticed that three variables—age, amount of experience and length of service in the present school—move together consistently. Shortness of experience and of service in the present school are inevitable corollaries of youth. Greater age, however, is not necessarily related to length of service in the present school or even to length of experience. In respect of five of the seven aspects of development, the teachers were discriminated on these three variables. The key to one dimension of these three variables may be simply youth. The other dimension may represent a particular combination of attributes which gain significance from their conjunction; thus, it may be the combination of age with long experience and with establishment in a particular school which differentiates this group from others, in respect of some of their opinions.

These two groups, then, were polarized on their ratings of five of the seven aspects of development. The young attached more importance to aesthetic, emotional/personal and social development; the older, experienced, established teachers attached more importance to moral and spiritual/religious development.

That the conjunction of age, experience and establishment may produce a characteristic attitude among teachers is perhaps underlined by the fact that head teachers (who are likely to have one or two of these characteristics but not necessarily all three), in contrast to other senior colleagues, resembled class teachers in the extent to which they favoured emotional/personal development. It will be remembered that this similarity between head teachers' opinions and those of class teachers, in opposition to the opinions of other senior staff members, also occurred in their preference for an individually oriented concept of the broad purposes of primary education (see p. 41). These results may indicate that the opinions of older teachers, which tend to differ sharply from those of younger teachers, are not necessarily a reflection of greater age and experience but of a different climate of educational opinion at the time of acquiring them; head teachers may be characterized by their capacity to absorb changes in educational opinion. In respect of the importance accorded to moral and spiritual/religious development, however, head teachers do align themselves with their other senior colleagues in opposition to junior members of staff. This may suggest that heads tend to take a more middle view of what is important in primary education, or indeed may reflect particular characteristics of the role of heads as opposed to other teachers.

As with the question on broad purposes of primary education, graduates tended to line up with younger teachers. The possession of higher qualifications, specifically in education, was associated with attaching importance to emotional/personal development and with rating physical development as least important. Physical development was one of the aspects of development most frequently rated as of least importance. Those with higher qualifications were the only sub-group of the sample to do so significantly more often than any other. Teachers accepted for diploma and higher degree courses are generally those with at least five years' experience and often more, and are consequently older. It is worthy of note that, subsequent to these courses, they apparently detach themselves from other older, more experienced teachers in the importance they attach to emotional/personal development, when they become similar in opinion to younger, less experienced teachers.

The one other sub-group with a significant preference for emotional/ personal development was that of single as opposed to married teachers. Marital status appeared to polarize opinion on this issue as on that of intellectual development. Particularly since married teachers are joined by part-time teachers in their view of intellectual development, it is reasonable to suppose that the differentiating factor is not marriage in itself, but having children. Half the sample rated intellectual development as one of the two most important aspects of development; but married and part-time teachers did so significantly more often than single and full-time teachers. It may be that having children of their own tends to alter teachers' concept of the function of schools; they may possibly come to decide that emotional/personal development can be coped with at home and change their emphasis to intellectual development as the responsibility of the school.

Reference

1   P. H. Hirst and R. S. Peters. *The Logic of Education*. Routledge, 1970, pp. 49–52.

8 The teacher's role

INTRODUCTION

The role of the teacher in primary education has changed considerably in recent years. Razzell[1] graphically describes the dimensions of these changes in writing about junior school teachers. Blackie[2] observes the same kinds of changes in describing modern primary education for the benefit of parents and others who are non-teachers. Blyth[3] makes more formal reference to changes in the role of the teacher. The sources of influence upon the teachers' role and the pressures towards change are usefully overviewed by Musgrove and Taylor.[4] The important implication of this review is that each individual teacher is subject to a personal combination of influences, which are modified by his own perception of them and his reaction to them.

It is a matter of common observation that teachers do execute their role in different ways. Discussions with teachers suggested that there are three particular areas of difference: these relate to the principles of selecting curriculum content, to the chosen nature of children's participation in learning and to the teacher's task in promoting learning. Section IV of the questionnaire consisted of paragraphs written to illustrate five different role conceptions (see p. 23); each one contained a reference to curriculum content, the children's part in the learning process and the teacher's task.

The differences illustrated by each paragraph are commonly described as varying along a 'traditional–progressive' dimension. These labels will be adopted as convenient abbreviations for the paragraphs. They are used purely descriptively and not evaluatively. 'Traditional' is taken to refer to a long-established role style, 'progressive' to a more recently developed style, and 'moderate' to a style which contains elements of both.

The paragraphs were placed in the questionnaire in random order but are given below in traditional–progressive order.

Most traditional (3)
There is an ordered body of knowledge and skills that should be taught in the primary school.

This is best taught in logical progression, and most economically to groups of children of roughly equal ability in a quiet, orderly atmosphere.

The teacher's task is to have full knowledge of what he wants his children to know, to be capable, by analysis and experience, of presenting it to them interestingly in as well-programmed a manner as possible, and to set the pace of learning.

Traditional (5)
There are certain basic language and number skills that should be taught in the primary school.

As well as these there are certain other areas of knowledge that should form part of the curriculum.

The teacher's task is to present work in each area of knowledge as stimulatingly as possible so that each child can learn as much as he is capable of.

Moderate (1)
There are certain basic language and number skills that should be learned through structured teaching.

The remainder of the children's learning can best be guided by a mixture of children's and teacher's choice.

The teacher's task is to teach the basic skills as individually as possible and to encourage and stimulate children to use them effectively and imaginatively in all other work.

Progressive (2)
Children learn better when involved in individual work that absorbs them and this is fostered by giving children as much freedom of choice as possible in what they learn, when and how.

To enable effective choices to be made, certain skills have to be mastered.

The teacher's task is to provide stimulating opportunities to learn and practise the basic language and number skills in order to have the tools to use in their self-chosen inquiries.

Most progressive (4)
Children only really learn what they want to learn—when not knowing becomes an obstacle to doing what they want to do.

Learning, therefore, takes place most effectively when children are involved in individual inquiries of their own choice; thus the children's interests and needs as they arise constitute the curriculum.

The teacher's task is to create a psychological environment in which inquiry can arise and a physical environment rich and stimulating enough to enable it to be pursued successfully at the child's own pace.

FINDINGS

The teachers were first asked to indicate their degree of agreement or disagreement with each description (on a five-point scale from A = strongly agree to E = strongly disagree). The results appear in Table 8.1. On the whole, the teachers were prepared to commit themselves to agreement or disagreement with each role. In regard to the three middle roles, at least five teachers out of every six were prepared to opt one way or the other. The

Table 8.1 Percentages of the sample indicating five degrees of agreement/disagreement with each of 5 descriptions of the teacher's role*

Degree of agreement/ disagreement	Role				
	Most trad- itional (3)	Traditional (5)	Moderate (1)	Progres- sive (2)	Most pro- gressive (4)
Strongly agree	15·7	30·8	48·2	24·5	14·4
Agree	26·5	43·7	42·2	45·1	30·8
Neither agree nor disagree	23·6	15·4	8·0	15·0	24·8
Disagree	26·3	8·5	1·5	13·5	26·0
Strongly disagree	7·9	1·6	0·1	1·9	4·0
TOTALS	100·0	100·0	100·0	100·0	100·0

* From Appendix D, Table D.17.

highest level of non-commitment, almost one teacher in every four, occurred in respect of the two extreme roles.

The highest level of agreement centred on the moderate role, with over 90% of the teachers either agreeing or strongly agreeing. A very high level of agreement was also given to the two roles on either side of the middle one; over two-thirds of the sample either agreed or strongly agreed with the progressive role and almost three-quarters with the traditional role. The percentage of the sample agreeing or strongly agreeing with the two extreme roles fell away to rather less than half. Looking only at those who registered strong agreement with each role, the picture is very similar. Most strong agreement was accorded to the moderate role, with the traditional roles having a slight edge over the progressive roles.

The teachers were very markedly less ready to disagree with any of the roles but the two extreme roles elicited the highest level of disagreement; about one-third of the sample disagreed or strongly disagreed with each of these. Disagreement with the moderate role was negligible at 1·6%. Strong disagreement with any role was unusual; the most traditional role was accorded most strong disagreement and that from only one in twelve teachers.

In summary, all five roles received agreement or strong agreement from at least 40% of the sample. The most traditional and most progressive roles were accorded most disagreement, in each case by approximately one-third of the sample. The moderate, traditional and progressive roles achieved very high levels of agreement, between two-thirds and 90% agreeing with

A.P.E.—3

each of them. Fewer than half the sample (42·2% and 45·2% respectively) agreed with the most traditional and most progressive roles. Fewer than one in six teachers were prepared to give strong agreement to either of these. These results indicate that the majority of teachers are prepared to agree with any of these five roles except an extreme one.

In conclusion, the teachers were asked to indicate which of the five role descriptions was closest to their own approach to teaching (Appendix D, Table D.18). The results were as shown in Table 8.2. As might be expected,

Table 8.2   Percentages of the sample selecting each of 5 role descriptions as closest to their own approach

Role	% of sample
Most traditional (3)	8·9
Traditional (5)	20·3
Moderate (1)	45·6
Progressive (2)	17·1
Most progressive (4)	8·1
TOTAL	100·0

the distribution of the teachers on this measure was very similar to their over-all distribution on agreement and disagreement with the roles. Much the largest number (45·6%) opted for the moderate role as closest to their personal approach to primary education. Around one in five (20·3% and 17·1% respectively) opted for the traditional and progressive roles. Only 17% opted for either of the extreme roles and divided almost equally between the two. Overall, the traditional roles were closest to the personal approach of marginally more teachers than were the progressive roles. Again, a picture of moderation emerges, with a general avoidance of extreme approaches of either kind.

ROLES AND BIOGRAPHICAL VARIABLES

The biographical compositions of the parts of the sample choosing each role were examined for significant features. Table 8.3 shows the results. A number of interesting features arise from examination of the sample sub-groups who preferred each role significantly more often. The now familiar combination of age, experience and length of service in the present school separated out sections of the sample in their preference for four out of the five roles. The older, the more experienced and those who had served for longer in their present school agreed significantly more often with the traditional and moderate roles than did their opposite numbers. Neither group, older or younger, agreed significantly more often with the progressive role; this is possibly the meeting ground where age and its associated characteristics are not particularly relevant. The young, the less experienced and those with shorter service in their present school, however, emerged as significantly more in favour of the most progressive role. In summary, the younger had a clear preference for a very progressive approach to teaching, and the older for approaches varying from moderate to very traditional; thus, the views of the

Table 8.3 Sub-groups of the sample agreeing with each of 5 descriptions of the teacher's role significantly more often

Role	Sub-group	Significance level
Most traditional	Older	0·001
	More experienced	0·001
	Longer in present school	0·001
	Certificated teachers	0·001
	Those without higher qualifications	0·05
Traditional	Older	0·001
	More experienced	0·001
	Longer in present school	0·001
	Married	0·001
	Certificated teachers	0·05
Moderate	Older	0·001
	More experienced	0·001
	Longer in present school	0·05
	Women	0·05
	Certificated teachers	0·05
	Higher positions	0·05
Progressive	Women	0·001
	Higher qualifications	0·001
	Certificated teachers	0·05
Most progressive	Younger	0·001
	Less experienced	0·001
	Shorter time in present school	0·001
	Women	0·01
	Those not employed outside teaching*	0·01
	Certificated teachers	0·05
	Higher qualifications	0·05

* Those who had *not* had two years or more of continuous paid employment other than teaching.

older were more varied except in their marked disagreement with very progressive approaches.

Women were distinguished by their disagreement with traditional roles, and preferred moderate and progressive roles significantly more often than men. Clearly, men appear to be more traditional and women more progressive in their approaches to teaching.

In respect of three roles out of the five, the possession of higher qualifications distinguished teachers in the sample in their levels of agreement with different roles. Higher qualifications were defined as 'higher degree, advanced diploma, etc. in education'. Only a very small minority of the sample had such qualifications but it is worthy of note that they significantly more often opted against the most traditional role and in favour of the progressive and most progressive roles. Remembering that those with higher qualifications would certainly not have been in the younger age groups and would have had some years of experience, it must be noted that they therefore tended to deviate from the pattern clearly established for their contemporaries generally and, in opinions about approaches to teaching, aligned themselves with their younger, inexperienced colleagues. It is interesting to speculate whether these opinions are characteristic of teachers who choose to take higher qualifications in education or whether courses leading to higher qualifications tend to modify opinions about education in these quite marked ways.

Three other groups stood out in their preferences for particular roles. Married teachers agreed with a traditional role significantly more often than single teachers. The link may reasonably be assumed to be teachers having children of their own; it is interesting that this may give rise to a preference for more formal approaches to teaching. Position distinguished the teachers only in their attitude towards the moderate role, which was just significantly more often preferred by those in senior positions than by class teachers. This moderate position may be in line with earlier results, which indicated some tendency for head teachers to align themselves at times with older colleagues and at other times with younger ones. The experience of an appreciable period of paid employment outside teaching appeared to have some relationship with disagreement with the most progressive role; it may be that this, like teachers having children of their own, gives rise to a different orientation to education and its methods.

It must be noted that all five roles were favoured significantly more often by non-graduate, as opposed to graduate, teachers. This is a curious result; one interpretation may be that certificated teachers simply tend to be more emphatic in their opinions about approaches to teaching.

The data were examined for sub-groups that significantly more often selected different roles as closest to their personal approach to teaching. This is an important area of the data because here the teachers were asked not to indicate broad levels of agreement or disagreement with different approaches to teaching, but to declare their own personal position. Traditional, as opposed to progressive, approaches were significantly preferred by five sub-groups of the sample. The results are given in Table 8.4.

As might be expected on the basis of the earlier data, the combination of

Table 8.4 Sub-groups of the sample significantly preferring
traditional and progressive roles respectively as
closest to their own

Traditional roles	Progressive roles	Significance level
Older	Younger	0·01
More experienced	Less experienced	0·01
Longer in present school	Shorter time in present school	0·001
Without higher qualifications	With higher qualifications	0·001
Married	Single	0·01

age, experience and length of service in the present school appeared again.
Interestingly, the highest correlation (significant beyond the 0·001 level) of
the three was that with length of service in the present school. This is in
accord with earlier results, which have indicated that long establishment in a
particular school may be a most pervasive factor in establishing particular
attitudes towards education. Alternatively, it may indicate that those with
more traditional attitudes tend to give long periods of service in a particular
school. In any event, this is an interesting result, meriting further investigation.

Higher qualifications appeared again as a variable discriminating those who
choose to teach in a more progressive way from teachers whose chosen
approach was more traditional. As suggested earlier, preference for more
progressive teaching approaches may characterize those who choose to do
advanced courses or may be the effect of the courses themselves. In either
case, the association was strongly marked, with a correlation significant
beyond the 0·001 level.

Finally, the married teachers emerged as more generally in favour of
traditional approaches to teaching and the single in favour of progressive
approaches. It may be, as suggested earlier, that marriage and children tend
to alter a teacher's opinions about teaching. On the other hand, remembering
that the great majority of married teachers are women, it may be that domestic
responsibilities outside school tend to influence these teachers to adopt a role
which is possibly less demanding. Whichever is the solution, it is of some
interest that a personal factor such as marriage, which is quite extraneous to
the teacher's professional role, may possibly tend to affect her attitudes
towards it.

ROLES, BROAD PURPOSES AND ASPECTS OF DEVELOPMENT

The responses of the teacher's role question were examined for associations
with responses to the questions discussed in Chapters 6–7, covering the
broad purposes of education and the aspects of development. Table 8.5 gives
the significant relationships.

Table 8.5 Significant relationships between agreement with each of
5 teacher's roles and support for (i) 2 broad purposes of
primary education, (ii) 7 aspects of development

| Role | Most important | | Least important | |
	Purpose/aspect	Signif.	Aspect	Signif.
Most traditional	(i) Societal	0·001		
	(ii) Moral	0·001	(ii) Aesthetic	0·001
	Physical	0·01	Emotional/	
	Spiritual/		personal	0·001
	religious	0·001		
Traditional	(i) Societal	0·001		
	(ii) Intellectual	0·05	(ii) Aesthetic	0·001
	Moral	0·01	Emotional/	
	Physical	0·05	personal	0·001
	Spiritual/		Social	0·05
	religious	0·001		
Moderate			(ii) Aesthetic	0·05
Progressive	(i) Individual	0·001		
	(ii) Emotional/		(ii) Intellectual	0·001
	personal	0·001	Moral	0·05
Most progressive	(i) Individual	0·001		
	(ii) Aesthetic	0·001	(ii) Intellectual	0·001
	Emotional/		Moral	0·05
	personal	0·001		

The table shows that there were clear and marked relationships between
the kind of approach to teaching which teachers selected, their opinions about
the broad purposes of education, and the aspects of children's development
which they considered respectively as most and least important in education.
As might be expected, the group whose opinions about the teacher's role had
least pattern of coincidence with their opinions on other issues were the
moderates. They were distinguished only by their rejection of aesthetic
development. This result suggests that, with this one exception, the opinions
of the moderates vary from one item to another more than do those of other
groups.

In several respects, the traditionalists and the progressivists were polarized
in their opinions. Two broad purposes of primary education were described
and the teachers asked to indicate the relative weight they would give to each.
The traditionalists weighted one purpose and the progressives the other; all
relationships between the opinions were significant beyond the 0·001 level.
The traditionalists' view was most often that the main broad purpose of
primary education is to prepare children to fit into society, equipping them

with appropriate skills and attitudes. The progressives much more frequently thought that the main broad purpose of primary education is to foster children's individuality and independence, enabling them to discover their own talents and interests and arrive at their own attitudes towards society. The striking clarity of this result does suggest strongly that teachers' opinions about modes of teaching are firmly rooted in their fundamental views about the aims of education.

The traditionalists and the progressives tended to be equally opposed in their opinions about which aspects of children's development were respectively most and least important in primary education. Comparison of the two traditional groups with the two progressive groups shows that four of the seven aspects of development were actually reversed in being rated as most and least important significantly more often by each of them. This suggests not merely a variation of opinion but an actual opposition. The traditionalists tended to rate intellectual and moral development as of most importance, the progressives as of least importance. At the same time, the progressives more frequently rated aesthetic and emotional/personal development as of most importance and the traditionalists rated them as of least importance. This is a compelling result which merits further investigation. It suggests a real and important cleavage of opinion between teachers who may well be working successively with the same group of children. Perhaps most striking is the progressives' tendency to relegate intellectual development to a place of least importance; it should just be borne in mind that, as will be shown later, intellectual development may have been open to a variety of interpretations which makes this particular result more equivocal.

Interesting too is the preference of the traditionalists for physical and spiritual development, two aspects about which apparently the progressives tended not to feel strongly in either direction. It should also be noted that social development appeared only once—just significantly rated as least important by the traditional group. On the whole, social development did not appear to be a contentious issue, in that attitudes towards it did not discriminate between the traditionalists and the progressives.

Finally, responses to the questions about the broad purposes of primary education and the seven aspects of development were compared with the teachers' choice of a role description as closest to their own teaching approach. The results are shown in Table 8.6 (p. 56).

The picture is virtually identical with that which emerged from the question asking the teachers to indicate their level of agreement or disagreement with each of the roles. The whole picture can now be drawn together in the shape of a summary. Those teachers who considered that the broad purpose of primary education is to equip children with skills and attitudes, which will enable them to fit effectively and competently into society, tended to stress as most important children's intellectual, moral, physical and spiritual

Table 8.6   Significant relationships between choice of a personal role
(traditional/progressive) and support for 2 broad purposes of
primary education and 7 aspects of development

	Traditional roles	Progressive roles	Signif.
	Favour societal purpose	Favour individual purpose	0·001
Aspects of develt.			
Aesthetic	Least important	Most important	0·001
Emotional/personal	,, ,,	,, ,,	0·001
Intellectual	Most important	Least important	0·001
Moral	,, ,,	,, ,,	0·001
Physical	,, ,,	,, ,,	0·01
Spiritual/religious	,, ,,	,, ,,	0·01

development; they also tended to choose to work in a more traditional,
teacher-directed manner with the accent on the acquisition of basic skills and
knowledge to specified levels of achievement. Those teachers who considered
that the broad purpose of primary education is to develop children's independence and individuality, enabling them to discover their own talents and
interests and to arrive at their own enjoyment and attitudes towards society,
were markedly inclined to stress as most important the aesthetic and
emotional/personal aspects of development; they tended to choose to work
in a more progressive, child-centred manner with the accent on inquiry and
the acquisition of the basic skills as the children require them and at their own
pace. The former group tended to be the older, more experienced, more
established married teachers and the latter tended to be the younger, less
experienced, less established, single teachers and those with higher qualifications in education.

These findings are intuitively acceptable in that they create two meaningful,
consistent and coherent pictures of two conceptions of education, its purposes
and methods. Over-simplification of these important issues should be
avoided; however, these findings appear to suggest strongly that a long-
suspected difference of opinion between teachers may be a real, and possibly
fundamental, cleavage.

References

1 A. G. Razzell. *Juniors : a Postscript to Plowden.* Penguin, 1968.
2 J. Blackie. *Inside the Primary School.* New imp. HMSO, 1969, Chapter 4.
3 W. A. L. Blyth. *English Primary Education.* Routledge, 1965, Chapter 7.
4 F. Musgrove and P. H. Taylor. *Society and the Teacher's Role.* Routledge, 1969,
   Chapter 1.

9 Aims of primary education

INTRODUCTION

Seventy-two aims for primary education had been derived from the earlier work with teachers (see Chapter 2). These seventy-two aims were put into section III of the questionnaire in random order and the sample teachers were asked to rate them. They were asked to assign a zero to any aim which they thought should *not* be an aim of primary education and otherwise to assign one of the following scores:

5   I think that this aim is of the *utmost importance* in primary education.
4   I think that this aim is of *major importance* in primary education.
3   I think that this aim is *important* in primary education.
2   I think that this aim is of *minor importance* in primary education.
1   I think that this aim is of *no importance* in primary education.

The teachers were asked to bear in mind children in their own school, in the middle range of ability, and at the end of their primary education.

MEAN SCORES ASSIGNED TO EACH AIM

Table 9.1 (p. 58) shows the average score given to each aim by the sample of 1513 teachers (see Appendix D, Table D.16). It also shows the number who thought that each aim should not be an aim of primary education. For convenience, the statements of aims are abbreviated. The numbers in the 'Aim' column refer to the list of aims as given in the questionnaire (Appendix B, pp. 177–83). Reference to this list will give the full text of each statement. The aims are given in descending order of mean score assigned. The means are grouped in intervals of 0·5 either side of each score. Thus the first eight aims, with an average score between 4·0 (major importance) and 4·5, fall in the group called 'major importance (upper)'; the next group contains items with average scores between 4·0 and 3·5 and is called 'major importance (lower)', and so on.

On average, 98·4% of the sample agreed that every aim was an acceptable aim of primary education, i.e. gave each aim a score of between one and five and did not use the zero indicating that they thought it 'should not be an aim

Table 9.1 Rank order of 72 aims of primary education scored by the sample

Rank	Aim No.	Description	Mean	SD*	No. thinking should *not* be an aim
		Major importance (upper)			
1	58	Happy, cheerful and well balanced	4·47	0·78	3
2	26	Read with understanding	4·46	0·71	0
3	24	Acquire moral values	4·36	0·77	2
4	12	Read fluently and accurately	4·34	0·81	3
5	13	Enjoyment in school work	4·32	0·76	0
6=	7	Individuality	4·09	0·94	9
6=	25	Careful and respectful of property	4·09	0·85	1
8	43	Courtesy and good manners	4·00	0·87	1
		Major importance (lower)			
9	66	Tolerance	3·97	0·88	0
10=	47	Enthusiastic and eager	3·96	0·91	7
10=	21	Convey meaning clearly through speech	3·96	0·82	0
12	3	Acquire information other than by reading	3·93	0·84	0
13=	50	Listen with concentration and understanding	3·91	0·89	3
13=	27	Kind and considerate	3·91	0·88	4
15=	4	Everyday maths	3·89	0·88	1
15=	55	Wide vocabulary	3·89	0·84	0
17	18	Obedient	3·87	0·90	13
18=	40	Self-confident	3·85	0·91	7
18=	11	Enjoyment in leisure interests	3·85	0·91	5
20=	31	Know moral values	3·82	0·93	9
20=	29	Arithmetic—4 rules	3·82	0·88	1
22	38	Control behaviour and emotions	3·81	0·84	1
23	9	Make reasoned judgements and choices	3·73	0·91	11
24	65	Questioning attitude	3·72	0·93	10
25	8	Write legibly	3·71	0·84	0
26	64	Community responsibility	3·70	0·90	7
27	23	Principles of health, hygiene and safety	3·67	0·90	5
28=	20	Behave appropriately	3·65	0·93	5
28=	30	Good social mixer	3·65	0·88	6
30=	56	Acquire information from written material	3·64	0·88	8
30=	60	Inventiveness and creativity	3·64	0·89	1
32	57	Plan independent work	3·63	0·92	8
33	5	Correct spelling	3·59	0·88	3
34	71	Modern maths	3·57	0·90	6
35	59	Deal with emergencies	3·35	0·97	8
36	17	Industrious, persistent and conscientious	3·52	0·91	15
		Important (upper)			
37=	28	Engage in discussion	3·49	0·83	10
37=	15	Observe	3·49	0·88	3
39	1	Communicate feelings through some art forms	3·44	0·93	1
40=	51	General knowledge of local environment	3·43	0·88	0

* Standard deviation.

Table 9.1—*cont.*

Rank	Aim No.	Description	Mean	SD	No. thinking should *not* be an aim
40=	39	Write interestingly	3·43	0·79	1
42	53	Swim	3·33	1·05	23
43	54	Techniques of some arts and crafts	3·31	0·85	1
44=	34	Write clear and meaningful English	3·30	0·93	13
44=	46	Personal appreciation of beauty	3·30	0·83	4
46	14	General knowledge	3·26	0·82	7
47	45	Adaptable and flexible	3·25	0·93	20
48	67	Behave in accordance with Christian religion	3·20	1·10	89
49	32	Speak in a clear and fluent manner	3·18	0·91	18
50	22	Form a considered opinion	3·16	1·01	89
51=	42	Basic grammar	3·14	0·93	27
51=	19	Behave in accordance with own religion	3·14	1·10	107
53	6	Knowledge of the Bible and Christian beliefs	3·08	0·99	38
54	52	Understand own emotions	3·07	0·94	40
55=	69	Play a part in own development	3·06	0·99	52
55=	48	Understand aesthetic experiences	3·06	0·84	13
57=	37	Critical and discriminating	3·03	0·97	24
57=	44	Maintain lasting relationships	3·03	0·99	96
		Important (lower)			
59	33	Precise and economic body control	2·95	0·76	17
60	63	Play a variety of games	2·93	0·82	6
61	72	Movement and gymnastic skills	2·92	0·76	6
62	62	Simple science	2·91	0·81	13
63	41	Sex education	2·89	0·99	98
64	2	Understanding of how body works	2·86	0·85	16
65	70	Listen to and enjoy a range of music	2·83	0·80	19
66	16	Knowledge and skill for simple music-making	2·76	0·80	7
67	36	Understanding of modern technology	2·73	0·76	16
68	10	Spiritual awareness	2·61	1·01	137
		Minor importance (upper)			
69	35	Ordered subject knowledge	2·44	0·80	89
70	61	Knowledge of world religions	2·35	0·89	154
71	49	Play a musical instrument	2·20	0·70	65
		Minor importance (lower)			
72	68	Second language	1·97	0·78	229

of primary education'. This may be taken to confirm the validity of the whole set of seventy-two aims.

The difference between any two adjacent ranks in respect of average score assigned is negligible. Therefore it is not the strict order which should be examined but the broad relative positions of different kinds of aims. At the same time, it should be remembered that no restriction was put upon the number of high scores which the teachers might assign and thus the rank order does reflect a discrimination among the teachers about the relative importance of different aims.

Eight aims achieved a mean score above 4·00, that is, between 'major importance' and 'utmost importance'. Three of these were concerned with the child's personal attributes and stated that he should be 'happy, cheerful and well balanced', that he should 'find enjoyment in a variety of aspects of school work and gain satisfaction from his own achievements', and that he should be 'an individual, developing in his own way'. High on the teachers' priorities, then, was that children should find school a route to personal satisfaction. Three further 'top' aims were concerned with children's social and moral development. These were that the child should be 'beginning to acquire a set of moral values', that he should be 'careful with and respectful of both his own and other people's property' and that he should know how to 'behave with courtesy and good manners both in and out of school'. There seems here to be some accent on formal good behaviour. The two other aims to achieve this high average score were both concerned with the skill of reading. Teachers' general priority aims, then, appear to be 'good behaviour', reading and a personal enjoyment of school.

The next group of twenty-eight aims which achieved an average score approaching 'major importance' reveals a very similar pattern. The twenty-eight aims in this group are divided almost equally between the same three areas—personal development, social and moral behaviour, and the basic skills. In respect of the child's personal development, the teachers placed great stress on his being enthusiastic and eager to put his best into all activities, controlling his behaviour and emotions, having a questioning attitude towards his environment, being able to plan independent work and organize his own time, and knowing how to deal with emergencies. The picture seems to be of an outgoing and confident child who is controlled and purposeful. The major aims relating to social and moral development were a mixture of positive, outgoing qualities and rather conformist ones. The teachers emphasized the child being tolerant, kind and considerate, developing a sense of community responsiblity and being a good social mixer. At the same time they stressed the child knowing the common moral values, knowing how to behave appropriately in a variety of situations, being obedient, industrious, persistent and conscientious.

Reading was undoubtedly considered the major basic skill, both aims relating to reading having appeared in the first eight. Ten other basic skills appeared in the next most important group of aims. First came the aim that the child should be able to 'convey his meaning clearly and accurately through speech' and this was closely followed by being able to 'listen with concentration and understanding'. Alongside these two came the aim that the child should 'know how to acquire information other than by reading; for example by asking questions, by experimenting, from watching television'. This aim too has a strong oral element and it is clear that the teachers placed great stress on oracy, making it second in importance only to reading. Close behind came the aim that 'the child should have a wide vocabulary', emphasizing again the teachers' concern with effective oral communication.

In this same highly placed group of basic skills were two other elements, related respectively to literacy skills and to mathematics. One of the three literacy aims was an extension of reading and was concerned with the child 'developing the skills of acquiring knowledge and information from written material'. The other two were concerned with legible writing and correct spelling. All three aims relating to mathematics appeared in this group of aims approaching major importance. The difference between the placings of the three was marginal but everyday maths ('the child should know how to use mathematical techniques in his everyday life') came first, followed by the child knowing 'how to compute in the four arithmetic rules', and the modern maths statement ('the child should know how to think and solve problems, mathematically') came last of the three.

Two other aims appeared in this highly placed group. The first of these, that the child should be 'developing the ability to make reasoned judgements and choices, based on the interpretation and evaluation of relevant information', was the only more complex intellectual skill to receive much emphasis. The other aim to appear in this group was that the child should be able to 'apply the basic principles of health, hygiene and safety'.

It so happens that these first two groups of aims took up the first half of the rank order. Remembering that the vast majority of the teachers agreed with all of the aims, this first half of the rank order can be taken to indicate their major emphases. As shown above, these major emphases fell into three clear areas. First was the area of personal development, which had three strands. The first strand seemed to be that of the child's general sense of well-being and positive orientation towards school, consisting of enjoyment and satisfaction in all activities. A positive and purposeful approach to leisure activities was an out-of-school extension of this general aspiration. The second strand was the child's sense of assurance and competence. This was exemplified by the aims referring to self-confidence, sense of personal adequacy, ability to deal with the environment at an appropriate level and cope with emergencies, ability to control behaviour and emotions, to plan work independently and organize time. The third strand in this personal area was the development of the child's individuality, of his inventiveness and creativity, and of a questioning attitude towards the environment—three aims reflective of autonomy for the child.

The second priority area was that of social and moral development. Here the child was required to learn to behave in a socially acceptable way based upon a growing awareness of moral values, and to have a positive, kindly and confident involvement in social relationships.

The basic skills made up the third area of priority aims. The emphases here were first on reading, then on oracy and thirdly on mathematics.

Conspicuous by their complete absence among the priority aims were any references to the arts, music, physical education, religious education, sex education, science or a second language. Aims in all of these areas were congregated in the lower half of the rank order and most of them failed to reach even an average rank of 'important'. It must not be forgotten that the teachers did accept aims in these areas as valid aims for the primary school but, against that background, the low level of importance accorded to them merits serious consideration. Free to accord as many high scores as they wished, the teachers have clearly discriminated against aims in these areas.

Equally surprising is that aims relating to the skills of communicating through writing also appear in these less important groups. So, too, do aims concerning the development of intellectual autonomy such as forming a considered opinion and being critical and discriminating.

How the teachers collectively stressed the importance of different aims is shown in Table 9.2.

Table 9.2   Relative importance of different aims

Curricular aims related to:	Personal aims	Social/moral aims
	Utmost importance	
Reading	Happiness Individuality Positive attitudes to school	Good behaviour
	Very important	
Oracy Mathematics	Outgoingness Confidence Control Purposefulness	Positive attitudes to others Conformity Good work attitudes
	Less important	

Literacy (except
  reading)
General knowledge
Religious knowledge
	Self-knowledge
	Independence of
	  mind
	Decision-making
		Religion-based
		  behaviour
		Social effectiveness

	Not very important	
Physical education Science and technology Sex education Music Second language		

By way of summarizing the teachers' emphasis in a different way, Table 9.3 shows the percentage of aims concerned with each area of the child's development which occurred in each quarter of the rank order. Intellectual aims were fairly evenly spread throughout the rank order. Emotional/personal and social+moral aims were clearly concentrated towards the top of the rank order and physical, aesthetic and spiritual/religious ones towards the bottom. This ordering matches that of the aspects of development selected by the teachers overall as of most and least importance (see pp. 42–3).

Table 9.3 Percentages of aims in seven areas of development occurring in each quarter of the rank order

Area of development	Quarter of the rank order				TOTALS
	1st	2nd	3rd	4th	
Social ⎱ Moral ⎰	40·00	40·00	13·00	7·00	100·00
Emotional/ personal	35·72	35·72	21·42	7·14	100·00
Intellectual	30·43	21·70	26·17	21·70	100·00
Physical	0·00	14·30	14·30	71·40	100·00
Aesthetic	0·00	12·50	37·50	50·00	100·00
Spiritual/ religious	0·00	0·00	60·00	40·00	100·00

Consideration will now be given to the pattern of the teachers' rejection of aims as indicated by their assigning of the zero, meaning that they thought a statement 'should not be an aim of primary education'. Of the seventy-two aims, only eight were not rejected by anyone. These eight were:

read with understanding;
enjoyment in school work;
tolerance;
convey meaning clearly through speech;
acquire information other than by reading;
wide vocabulary;
write legibly;
general knowledge of local environment.

The remaining sixty-four aims were rejected by numbers of teachers ranging from one to 229. It should be remembered that some aims may well have been rejected not because teachers thought them undesirable but because they thought them unrealistic, in that they would be very difficult or impossible to achieve. An example of such an aim might be that the child should be able to play a musical instrument. Nevertheless, note should be taken of the aims which were rejected with some frequency. Five per cent of the sample was arbitrarily chosen to represent an appreciable minority. In no case did a majority of the sample reject an aim. Nine aims were rejected by more than 5% of the sample; these are given in Table 9.4.

Table 9.4   Appreciable percentages of the sample rejecting certain aims

Aim	% rejecting
Second language	15·14
Knowledge of world religions	10·18
Spiritual awareness	9·05
Behave in accordance with own religion	7·07
Sex education	6·48
Maintain lasting relationships	6·35
Behave in accordance with Christian religion	5·88
Form a considered opinion	5·88
Ordered subject knowledge	5·88

As might be expected, six of these nine refer to the currently fairly contentious issues of religion, sex education and second language. Neither is it surprising that, in the current climate of educational thought, ordered subject knowledge in, for example, history and geography should be rejected by an appreciable minority. The aim concerned with forming a considered opinion continued with the statement that the child should be prepared 'to act upon it even if this means rejecting conventional thought and behaviour', and it is probably this last phrase which made it a candidate for rejection by a fair number of primary school teachers. That 'the child should be able to maintain lasting relationships with a few close friends' should have been rejected by ninety-six teachers is perhaps more surprising, but it may well have been judged not to fall within the province of the primary school.

It will be noted that the incidence of rejections generally follows the rank order fairly closely. The less importance was given an aim by the sample as a whole, the more frequently was it also actually rejected. Thus, on the whole, the teachers who actually rejected aims were not so much at variance with the remaining teachers as holding the same kinds of opinion more strongly.

GROUPS OF AIMS

The data presented so far in this chapter can be taken only as a broad indication of general emphases. The teachers have been treated as one group, whereas evidence presented in earlier chapters has shown clearly that marked differences of opinion exist between them. It is necessary to be able to create a picture of each individual teacher's opinions about aims, and thus to see what kinds of groups of teachers hold similar opinions to one another. Because seventy-two is an unmanageably large number of aims to characterize a teacher by, the aims need to be grouped in some way. Originally the aims were grouped according to whether they referred to knowledge, skills or qualities and according to which aspect of the child's development they concerned (see p. 18). However, these need not necessarily be the ways in which teachers would group them. In order to find out how teachers would group them, it is possible to perform a statistical operation known as factor analysis showing up which aims the teacher consistently scored in a similar pattern, and thus suggesting that the teachers saw some similarity between those aims.

This analysis (Varimax solution, see Appendix E) showed up seven groups of aims. Each group, or factor, has been given a title which seems to describe its content. The factors are given in Table 9.5 (p. 66), and discussed below.

Twenty-three of the seventy-two aims had been thought to relate simply to the child's intellectual development. The teachers were much more discriminating than this, and the factor analysis revealed that they perceived these aims as falling into three clear-cut groups. Similarly, although two factors were clearly related to emotional/personal and social/moral development respectively, a number of aims thought to belong in these categories were distributed among other groupings. Only one factor, the spiritual/religious one, coincided almost exactly with a group as it had been conceived previously.

Most of the intellectual aims were distributed among three factors, revealing three quite different conceptions of the nature of education relevant to intellectual development. The existence of these different conceptions may, in part at least, account for the low importance given to intellectual development by some teachers, as noted in the last section. The first of these factors is almost wholly composed of rather formal basic skills. Two non-intellectual aims are associated with this factor: that the child should be generally obedient and that he should be industrious, persistent and conscientious. It is interesting that these two particular exemplifications of good, conformist behaviour should be associated with competence in the basic skills.

The second factor is a mixture of intellectual and emotional/personal aims, and this juxtaposition suggests that the latter were, in fact, conceived in an intellectual sense. For example, forming a considered opinion was originally thought of as an activity relating to the development of the individual as a whole person, but it may be inferred that the teachers saw this as a specifically intellectual activity. This whole group of aims seem to add up to a concern for the ability of the child to function independently and autonomously in the intellectual sphere. It is worthy of note that almost every aim with a connotation of independent activity on the part of the child appeared in this intellectual group; an inference may be drawn that, while independence of thought might be encouraged, personal and social behaviour is more generally required by teachers to be conformist.

The third conception of intellectual development, as revealed by the

Table 9.5 Seven factors identified from analysis of scores on 72 aims of primary education

Aim		Factor loading*
No.	Description	
	Factor I Basic skills (variance† 6·95%)	
29	Arithmetic—4 rules	−0·680
5	Correct spelling	−0·601
12	Read fluently and accurately	−0·561
26	Read with understanding	−0·558
8	Write legibly	−0·551
71	Modern maths	−0·511
4	Everyday maths	−0·466
42	Basic grammar	−0·465
55	Wide vocabulary	−0·454
17	Industrious, persistent and conscientious	−0·453
50	Listen with concentration and understanding	−0·429
18	Obedient	−0·427
56	Acquire information from written material	−0·425
34	Write clear and meaningful English	−0·421
21	Convey meaning clearly through speech	−0·417
	Factor II Intellectual autonomy (variance 6·93%)	
9	Make reasoned judgements and choices	−0·616
22	Form a considered opinion	−0·528
7	Individuality	−0·505
3	Acquire information other than by reading	−0·497
57	Plan independent work	−0·490
15	Observe	−0·478
65	Questioning attitude	−0·474
2	Understanding of how body works	−0·421
14	General knowledge	−0·415
69	Play a part in own development	−0·415
	Factor III Intellectual competence (variance 4·54%)	
35	Ordered subject knowledge	−0·580
36	Understanding of modern technology	−0·517
34	Write clear and meaningful English	−0·504
37	Critical and discriminating	−0·498
32	Speak in a clear and fluent manner	−0·460
42	Basic grammar	−0·405

* The measure of the correlation of each item with the factor. A perfect correlation would be 1·0. Any loading of over 0·4 indicates an acceptable degree of relationship.
† The amount of difference between teachers' opinions accounted for by the factor.

Table 9.5—*cont.*

Aim		Factor loading
No.	Description	
	Factor IV Personal (variance 5·88%)	
40	Self-confident	+0·571
47	Enthusiastic and eager	0·534
45	Adaptable and flexible	0·509
46	Personal appreciation of beauty	0·490
38	Control behaviour and emotions	0·474
58	Happy, cheerful and well balanced	0·460
66	Tolerance	0·443
44	Maintain lasting relationships	0·405
	Factor V Social/moral (variance 6·53%)	
25	Careful and respectful of property	+0·661
23	Principles of health, hygiene and safety	0·619
20	Behave appropriately	0·593
27	Kind and considerate	0·587
31	Know moral values	0·586
24	Acquire moral values	0·530
43	Courtesy and good manners	0·502
59	Deal with emergencies	0·463
18	Obedient	0·441
30	Good social mixer	0·432
	Factor VI Spiritual/religious (variance 4·37%)	
10	Spiritual awareness	+0·791
6	Knowledge of the Bible and Christian beliefs	0·782
67	Behave in accordance with Christian religion	0·756
19	Behave in accordance with own religion	0·638
	Factor VII Cultural (variance 6·77%)	
54	Techniques of some arts and crafts	+0·618
63	Play a variety of games	0·577
70	Listen to and enjoy a range of music	0·576
49	Play a musical instrument	0·530
72	Movement and gymnastic skills	0·526
16	Knowledge and skill for simple music-making	0·502
1	Communicate feelings through some art forms	0·498
51	General knowledge of local environment	0·481
60	Inventiveness and creativity	0·479
62	Simple science	0·469
53	Swim	0·455
68	Second language	0·424
46	Personal appreciation of beauty	0·409

component aims of factor III, may be summed up as referring to intellectual competence. (We are indebted to Douglas Hubbard, of the Sheffield Institute of Education, for this suggestion.) This seems to be a group of higher basic skills consisting of clear, meaningful and correct speech and writing, ordered knowledge both of the traditional subjects and of the modern world, and a critical and discriminating attitude.

The fourth factor clearly relates to personal development. Interestingly it includes aims which may be thought to be relevant to social development but which the teachers have seen to be related to the kind of person whom they hope to see emerging from the primary school. The child characterized by this factor is assured, happy, controlled and positive in his attitudes to others.

The social/moral factor (V) is clearly concerned with the polite, well-behaved, responsible child. It is interesting that the item requiring the child to 'know how to apply the basic principles of health, hygiene and safety' is seen in a specifically social sense.

There were five spiritual/religious aims and four were taken up to consti-tute factor VI. The one which does not appear refers to the child having some knowledge of the major world religions, and it would seem that this was not seen to be particularly relevent to religious development.

Finally, factor VII, which has been named 'cultural', is composed of a very mixed group of aims involving references to the arts, music, physical education, general knowledge of the local environment, science and a second language. That this miscellaneous group should find their way into a single factor, indicating that the teachers tended to respond to them in a similar way, does appear to bear out the impression gained from examining the rank order of aims, that teachers seem to distinguish all these areas from the basic skills core of primary education. They seem to regard them as a rather homogeneous group of enrichment, or perhaps peripheral, subjects. Clearly there is some kind of basic similarity in the teachers' minds between these essentially disparate areas and, in view of the placement of these items in the rank order, it may be a similarity in lack of importance.

GROUPS OF AIMS AND BIOGRAPHICAL VARIABLES

In order to characterize the opinions of each teacher and thence to discover the common factors between teachers holding similar opinions, the following procedure was adopted. First, the average score which each individual teacher gave to the aims within each factor was calculated. The range of average scores given to each factor was then divided into four equal parts. The whole sample of teachers was then divided into four groups on each factor, according to whether their average scores lay within the first, second, third or fourth quarter of the range. Thus, teachers in the first group were those who had given a very high average score to the aims within that factor and so on. For each factor the composition of each group of teachers was then examined to see if it included significant numbers of any particular sub-group of the sample. The composition of the groups was examined in terms of both biographical information and responses to other questions (those relating to the broad purposes of primary education and to the rating of aspects of development as most/least important). Table 9.6 (p. 70) shows the significant relationships between biographical variables and high scoring on each factor.

No sub-groups of the sample on biographical variables rated either the intellectual competence or the cultural factors significantly higher. The remaining five factors were significantly preferred, in thirty-six cases, by different sub-groups of the sample. All are shown in Table 9.6; the more interesting of these will be discussed below.

Significant emphasis tended to be placed upon the basic skills by the trained, non-graduate teachers who had not sought higher qualifications in education, who had longer teaching experience, and who had given long service to a particular school. These teachers are likely to represent the core of the primary teaching profession. Their younger, less experienced, more mobile colleagues tended to stress, in this intellectual connection, the development of independent thought. In this they were joined by just significant numbers of those who had had appreciable experience of employment other than teaching and those who had previously taught adults. Competence in the basic skills and independent thought are obviously not mutually exclusive; indeed, many of the former are a pre-requisite for the latter. Yet a distinction between them in the minds of teachers is clearly apparent from the separation of the aims into two factors and from the preference of different groups of teachers for each of them. It is particularly interesting that close acquaintance with work outside the primary school tended to be among the attributes of those who preferred intellectual autonomy to competence in the basic skills, while those with the alternative preference had longer primary school careers.

The older teachers with longer experience who were longer established in particular schools were those who together significantly preferred the personal, social/moral and spiritual/religious aims. There is some anomaly in relation to the personal factor, in that it was the younger teachers who had significantly rated emotional/personal development as one of the two most important aspects of development, while it was now the older teachers who were strongly inclined to prefer aims which can reasonably be supposed to relate to personal development. However, the younger teachers' conception of emotional/personal development is likely to be different from that defined by the aims grouped within this factor. These aims relate to confidence, happiness, control and positive attitudes to others. Given the younger teachers' preference for the intellectual autonomy factor, it may well be that their conception of personal development is something of a much more intellectual nature. Indeed, half of the ten aims within the intellectual autonomy group had been originally classified as emotional/personal. Aims within the social/moral factor

Table 9.6 Sub-groups of the sample scoring higher on each of 7 aims
factors significantly more often

	Factor	Sub-group	Signif. level
I	Basic skills	Longer in present school	0·001
		Married	0·001
		Certificated	0·001
		More experienced	0·01
		Without higher qualifications	0·05
		Previous lower junior experience	0·05
II	Intellectual autonomy	Less experienced	0·001
		Shorter time in present school	0·001
		Younger	0·01
		Experience other than teaching	0·05
		Teaching adults	0·05
III	Intellectual competence	(No significant relationships)	
IV	Personal	Older	0·001
		More experienced	0·001
		Longer in present school	0·001
		Higher positions	0·001
		Previous nursery experience	0·001
		Women	0·01
		Graduates	0·01
		Teaching younger children	0·01
		Higher qualifications	0·05
		Previous infant experience	0·05
		Special responsibility for maths	0·05
V	Social/moral	Older	0·001
		More experienced	0·001
		Longer in present school	0·001
		Previous lower junior experience	0·05
		Special responsibility for music	0·05
VI	Spiritual/ religious	Older	0·001
		More experienced	0·001
		Longer in present school	0·001
		Higher positions	0·001
		Previous infant experience	0·001
		Special responsibility for religious education	0·001
		Previous secondary experience	0·01
		Teaching younger children	0·01
		Special responsibility for music	0·01
VII	Cultural	(No significant relationships)	

were heavily biased towards the moral, and the older teachers' preference for this factor is consistent with their 'most important' rating of moral development. Similarly, their preference for the spiritual/religious factor had been foreshadowed by their earlier emphasis on this area of development.

As might well have been anticipated, teachers working with younger children tended to emphasize personal aims more often than teachers of older age groups, as did those who had previously taught younger children. Perhaps more surprising was the tendency of the teachers of younger children to emphasize spiritual/religious aims. It is interesting that it was those with previous experience of teaching lower juniors who significantly tended to stress the basic skills. It may be that this is the stage in the primary school at which growing competence in these skills is seen to be most necessary, thus influencing the teachers' assessment of important aims for the end of primary education.

Of the seven factors, the spiritual/religious approximates most closely to a specialism, and it was indeed significantly preferred by the specialist teachers of religious education. There may be several explanations but no obvious one for the emphasis placed by teachers of music on the social/moral and spiritual/religious factors and by teachers of maths on the personal one.

In summary, it seems that most of the highly significant differences of opinion were tied in with one group of related biographical variables. These were age, experience and length of service in the present school. The polarization was between the younger and the older, the less and the more experienced, and the mobile and the established. The data show quite compellingly that these polarized groups tend to give a high rating to rather different kinds of aims. The findings do not show that any groups rejected aims valued by other groups, but that they tended to consider them as less important. The older, more experienced, established teachers tended to put their emphases on competence in the basic skills, confidence, control, positive attitudes to others and good behaviour, with some consciously moral and religious basis. The younger, less experienced, mobile teachers tended instead to stress intellectual and personal independence.

GROUPS OF AIMS AND BROAD PURPOSES

High average scoring on each of the seven factors was compared with responses to the question asking for the sharing of five points between two broad purposes of primary education. Table 9.7 (p. 72) shows the results.

Preference for the intellectual competence factor was significantly related to neither purpose. Preference for the other six factors was, and in each case this was in the direction which might have been predicted. This clear-cut result underlines the sharp distinction between the two broad purposes and points to a real disparity in aims between teachers subscribing to each of these two conceptions of the basic purpose of primary education. Those who subscribed

Table 9.7   Significant relationships between preference for one of
2 broad purposes of primary education and emphasis
on 7 aims factors

	Factor	Significance level	
		Societal purpose: equipping child with skills and attitudes appropriate to society	Individual purpose: devin. of child's individuality and independence
I	Basic skills	0·001	—
II	Intellectual autonomy	—	0·001
III	Intellectual competence	—	—
IV	Personal	—	0·001
V	Social/moral	0·001	—
VI	Spiritual/ religious	0·001	—
VII	Cultural	—	0·01

to the view that the major purpose of primary education is to equip the child, both practically and socially, to fit into society strongly tended to emphasize aims relating to the basic skills, to the social/moral and to the spiritual/religious areas. By contrast, those who believed that primary education is most concerned with the development of individuality and independence were markedly inclined to emphasize aims in the intellectual autonomy, personal and cultural areas.

GROUPS OF AIMS AND ASPECTS OF DEVELOPMENT

Lastly, the data were explored for significant relationships between emphasis on aims within each of the seven factors and the rating of the seven aspects of development as most and least important respectively. Table 9.8 shows the significant relationships.

The first comment which might be made upon these results concerns the high frequency of coincidence between the groups of aims to which teachers subscribed and the aspects of development which they rated as most important. This evidence suggests, as did that relating factors to broad purposes of education, that there is a close and logical connection between teachers' basic conceptions of the nature of primary education and the aims which they support. Those who emphasized aims within the basic skills and intellectual competence groups tended to rate intellectual and moral development as the two most important aspects of the child's development. Emphasis on social/moral and spiritual/religious aims was associated with selecting moral and spiritual/religious development as the most important aspects. Those who

Table 9.8   Significant relationships between emphasis on 7 aims factors and support for 7 aspects of development

	Factor	Most important aspects	Signif. level	Least important aspects	Signif. level
I	Basic skills	Intellectual Moral	0·001 0·01	Aesthetic Emotional/ personal	0·001 0·001
II	Intellectual autonomy	Emotional/ personal	 0·001	Physical Spiritual/ religious	0·001 0·05
III	Intellectual competence	Intellectual Moral	0·05 0·05	Social	0·001
IV	Personal	Aesthetic Emotional/ personal	0·001 0·001	Intellectual Physical	0·001 0·001
V	Social/moral	Moral Social Spiritual/ religious	0·001 0·05 0·001	Aesthetic Emotional/ personal Intellectual	0·001 0·01 0·001
VI	Spiritual/ religious	Moral Spiritual/ religious	0·001 0·001	Aesthetic Emotional/ personal Intellectual Physical Social	0·001 0·001 0·01 0·001 0·001
VII	Cultural	Aesthetic Emotional/ personal Physical	0·001 0·01 0·01	Moral Social Spiritual/ religious	0·01 0·05 0·01

rated the social/moral aims highly also tended to rate social development as most important. Those most highly concerned with personal, intellectual autonomy and cultural groups of aims all rated emotional/personal development as most important. The teachers most concerned with personal aims added aesthetic development as another most important aspect, and the teachers who subscribed to the cultural aims added both aesthetic and physical development to their assessment of what was most important.

Perhaps one of the most interesting features of this evidence is the association between stress on moral development and a high rating of basic skills aims, and the association between stress on emotional/personal development and a high rating of intellectual autonomy aims. That there were different conceptions of the nature of the education of the intellect was clear from the throwing up of three different groups of 'intellectual' aims by the factor analysis. What is now apparent is that subscribing to each of these is part of a much wider concept of the nature of education. This tends to confirm the earlier evidence, which demonstrated the relationship between preferences for different kinds of intellectual aims and different views of the basic purpose of primary education.

Of interest, too, is the clear association between aesthetic and personal education. Teachers who emphasized aims within the personal factor tended to select aesthetic development as one of the two most important aspects. Those who emphasized aims within the cultural area, which was largely concerned with the arts, stressed emotional/personal development as most important. This association may suggest a fairly general view of the arts as a route to personal development.

The highly significant relationships between high ratings of aims within different factors and choice of different aspects of development as most important throw some light upon the meaning ascribed by the teachers to the labels given to the aspects of development. Those who stressed basic skills and intellectual competence aims rated intellectual development as most important. Those who stressed intellectual autonomy aims did not. This may suggest that intellectual development may generally be given a rather formal, narrow interpretation, and may explain to some extent why little over half the sample thought that intellectual development was one of the two most important aspects.

An anomaly occurred in relation to emotional/personal development. Younger teachers rated it as most important significantly more often than older teachers. However, older teachers rated aims within the personal factor significantly higher than did younger teachers. This might suggest that the personal factor and the label 'emotional/personal development' had two different meanings. Yet those who gave a high rating to aims within the personal factor also rated the emotional/personal development as most important significantly more often. An explanation of this curious result is that there were, in fact, two age groups who rated emotional/personal development as most important, the younger group predominating overall. The older of these two groups went on to rate highly the aims within the personal factor and the younger to rate highly the aims within the intellectual autonomy factor. This would suggest that the two age groups were actually each making a different interpretation of the label 'emotional/personal development'.

Understanding of the meaning of subscription to particular groups of aims can be further increased by examining the aspects of development which these teachers tended to reject as of least importance. Perhaps most striking were those high on the spiritual/religious aims, who significantly more often rated every aspect other than spiritual/religious and moral development as of least importance. Teachers high on basic skills and social/moral aims joined in their rejection of emotional/personal and aesthetic development. Those high on cultural aims rejected social, moral and spiritual/religious development as of least importance. The teachers favouring intellectual autonomy rejected physical and spiritual/religious development, and those high on personal aims rated physical and intellectual development as of least importance.

Overall, with some discrepancies, there appears to have been a kind of antithesis between the basic skills, social/moral and spiritual/religious aims, on the one hand, and intellectual autonomy, personal and cultural aims on the other. This is an exact parallel to the way in which these aims were divided in relation to each of the two broad purposes of primary education.

10 School variables

INTRODUCTION

Data, taken from the head teachers' questionnaire, on the environment, type and organization of the school were compared with the responses to two sections of the teachers' questionnaire. Thus, it was possible to see whether working in any particular type of school was apparently related to opinions about the broad purposes of primary education, most and least important aspects of development and the teacher's role. Unfortunately, it was not possible in the available time to compare school variables with opinions about the seventy-two aims.

The most interesting feature of this area of the data is the lack of much strong relationship between the characteristics of schools and the opinions of teachers working within them.

ENVIRONMENT, SCHOOL ORGANIZATION AND TEACHERS' OPINIONS

The relationships between environmental and organizational variables and teachers' opinions are shown in Table 10.1.

Schools were classified (see p. 26) according to whether they were situated in counties or in county boroughs, the latter group being divided into three population size ranges. There were only two indications that the kind of area, in this sense, had any connection with teachers' opinions. Those working in county areas, which will tend to be rather more rural, significantly more often thought that intellectual development was one of the two most important aspects. At a just significant level they were joined in this by teachers in all-rural, as opposed to urban or suburban areas. Taken together, there is some suggestion here that rural teachers are more commonly concerned with intellectual development than teachers in towns and cities. Teachers in county areas were distinguished, too, by their slightly more usual preference for a progressive teaching role. On the whole, rural primary schools tend to be smaller; size, rather than geographical situation, may be the link with preferences for more informal, progressive teaching approaches. Indeed, it was in relation to teaching role that size of school, measured by numbers of

Table 10.1 Significant relationships between school environmental and organizational variables and teachers' opinions

School variable	Opinions	Signif. level
County area	Stress intellectual development	0·01
	Agree with progressive role	0·05
Rural area	Stress intellectual development	0·05
Middle class	Stress intellectual development	0·01
	Stress spiritual/religious development	0·01
Working class	Stress social development	0·01
Non-denominational	Stress aesthetic development	0·05
Denominational	Stress spiritual/religious development	0·001
	Agree with traditional role	0·05
	Agree with most traditional role	0·05
Infant	Agree with progressive role	0·001
	Agree with most progressive role	0·001
	Adopt progressive role personally	0·001
Junior	Stress moral development	0·001
	Agree with traditional role	0·05
With nursery classes	Agree with moderate role	0·05
Fewer staff	Stress aesthetic development	0·05
	Agree with progressive role	0·05
	Adopt progressive role personally	0·05
Fewer children	Agree with most traditional role	0·05
Head responsible for class	Agree with most traditional role	0·05

teachers, seemed most relevant to teachers' opinions. Teachers working as members of a smaller staff preferred a progressive teaching role just significantly more often than members of a larger staff. Equally, they tended more often to consider the descriptions of more progressive approaches as closest to their own approach. An inexplicable contradiction to this result is that teachers in schools with fewer children on roll tended to agree more often with the most traditional role; this relationship was again just significant. It would seem that these just significant relationships are covering up some other relevant factor, not detected by the questionnaire. The only other indication of the relevance of staff size was the slight tendency of members of smaller staffs to rate aesthetic development as of most importance. There have been repeated indications throughout the data of the association between preference for informal teaching approaches and stress on aesthetic development, and both seemed to be a little more common amongst smaller teaching groups.

School age range was one of the characteristics most significantly related to teachers' opinions, although much less often than might well have been expected. At the highest level of significance, teachers in infant schools, more often than teachers in junior schools, agreed with progressive approaches to teaching and chose one or other of the progressive descriptions as closest to their own approach. Teachers in junior schools just significantly preferred a traditional role. In short, there were strong indications that teachers in infant schools were emphatic in their preference for progressive approaches to teaching and teachers in junior schools just tended to prefer a more traditional approach. The junior school teachers distinguished themselves from infant teachers in one other respect. To a highly significant extent they more often selected moral development as one of the two most important aspects. Again, this association between the tendency to be more formal in approach and the tendency to stress moral development has shown up consistently throughout the data.

One curious result was the tendency for teachers in schools which had a nursery class or classes to prefer a moderate teaching role. This places teachers in schools with nursery classes between the very progressive infant schools and the more traditional junior schools. The indication is slight, but it may be worth considering whether teachers regard infant children who have been in the school from the age of three as 'older' than they regard children who have only been in school from the age of five. This hypothesis contains the assumption that a teacher's decision about an appropriate role depends to some degree on the age of the children being taught. This notion, however, has no support from any other aspect of the data.

Not surprisingly, teachers in church schools considered spiritual/religious development to be one of the two most important aspects very significantly more often than did other teachers. Other than this, teachers in these schools showed a slightly greater preference than their non-denominational colleagues for traditional and most traditional teaching roles. Teachers in non-denominational schools were distinguished only, and at a low level of significance, by the importance they attached to aesthetic development. Here again is the apparent opposition between concern for aesthetic development and formality.

The socio-economic background of the children with whom teachers were working appeared to have little relationship to differences in teachers' opinions. Teachers of more middle class children tended to select intellectual and spiritual/religious development as the two most important aspects of development. At the same level of significance, teachers of more working class children tended to consider that social development was most important. These were the only differences between teachers in different socio-economic areas. The stress placed by teachers of middle class children on spiritual/ religious development is more difficult to interpret, but their concern with intellectual development, and that of the teachers of working class children with social development, is very much what might be expected.

Only one other variable was related to teachers' opinions, and that at a low level of significance. Teachers in schools in which the head had full-time or nearly full-time responsibility for a class were marginally more often in favour of a very traditional teaching role. The likely connection is that such schools tend to be small, and one piece of earlier evidence indicated a tendency of teachers in smaller schools to be more traditional. Nonetheless, the evidence for the relationship between size of school and tendency towards traditional attitudes on the part of the staff is conflicting and demands further examination.

The parents' attitude to the school and the adequacy of the schools' building and equipment—both as judged by the head teacher—appeared to bear no relation to teachers' opinions. Neither did the size of classes within schools. In summary, the lack of relationship between characteristics of the school and teachers' opinions, at least on this evidence, is striking and perhaps unexpected. The only results to reach the highest level of significance are, for the most part, those which could have been predicted with confidence. Teachers in infant schools showed a strong tendency to prefer progressive teaching roles; teachers in church schools stressed spiritual/religious development significantly more than other teachers and, less predictably, teachers in junior schools markedly tended to emphasize moral development.

ORGANIZATIONAL CHOICES AND TEACHERS' OPINIONS

The examination now turns to the relationships between organizational choices, presumably made for the most part by the head teacher, and the opinions of teachers. Table 10.2 (p. 80) shows the significant relationships between schools characterized by particular organizational choices and the opinions of teachers within them.

In schools in which the head teacher planned the work of individual classes to a greater extent, the staff were very significantly more likely to agree with the most traditional teaching role. There is a hint worthy of exploration here, although this can only be extremely tentative, that where heads exert more control over teachers, they in their turn choose to exert more control over children. Equally, in schools where there were no formal meetings between the head and the whole staff, teachers were significantly more likely to opt for a traditional role. Where regular formal staff meetings were held, teachers were more likely to choose more progressive roles. Again, it might be hypothesized that where head–staff relations may be more democratic, as evidenced by the holding of joint meetings, then teachers choose to adopt a more democratic role with children. This may be a very complex relationship, with a number of possible interpretations. More progressive teachers may seek schools in which they will be given opportunities to participate in planning. A

Table 10.2   Significant relationships between organizational choices and
teachers' opinions

Organizational choice	Opinions	Signif. level
Head plans class work	Agree with most traditional role	0·001
Staff meetings	Adopt progressive role personally	0·05
No staff meetings	Agree with traditional role	0·001
	Agree with most traditional role	0·001
Vertical grouping	Agree with progressive role	0·01
	Adopt progressive role personally	0·01
No vertical grouping	Stress spiritual/religious development	0·05
Team teaching	Agree with most progressive role	0·01
	Agree with progressive role	0·001
	Agree with moderate role	0·05
	Adopt progressive role personally	0·001
No team teaching	Agree with traditional role	0·05
	Agree with most traditional role	0·01
Unstreamed	Stress individ. purpose of prim. educ.	0·05
	Emotional/personal aspect of development most important	0·001
	Moral aspect of devc lt. least important	0·05
	Spiritual/religious aspect of development least important	0·01
	Disagree with traditional role	0·01
	Disagree with most traditional role	0·01
	Adopt progressive role personally	0·05
Streamed	Stress societal purpose of prim. educ.	0·01
	Aesthetic aspect of development least important	0·01
	Emotional/personal aspect of development least important	0·01
	Moral aspect of development most important	0·01
	Disagree with most progressive role	0·001
	Disagree with progressive role	0·001
	Agree with traditional role	0·001
	Agree with most traditional role	0·001
	Adopt traditional role personally	0·001

more progressive mode of teaching on the part of the majority of staff in a
school may make joint consultation with the head more necessary. Whatever
underlies the relationship, the indication arising from this evidence that the
style of head–staff consultation, and the involvement of teachers in planning,

has some association with teachers' attitudes towards their role is likely to have important implications for head teachers' perceptions of their own role.

A slight relationship was found between the practice of vertical grouping and preference for more progressive roles. This is hardly surprising since vertical grouping obviates formal lessons and is, in part, based on a concept of stage rather than age, as the criterion of learning progress. Absence of vertical grouping showed a slight relationship with emphasis on spiritual/ religious development. Earlier data have generally shown an emphasis on spiritual/religious development to be associated with more formal and traditional opinions, and if a change to vertical grouping is an indication of more informal and progressive approaches, then this finding is consistent.

The practice of team teaching appears to be strongly related to teachers' role preferences. Teachers in team teaching situations agreed significantly more often than teachers in ordinary class situations with the most progressive, progressive and moderate roles; they also thought very significantly more often that the progressive role descriptions were closest to their own approach to teaching. Non-team teaching teachers significantly more often agreed with more traditional roles. It may be simply that teachers who prefer a more progressive role are more ready to experiment with a quite new teaching concept. There may be an interesting link back to the indications arising from the data on the style of head–staff consultation. It may be that teachers who prefer, or are encouraged, to work more co-operatively with their colleagues are able or willing to work more co-operatively with children. Once again, it is possible that the style of relationships among staff may have important implications for their attitudes towards children and teaching. This is not much beyond the stage of conjecture but it is consistent with the social psychological literature covering the effects of authoritarian leadership on group relationships.

Of all the organizational variables, streaming or non-streaming appeared to be by far the most important in differentiating teachers' opinions. In keeping with the findings of the National Foundation for Educational Research [1] teachers in streamed schools tended to show marked preference for more traditional teaching roles. At the highest level of significance they more often disagreed with progressive roles, agreed with traditional roles and thought one or other of the traditional role descriptions nearest to their own approaches. To a lower level of significance, teachers in unstreamed schools disagreed with traditional roles and chose a progressive role as nearest to their own. Teaching in a streamed or an unstreamed school was the only variable associated with the broad purposes of primary education. As might be expected, teachers in streamed schools tended to prefer the socially oriented concept of educational purposes, and teachers in unstreamed schools the individually oriented purpose.

Teachers in streamed schools, furthermore, tended to rate the moral aspect of development as of most importance and aesthetic and emotional/personal development as of least importance. On the other hand, teachers in un-streamed schools tended, at the highest level of significance, to rate emotional/personal development as most important and, at a lower level, to rate moral development as least important. Teachers in streamed schools thus tend generally to conform to the more formal and traditional patterns, as evidenced by earlier data.

As remarked at the beginning of this chapter, it is perhaps surprising that differences in teachers' opinions are not more frequently related to differences in school type, environment and organization. The most important school variables appear to be school type (infant or junior) and the existence or otherwise of streaming. The differences in opinion generally most frequently related to school variables are concerned with teaching role. Although these differences are highly predictable, it is useful confirmation to see the repeated preference for progressive roles by teachers in schools which have engaged in recent innovation in the shape of de-streaming, vertical grouping and team teaching. Perhaps the most interesting feature of the data is the indication, albeit slight, of some relationship between the organizational style of staff relationships and attitudes towards teaching approaches.

Reference

1   'The organisation of junior schools and effects of streaming: National Foundation for Educational Research: a preliminary report'. In Central Advisory Council for Education (England), *Children and their Primary Schools* [Plowden Report], vol. 2, *Research and Surveys*. HMSO, 1967, Appendix 11.

11 Summary and conclusions

The purpose of this main study has been to discover what primary school teachers think are the aims of primary education, and which are more or less important. It was expected that teachers would differ from one another in their opinions. In order to explore what factors might be associated with these differences, questions were asked about the environment and organizations of the schools, the teachers' biography, and their opinions about the fundamental purposes of primary education, the importance of various aspects of development, and their own role.

It must be remembered that what the evidence has shown are trends, tendencies and indications. There are many teachers who fit no pattern and conform to no particular type. They hold independent opinions, blending different points of view. That having been said, there are still very marked differences of opinion amongst this representative sample of teachers, suggesting that distinctively different schools of thought about educational aims and practice do exist within the profession. For the purposes of this summary, only relationships significantly beyond the 0·001 level will be discussed. These are the relationships which are sufficiently marked to have a less than one in a thousand probability of having occurred by chance, and they would be the priority targets for any further investigation.

Twelve questions were asked about the teachers' personal background. These dealt with sex, age, marital status, employment other than teaching, initial and subsequent qualifications, length of teaching experience, length of service in the present school, full-time or part-time status, position in school, special responsibilities, age range taught and age ranges previously taught.

The teachers were grouped according to their responses on twenty-one questionnaire variables. The variables were the broad purpose of primary education, seven aspects of development, seven groups of aims, five teachers' roles and the choice of personal role. These groups were explored for any significant characteristics in their biographical composition.

There were very few differences of opinion between men and women teachers, and only one which reached the highest level of significance. This one difference concerned the marked preference of women for a progressive teaching role. At lower levels of significance, women preferred both very progressive and moderate roles. In short, there are strong indications that women are generally less traditional than men in their approaches to teaching. This might be thought to be related to the almost exclusive incidence of women as opposed to men teachers in infant schools, where more informal approaches to teaching are of much longer standing than in junior schools. However, assuming that every infant teacher in the sample was a woman, which would be a slight over-estimate, there were still very nearly as many women junior as women infant teachers (567 compared with 573) in the sample. It would seem that this greater tendency to informality and progressivism is likely to be a characteristic of women, irrespective of the age group they teach.

Married teachers were twice significantly distinguished from single teachers in their opinions. They tended to give markedly more emphasis to the basic skills group of aims and showed a widespread preference for a traditional teaching role. Filling out this picture, although to a less marked extent, they also tended to consider intellectual development as one of the two most important aspects and, in direct opposition to their unmarried colleagues, emotional/personal development as one of the least important. Overall, married teachers tended to be more often formal and traditional in their opinions than the single teacher. Married teachers would have tended to be at least a little older than the single. Age has proved to be a most important variable in distinguishing teachers' opinions. Perhaps more important in this connection, however, is the likelihood that many of the married teachers were also parents. It is an interesting possibility that parenthood may change crucially teachers' opinions about desirable purposes and methods in education. It could be hypothesized, on the basis of this evidence, that becoming a parent may make teachers more aware of the educative potentialities of the home and thus that the role of the school in education can, or should, be more restricted to functional activities in the cognitive realm.

Some indications have occurred throughout the data of more rejection of formality on the part of graduate, as opposed to certificated, teachers. This was perhaps epitomized in two results which reached the highest level of significance. Graduate teachers tended significantly more often to give a lower rating to the basic skills group of aims, which the certificated teachers tended to emphasize strongly. Alongside this, the graduates much more often disagreed with a very traditional mode of teaching. The more highly educated teachers thus showed some tendency to be less formal and narrow in their conception of educational aims and methods. Nevertheless, it should be remarked that the aims grouped within what has been called the basic skills factor concern competence in a number of tools essential to success in the present education system. It is interesting that those teachers who had enjoyed

greater formal success in the education system tended to be rather less concerned with transmitting competence in those areas than were the certificated
teachers. However, these indications should be regarded with caution, since
graduates formed a very small minority of the sample and other factors may
have been at work; for example, it may have been that the graduates were also
very largely young teachers.

The small number of teachers with higher degrees, diplomas, etc. in
education tended to follow a similar pattern. At a lower level of significance,
they tended to put less emphasis on the basic skills. To a highly significant
extent they agreed with a progressive mode of teaching and indicated that they
adopted a progressive role in their own teaching and disfavoured traditional
roles. As pointed out earlier, this is particularly interesting since teachers
taking advanced courses tend to be older and more experienced and are thus
somewhat at variance with their contemporaries. Whether these opinions are
cause or effect of undertaking advanced courses in education is unanswerable
at this point. However, in the light of the James[1] proposals for increased
provision of academic courses for practising teachers, this indication is well
worth further exploration.

It would not have been surprising if status had been a variable which
distinguished teachers in their opinions. Opinions about education might
reasonably be expected to be different among those who seek and secure
promotion and those who do not. Or, again, it might be expected that those
in higher positions might have a different perspective about education, since
their responsibilities widen with each promotion beyond one particular group
of children. However, of the twenty-one possibilities for differences of
opinion, position in school distinguished the sample of teachers on only eight
occasions. Of these, only three were at the highest level of significance. Class
teachers tended, just significantly, to emphasize the individualistic concept
of the broad purposes of primary education more than did their senior
colleagues. Senior staff tended to prefer the moderate teaching role. Otherwise,
the differences between junior and senior teachers were all concerned with the
broad area of personal and social education; there were no differences in
relation to aims in the academic sphere of education. In line with their
preference for the individually oriented purpose of education, the class
teachers tended to stress emotional/personal and social development. Their
senior colleagues, by contrast, stressed moral development. However, the
teachers in higher positions stressed the personal group of aims much more
than the class teachers, and at the highest level of significance. These were the
aims concerned with self-confidence, self-control and positive attitudes to
school and to social relationships. Most interesting is that the senior teachers
emerged as generally far more concerned with spiritual/religious development
and placed more emphasis on the spiritual/religious group of aims. This is an
area markedly disfavoured on the whole by the class teachers. In the present

climate of uncertainty about religious education, it appears very much as if the fort may be being held by the senior teachers. It is clear from the data that older, more experienced teachers generally tended to stress spiritual/ religious development as a most important aspect of primary education. That senior teachers in particular did so may simply reflect their organizational, obligatory concern with this area. There is an ambiguity about this area of the data since, in respect of the broad purposes and emotional/personal development, the head teachers reversed the trend and held opinions similar to those of the class teachers. As there may be special reasons for the major area of difference between teachers of different status, i.e. the traditional responsibility of senior teachers for religious education, position seems to have limited bearing on teachers' opinions.

It might well have been expected that the age ranges which teachers current- ly and had previously taught would differentiate them in their opinions about aims and methods. In the event, this appeared to be almost always irrelevant. At the lowest level of significance, teachers of particular age groups were rarely distinguished in their opinions, and only twice at the highest level of significance. Teachers with previous nursery experience stressed the personal group of aims and those with previous infant experience stressed the spiritual/ religious group of aims. The nursery teachers' view is completely consistent with what is now known about the opinions of nursery teachers generally with regard to the aims of nursery education.[2] The infant teachers' concern with spiritual/religious aims, which is significantly greater than the concern of the teachers of any other age group, does not seem to be amenable to any obvious explanation.

Teachers' specialisms, in the shape of subjects for which they take responsi- bility with more than one class of children, were in only one case significantly related to aims to which they gave preference. The specialist teachers of religious education strongly emphasized the spiritual/religious group of aims. This again appears to be a special case. It is interesting that, otherwise, special interest in a subject appears not to give rise to an emphasis on aims related to that subject. This certainly supports the traditional picture of the primary teacher as a general practitioner, despite the organizational move towards some specialization.

In respect of no less than two-thirds of these opinion variables, the sample was differentiated on the dimensions of age, length of teaching experience and length of service in the present school. In most cases, differences showed on all three dimensions together and always in the same direction, i.e. older, more experienced, more established teachers were aligned in opposition to the younger, less experienced, less established ones. This conjunction appears to be the outstanding dimension along which opinions differed, and was im- mensely more important than sex, marital status, training, qualifications position and age groups currently and previously taught.

The older, more experienced, more established teachers strongly preferred a socially oriented concept of education concerned with equipping the child, both personally and practically, to fit into society; they emphasized moral and spiritual/religious development as the two aspects most important in primary education; they markedly preferred traditional and very traditional teaching roles and emphasized aims related to the personal, social/moral and spiritual/religious areas. The younger, less experienced, less established teachers, while still tending on the whole to give more weight to the socially oriented purpose of education, were inclined to give much more room to the individually oriented purpose than their older colleagues; they stressed emotional/personal development as a most important aspect and strongly favoured a progressive teaching role. While by no means every teacher fitted this pattern, the differences were significant at the highest level. The longer established teachers strongly favoured the basic skills group of aims, while the less established and the less experienced favoured the intellectual autonomy aims.

In most cases the changes of opinion occurred regularly with increased age, longer experience and longer service in the present school. There were no very marked points at which opinions changed. However, there was some slight indication that the change of preference from a more progressive to a more traditional teaching role tended to occur as early as around the end of the probationary year. In respect of length of service in the present school, there was a large mobile element in the sample. Of the approximately three-quarters of the sample with more than three years' experience, something of the order of 45% had spent less than three years in their present school. Examining the sample by lengths of service in the present school reveals that in almost every case the largest differences in opinion tended to be between those who had served for more than three years in the school and those who had served for less. The 500 or so teachers who had changed school within the previous three years will by no means necessarily have been the youngest or the least experienced. Yet there is some indication here that they tend to retain the outlook of the newer entrants to the profession. It is clear that there may possibly be some important connection between a teacher's mobility and his opinions about educational aims and methods. This certainly merits further exploration.

It must be said again that many teachers do not fit the pattern outlined above, but that there is a pattern is clear from this evidence. The pattern, or the dimension around which all the differences seem to cohere, appears to be one of control. One end of the dimension, which tends to be more favoured by the older, more experienced teachers, is that in which the teacher has control of what shall be learned, when and how. Closely associated with this is the teacher's concern that the child shall be controlled by adherence to established moral values and religious conviction. The other end of the dimension, which tends to be favoured by the younger and less experienced teachers, is that in which much more control is put into the hands of the child in regard to what he learns, when and how. There is a concern to develop autonomy, both intellectually and personally.

That patterns of opinion tended to be so repetitively associated with age, experience and length of service in a particular school may partly explain why opinions showed little relationship with different environmental and organizational features of schools. Generally, school staffs are probably composed of teachers of different ages and different lengths of experience, who have served in the particular school for different lengths of time. This is likely to mean that different opinion patterns will exist among each staff group. The only opinions which tended to unite some staff groups related to progressive roles (preferred by infant school teachers), moral development (stressed by junior school teachers) and spiritual/religious development (stressed by teachers in church schools).

More strongly marked associations emerged between opinions and the organizational choices which had been made within schools. These opinions related almost exclusively to the teacher's role. Specifically, those in team teaching situations widely preferred a progressive role. More emphatically still, teachers in ability streamed schools expressed their disagreement with progressive roles and their preference for traditional roles. The most far-reaching implications may stem from the last indication in this area. This concerned the significant tendency of teachers in schools in which the head took a large responsibility for planning work for individual classes, and in which no staff meetings were held, to prefer very traditional roles. There may, of course, be a number of possible explanations for this finding. However, that a low level of formal participation by teachers in planning may give rise to a more controlled, teacher-directed style of teaching is a reasonable hypothesis and worth further exploration.

The two descriptions of different broad purposes of primary education were very simple characterizations. Both raise several questions of meaning and definition. They were written as paragraphs in order to convey an overall picture or essence. The teachers could only respond to them globally—in other words, to the essence of each. The ways in which teachers answered this question could only show very broadly the emphasis of their stand in relation to the whole nature of education. The two paragraphs characterized the nature of education, on the one hand, as a social process by means of which children are brought to function effectively in, and subscribe to, the values of the society as it is seen by the teacher; on the other hand, as an individualized process, concerned with enabling the child to be independent through the development of his personal capacities and his own attitudes. The teachers were required to show only which of these they emphasized more than the other. The meaning and the implications of emphasizing either of these ideas more than the other can be filled out by examining how this related to responses to other questions.

The societal and the individualistic patterns take on a great deal of detail when the aims to which these teachers primarily subscribed are examined. These aims are the means by which the teachers presumably see their basic purposes being achieved.

Looking first at the intellectual sphere, there is a strongly marked difference in the kinds of children the societal and the individualistic teachers hope to see emerging from their primary schools. There is a strong 'three Rs' flavour to the aspirations of the societal teachers. They most want children to read fluently, accurately and with understanding. They want them to write clear and meaningful, grammatical, correctly spelt English in legible handwriting. They want children to be able to do arithmetical computations and to cope with the mathematics of everyday situations. Beyond this basic level, they want children to be able to convey meaning clearly and accurately through speech with the use of a wide vocabulary, to know how to listen with concentration and understanding, to extract information from written material, and to think and solve problems mathematically. Within this same group of aims comes the desire for children to be obedient, industrious, persistent and conscientious. Here are the skills and qualities by means of which the societal teachers hope children will be able to join the adult society effectively and harmoniously.

In sharp contrast are the major aims of the individualistic teachers. Revealingly, the highest loadings within their chosen intellectual group of aims were upon the children making reasoned judgements and choices and forming a considered opinion. Here immediately is the notion of children using their minds in their own way, completely in line with these teachers' basic purpose of enabling children to develop their own attitudes towards society and their own chosen way of life. Continuing in this vein of autonomy for the child intellectually, the teachers want children to be able to observe, to have a questioning attitude, to know how to acquire information other than by reading—by asking questions, by experimenting and so on—and to have a wide general knowledge. Related to this area but on a wider scale, these teachers want children to be able to plan independent work, organize their own time, to play a part in their own development by recognizing their own strengths and limitations and setting their own goals, and of course to be individuals, developing in their own way. This group of aims much expands understanding of the autonomous role which the individualistic teachers think children should be enabled to take eventually in society.

In the other groups of aims which societal and individualistic teachers tend to stress to very different extents, there is the same kind of opposition, as was foreshadowed by their choices of different aspects of development to emphasize, simple as that question was. In respect of the kind of people that teachers hope primary education will help children to become, the societal stress conformity to accepted standards and the individualistic teachers concern themselves still with autonomy and a distinctively individual development.

The societal teachers want children to know the moral values shared by the majority of the society and to be beginning to acquire values on which to base their own behaviour. More than this, they want them to know the rules of acceptable social conduct; they think they should be courteous and well mannered, know how to behave appropriately in a variety of social situations, be careful and respectful of property and obedient. In this area, too, they think children should know how to apply the basic principles of health, hygiene and safety and how to deal with emergencies. On a more informal level, they want them to be good social mixers, who are both kind and considerate. The societal teachers also want a specifically religious basis to the good behaviour outlined above; they think children should have some knowledge of the Bible and of Christian beliefs and should behave in accordance with a religion. They hope, too, that children will be developing awareness of the spiritual aspects of prayer and worship.

In quite marked contrast with this wish for the child to conform to external accepted standards, the individualistic teachers want, above all, that children should feel self-confident and personally adequate. They want them to be happy, cheerful and well balanced, enthusiastic and eager, adaptable and flexible. They want them to feel able to cope with themselves and their environment. Socially, they want children to be tolerant, respecting and appreciating others and able to maintain lasting relationships. Here again is the emphasis on autonomy; aspirations for children being for their personal sense of assurance and positive approach to others.

Lastly, the individualistic teachers stressed a group of aims which were notably unpopular with many teachers. They hope for children to appreciate, enjoy, and participate creatively and skilfully in the arts, music and physical activities. They also want children to develop some understanding of simple scientific concepts and procedures, to have knowledge of their local environment and some early competence in a second language. In this last area, the individualistic teachers betoken a very much wider concept of the aims of primary education, extending their scope much beyond the central academic core of the societal teachers.

Consistent with their very different views of the aims of primary education, the societal and individualistic teachers see the process of teaching quite differently. The societal teachers see their task as deciding upon what children are to learn and closely directing the course of that learning. The individualistic teachers see teaching as a much more co-operative venture with children, who should have a measure of choice in what they learn and a much more active part in learning it.

The material presented above raises many questions. Since the purpose of this whole project was to examine and open up the question of what primary teachers are thinking about aims, and not to try to establish a set of ideal aims, it is to be hoped that these questions will be widely debated and new formulations made. Perhaps the point at which such re-thinking should begin is the apparent tendency for these two patterns of opinion to be opposed. What they appear to show is not an evolution of thought in education, but the reaction of one tradition against another. The individualistic pattern seems not so much to have developed from and built upon the societal one as to have relegated it to a place of significantly less importance. It is to be hoped that a basis for thinking has been provided in this report and some tools to do it with; it is a matter of urgency that each individual teacher, aware of the possibilities and conflicts, re-thinks his own aims of primary education.

References

1   Department of Education and Science. *Teacher Education and Training* [James Report]. HMSO, 1972.
2   P. H. Taylor, G. Exon, B. Holley. *A Study of Nursery Education* (Schools Council Working Paper 41). Evans/Methuen Educational, 1972.

Part two

Related exploratory studies

Opinions of tutors in colleges of education

12 Introduction

More than 95% of all primary school teachers are professionally educated and trained by tutors in colleges of education. Yet recent studies[1] have shown fairly consistently that tutors and teachers differ from one another in opinions about education in important respects. Underlining this, the studies have shown marked tendencies for students in training to become more similar in opinion to tutors and then, having started teaching, to move rapidly nearer to teachers in opinion. This has been attributed to the change of reference group from tutors to teachers and to the exigencies of teaching. The essence of the difference between tutors and teachers seems to be a greater liberalism, child-centredness and general progressivism among tutors.

The kinds of aim to which people subscribe are clearly reflective of their general educational opinions and attitudes. Liberal/conservative, child-centred/teacher-centred, progressive/traditional dimensions showed up clearly in the differences of opinion among primary teachers on the aims questionnaire used in the primary school investigation.

It was decided that it would be of considerable interest to parallel the survey of teachers' opinions of aims with one of tutors' opinions. This in itself would provide an important comparison. It would be expected that opinions would tend to be different and, specifically, in the ways shown by the studies previously referred to.

THE QUESTIONNAIRE

The questionnaire was identical to the one used with teachers with two exceptions. The biographical section I was appropriately altered to cover the different qualifications and career patterns of college tutors. In section III, while teachers had been asked to respond in terms of children in their own school, tutors were asked to respond in terms of children and primary education generally. The relevant parts of the questionnaire are reproduced in Appendix G. For the rest, see the primary teachers' questionnaire (Appendix B).

THE SAMPLE

The population of colleges of education from which the sample was drawn consisted of all colleges in England and Wales except those not concerned with primary work and specialist colleges. A random sample of one in ten colleges was taken, which gave rise to a sample size of fourteen. The composition of the sample in respect of size, sex composition and maintaining body is shown in Appendix H.

All members of the sample college staffs who worked with primary students, either through Education or Professional studies, were asked to complete the questionnaire. A total of 724 questionnaires were dispatched in accordance with information supplied by the colleges; 348 (48·1%) were returned completed. The percentage of completed returns from the teacher sample was 75·5%.

BIOGRAPHICAL DATA

Sex

Of the sample 68·0% were men and 111 were women (Appendix J, Table J.1). These proportions are very close to the national picture of 65% male staff in colleges of education.[2]

Age

Compared with the national proportions[3] the middle-aged group of 40–49 was appreciably over-represented at the expense of the 29 and under, and 30–39 age groups (Appendix J, Table J.2). There is no means of knowing whether the age distribution in the sample colleges was biased towards the older age groups or whether younger tutors more frequently refused to complete the questionnaire.

Qualifications

Some 36·2% of the sample were qualified by Teacher's Certificate and 63·8% by degree (Appendix J, Table J.3). Of the 213 graduates 26 were untrained. Graduates formed a rather higher proportion of the sample than they do of the national total, of whom 55% are graduates.[4] A total of 39·9% of the tutors held higher qualifications in Education and 30·7% in subjects other than Education (Appendix J, Table J.4).

Length of primary experience

Only those tutors actually teaching primary students were invited to complete the questionnaire. The distribution of responses to the question about length of primary teaching experience revealed something of a paucity of such first-hand experience (Appendix J, Table J.5). Little over one-quarter had any substantial experience, more than five years. Nearly a third had none at all. Another quarter had less than two years. It must be remembered that only half the relevant tutors in each of the sample colleges completed the questionnaire. On these grounds it must be considered whether the picture obtained from this question has been distorted by the low response rate. This is difficult to judge but it is, in fact, unlikely. As shown below, education departments were markedly over-represented in the sample as compared with subject departments. Primary teaching experience is generally rather more common among staffs of education departments than among other staff. The sample thus included those most likely to have primary teaching experience. Therefore, this may be a reasonably accurate picture of the general amount of primary teaching experience possessed by college of education staff.

Length of time spent teaching primary students
This may be generally synonymous with length of experience in colleges of education. Compatible with the probably lower rate of response from younger tutors, a minority of the sample had only short experience of teaching primary students (Appendix J, Table J.6). Nineteen (5·5%) had been doing so for less than a year and a further 67 (19·5%) for less than three years. By contrast, 206 (59·9%) had been teaching students for between four and ten years and as many as 52 (15·1%) for longer than ten years. The sample was thus largely composed of well-established tutors with substantial college experience.

Position
At 43·7% (Appendix J, Table J.7), senior lecturers were almost exactly represented in the sample, the national proportion being 42·7%.[5] Lecturers were distinctly under-represented in the sample (28·5% compared with the population of 37·6%) in favour of principal lecturers including heads of department (sample: 27·8%, population: 19·7%). This must be attributed to self-selection on the part of the questionnaire respondents. It is interesting that, in terms of completing and returning the questionnaire, a better response was obtained from the older, longer established, more senior staff of the sample colleges.

Department
As pointed out earlier, education departments were proportionately over-represented in the sample (Appendix J, Table J.8). Probably most education departments include between 20% and 25% of a college's total staff complement. More than one-third of this sample were members of the education department and, on average, nine members of this department in each sample college completed the questionnaire. Only those tutors concerned with the professional, as opposed to what is usually known as the personal, education of students were invited to complete the questionnaire. Thus the entire sample was directly concerned in the training of students for teaching in primary schools. It seems clear that those whose connection was through education, rather than a curriculum subject, were generally more willing to participate in an investigation concerned with primary education. Apart from this

bias towards education staff, all departments were represented in the sample. The better than average response from geography departments, usually rather small, is surprising and there would seem to be no obvious reason for it.

Primary age range of students taught
Only 4·1% of the sample (14 individuals) were wholly concerned with training infant students and the same number with junior students. Clearly, much the more common pattern was a combined infant/junior course, in which 220 members of the sample (64·0%) were engaged. A further 96 tutors (27·9%) were involved in junior/secondary courses.

Summary
There was some tendency for this sample of 348 college of education tutors to be older and holding more senior positions than might have been expected on the basis of the national proportions on these variables. Consistent with this was the tendency of the sample to be biased towards an appreciable length of service in colleges of education. The tutors were drawn from all subject departments but there was a proportionate over-representation of education staff. Less than half the sample had more than two years' experience of teaching in primary schools and very nearly a third had none.

References

1   For a convenient summary of the evidence see A. Morrison and D. McIntyre, *Teachers and Teaching*. Penguin, 1969, pp. 68–72.
2   Department of Education and Science. *Statistics of Education, 1968*, vol. 4, *Teachers*. HMSO, 1970, Table 37.
3   Ibid., Table 37.
4   Ibid., Table 37.
5   Ibid., Table 38.

13 Broad purposes of primary education and aspects of development

BROAD PURPOSES

As the teachers had been, the tutors were asked in section II.A of the questionnaire to share five points between two paragraphs each describing a purpose of primary education. The first paragraph described the purpose as equipping children with appropriate skills and attitudes which would enable them to choose an occupational role and to live harmoniously in society. The second paragraph described the purpose as enabling children to develop their own talents and interests, find their own enjoyment of life and arrive at their own attitudes towards society. Table 13.1 shows how the tutors distributed the score.

Table 13.1 Distribution of tutors' scores between 2 broad purposes of primary education*

Score	Societal purpose		Individual purpose	
	No.	%	No.	%
0	19	*5·6*	2	*0·6*
1	65	*19·1*	20	*5·9*
2	145	*42·6*	89	*26·2*
3	89	*26·2*	145	*42·6*
4	20	*5·9*	65	*19·1*
5	2	*0·6*	19	*5·6*
TOTALS	340	*100·0*	340	*100·0*

* From Appendix J, Table J.10.

As with the teachers (Table 6.1), a very small minority opted entirely for one purpose or the other. Just over two-thirds of the tutors, as opposed to nearly three-quarters of the teachers, balanced the two purposes as closely as possible by assigning a score of 2 to one and 3 to the other. Here the tutors and teachers were almost exactly reversed. The majority of the tutors weighted the individual purpose and the majority of teachers the societal purpose. Proportionately, slightly more tutors than teachers (25·0% as against 22·3%) clearly discriminated between the purposes by giving a score of 4 to one and a score of 1 to the other. While the teachers who did this divided equally between the purposes, the tutors were heavily weighted towards choice of the individual purpose.

Overall, the tutors gave a mean score of 2·09 to the societal purpose and 2·91 to the individual purpose. The teachers' mean scores were 2·62 and 2·38 respectively. There was thus a markedly greater tendency among the college tutors to weight the individual purpose than there had been among the teachers. Just marginally more than two-thirds of the tutors (67·3%) did so to varying degrees, as opposed to rather less than half (42·1%) of the teachers. Thus far, then, there is indication of the expected greater liberalism among tutors than among teachers.

ASPECTS OF DEVELOPMENT

Seven aspects of development were listed in section II.B of the questionnaire and the respondents asked to consider which, in the context of primary education, they considered the two most important and the two least important. Table 13.2 shows the results.

Table 13.2 Percentages of the tutors' sample judging each of 7 aspects of development as one of the two most important, one of the two least important, or neither*

Aspect of development	Most important	Neither	Least important	TOTALS
Aesthetic	11·6	47·2	41·2	100·0
Emotional/personal†	43·6	44·8	11·6	100·0
Intellectual	68·0	25·9	6·1	100·0
Moral	20·7	68·9	10·4	100·0
Physical	3·7	37·8	58·5	100.0
Social	46·1	45·7	8·2	100·0
Spiritual/religious	6·4	29·9	63·7	100·0

* From Appendix J, Table J.11.
† It should be noted that the questionnaire went out with a misprint of 'emotional/personal' as 'emotional/physical'. Addendum notices were sent out but did not always reach the respondents before the questionnaire had been completed.

Much the highest consensus was in rating intellectual development as one of the two most important aspects. This was approached by the rating of spiritual/religious development as one of the least important aspects. Following intellectual development there was most agreement about the importance of social and emotional/personal development. More than half the sample

(58·5%) considered physical development one of the two least important aspects, and an appreciable minority (41·2%) made the same assessment of aesthetic development.

With the one exception of intellectual development, considered most important by proportionately many more tutors than teachers, the tutors and teachers indicated very similar judgements in respect of this question. Table 13.3 shows the proportions of each sample (in descending order of size) rating each aspect of development as most important.

Table 13.3   Percentages of the tutors' sample and the primary teachers' sample rating each of 7 aspects of development as most important

| Tutors | | Teachers | |
Aspect	%	Aspect	%
Intellectual	68·0	Social	53·6
Social	46·1	Emotional/personal	53·6
Emotional/personal	43·6	Intellectual	52·9
Moral	20·7	Moral	22·7
Aesthetic	11·6	Spiritual/religious	7·5
Spiritual/religious	6·4	Aesthetic	6·2
Physical	3·7	Physical	3·6

The two samples seemed to be similarly constituted in regard to aspects of development. The same three aspects were most frequently thought to be most important by both samples; these were intellectual, emotional/personal and social development. Moral development occupied an almost identical position in each sample. While only one in five of both samples considered it most important, only one in ten considered it of least importance. In short, the majority of both samples gave it an intermediate position of neither most nor least importance. The same three aspects of development—aesthetic, spiritual/religious and physical—were mostly rarely thought to be most important by both samples.

The opinions of both tutors and teachers tended very largely to differ in degree rather than in kind. All but very small minorities in both cases rated each aspect of development as either of most importance or neither, or of least importance or neither. No aspect gave rise to anything approaching a division of opinion which would have been evidenced by roughly equal numbers considering an aspect respectively most and least important.

Different aspects of development, then, receive very similar emphasis from tutors and from teachers. Only intellectual development stands out as an aspect much more widely thought important by tutors than by teachers. It will be remembered that there was some evidence that intellectual development may have been frequently interpreted by teachers as having to do with the basic skills. It would be reasonable to suppose that tutors, probably more familiar with current educational literature, could have made a different interpretation. On the other hand, no alternative was given, in that none of the other six aspects of development could have been seen to relate to learning in the ordinary sense, except indirectly. In short, despite the possibility of different interpretation, it may be fairly concluded that rather more tutors than teachers showed concern with children's learning, in the intellectual sense.

14 The teacher's role

FINDINGS

The tutors were asked in section IV of the questionnaire to indicate their degree of agreement or disagreement with each of five descriptions of the teacher's role. Each description outlined a conception of the curriculum, the children's role in learning and the teacher's task. The descriptions varied along a dimension which, for convenience, has been called traditional–progressive. The sample of tutors distributed their ratings as in Table 14.1.

Table 14.1 Percentages of the tutors' sample indicating five degrees of agreement/disagreement with each of 5 descriptions of the teacher's role

Degree of agreement/ disagreement	Role				
	Most trad- itional (3)	Trad- itional (5)	Moderate (1)	Progres- sive (2)	Most pro- gressive (4)
Strongly agree	4·5	15·9	36·9	32·7	16·2
Agree	15·1	35·9	46·4	40·5	32·9
Neither agree nor disagree	22·3	27·2	14·6	18·2	22·8
Disagree	40·0	19·2	2·1	7·7	23·6
Strongly disagree	18·1	1·8	0·0	0·9	4·5
TOTALS	100·0	100·0	100·0	100·0	100·0

* From Appendix J, Table J.13.

About one in five tutors took the option not to commit themselves by checking 'neither agree nor disagree' in respect of four of the five roles. Rather fewer did so in respect of the moderate role. Overall, at least half the tutors were prepared to countenance any role except the most traditional. The most favoured was the moderate, followed by the progressive. An appreciable minority (one in five) disagreed with both the traditional and the most progressive roles. These findings perhaps present a rather unexpected picture. They indicate little in the way of strong enthusiasm for very progressive, or child-centred approaches; certainly there was a marked rejection of very traditional roles, but the majority favoured a moderate role followed by a reasonably progressive one.

Again, in respect of this question, the tutors did not appear to be markedly different in opinion from the teachers (Table 8.1). They had the same overall preference for moderation and were similarly disposed towards progressive approaches. Tutors differed most from teachers in that agreement with traditional roles was rather less common amongst them and disagreement with these roles was rather more common.

The tutors were asked to indicate which of these five roles was nearest to their own approach, which is presumably closest to the approach they advocate to students. Table 14.2 shows the findings, with those for the teachers

Table 14.2 Percentages of the tutors' sample and the primary teachers' sample selecting each of 5 role descriptions as closest to their own approach to primary teaching

Role	Tutors*	Teachers
Most traditional (3)	*1·6*	*8·9*
Traditional (5)	*14·2*	*20·3*
Moderate (1)	*40·9*	*45·6*
Progressive (2)	*29·7*	*17·1*
Most progressive (4)	*13·6*	*8·1*
TOTALS	*100·0*	*100·0*

*From Appendix J, Table J.14.

given for comparison. This question, requiring a personal commitment, drew out greater differences between tutors and teachers, although in both cases the majority opted for a moderate role. Certainly, the greater tendency of tutors to favour progressivism rather than traditionalism was more marked, although this was most evident in relation to the progressive rather than the most progressive approach.

In summary, these results indicate a strong moderate core among both tutors and teachers; otherwise, more tutors tended to lean towards progressivism, while the teachers were more equally divided but with a slight edge towards traditionalism.

ROLES, BROAD PURPOSES AND ASPECTS OF DEVELOPMENT

Data arising from this question on role were analysed for relationships with responses to the two section II questions on broad purposes of primary education and aspects of development.* The results are shown in Table 14.3.

Most striking is the relationship, at the highest level of significance, between agreement with every role and one or other of the two broad purposes of education. Those who agreed with both traditional roles and the moderate

Table 14.3   Significant relationships between agreement with each of 5 teacher's roles and support for (i) 2 broad purposes of primary education, (ii) 7 aspects of development

Role	Most important		Least important	
	Purpose/aspect	Signif.	Aspect	Signif.

Most traditional	(i) Societal
	(ii) Spiritual/
	   religious
		0·001
		
		0·05
			(ii) Emotional/
			   personal
				0·001

Traditional	(i) Societal
	(ii) Spiritual/
	   religious
		0·001
		
		0·05
			(ii) Emotional/
			   personal
				0·01

Moderate	(i) Societal	0·001		
Progressive	(i) Individual (ii) Social	0·001 0·01	(ii) Moral	0·01
Most progressive	(i) Individual (ii) Social	0·001 0·05		

one significantly more often weighted the societal purpose, and those who agreed with progressive roles the individual one. This appears clearly to associate broad aims or purposes and teaching methods in an intuitively logical way. Those who stressed the purpose of education as development of the individual chose child-centred modes of teaching, and those who stressed preparation for society chose much more teacher-directed approaches. Tutors and teachers were identical in this respect.

The relationships were fewer among the tutors than they had been among the teachers (Table 8.5). However, with one exception, such relationships as did appear had their exact counterparts among the teacher sample. As with the teachers, the traditionalist tutors favoured spiritual/religious development and relegated emotional/personal development to a place of least importance. Again, the progressive tutors considered moral development one of the two least important aspects. This near-polarization between spiritual/religious

* The measure of relationship used throughout the analysis was *G* (see Appendix F).

and moral development, on the one hand, and emotional/personal development, on the other, has become a familiar syndrome of all the data arising from the surveys. It does suggest that the traditionalists seem to see these in opposition. There is perhaps a flavour of the application of external behavioural standards in religious and moral development, absent from emotional/personal development, and this would tie in with the traditionalists' strong tendency to prefer the idea of education as a means of equipping children to fit into society. Stressing religious and moral development may be seen as a means to this, whereas stress on emotional/personal development may carry the implication of fostering individuality. In some confirmation of this possibility is the tendency of progressivists, who are inclined to emphasize the idea of education as a means to developing individuality, to disfavour moral development, considering it least important.

Interestingly, the progressive teachers stressed emotional/personal development, a relationship significant at the highest level. The progressive tutors, to rather less significant extents, tended to stress social development. However in respect of the tutors' choice of a role nearest to their own, as opposed to degree of agreement with all five roles, those choosing progressive roles tended to stress emotional/personal development, at a significance beyond the 0·01 level. Again, those choosing traditional roles tended, at the highest level of significance, to emphasize the societal purpose.

In summary, the largest single group of both tutors and teachers, 41% and 46% respectively, chose a moderate role as most like their own. Of the remainder, almost three-quarters of the tutors chose progressive roles and the teachers split almost equally with a slight edge towards traditional roles. There were highly significant tendencies among both tutors and teachers for those who chose traditional roles to favour the societal purpose of education and for those who chose progressive roles to favour the individual purpose. Among both groups there were marked tendencies for the traditionalists to emphasize spiritual/religious and moral development, and to consider emotional/personal development as least important, and for the progressivists to do the reverse. In contrast with the teachers, there were negligible associations between biographical characteristics of the tutors and their choices. However, the patterns of related choices were very similar in both samples, suggesting that, irrespective of personal background, certain educational opinions do tend to hang together consistently.

15 Aims of primary education

THE RANK ORDER OF SEVENTY-TWO AIMS

The tutors were asked to rate the seventy-two aims of primary education derived from the early project work with teachers. In the same way as the teachers' sample, the tutors were asked to assign a zero to any statement which they thought should not be an aim of primary education and then to use a five-point rating scale:

5   of the *utmost importance*;
4   of *major importance*;
3   *important*;
2   of *minor importance*;
1   of *no importance*.

Table 15.1 (p. 108) shows the 72 aims in mean rank order. The text of each aim is abbreviated and the full statement can be found in Appendix B, pp. 177–83. (See Appendix J, Table J.12 for full data on the scores.)

The comparison which follows, between the rank order of aims which emerged from the tutor sample and that emerged from the teacher sample (Table 9.1), must be regarded with very great caution. It is a simple initial exploratory exercise. The procedure is a crude one; the average score given by the whole of each sample to each aim has been calculated and, on that basis, the aims put into a rank order for each sample. More detailed analysis of the teacher sample has shown wide differences between individuals, all of which are blurred by this procedure. What shows up is an approximate picture of the trends of majority opinion. Moreover, the differences between the mean scores of adjacent ranks are negligible and thus only the patterns of placement of aims have any real meaning. Nevertheless, it is important to remember that no restriction was put upon the use of the five-point scale and respondents were not asked to compare one aim with another. They were asked simply to give each aim the score they thought appropriate. They were free to assign as many high scores as they chose, but both samples clearly discriminated in their use of the scale.

The first striking feature of the rank order which emerged from the tutors' sample was its remarkable similarity to the teachers' rank order. The correlation between the two was 0·87, significant beyond the 0·001 level. Close examination shows a feature of particular interest: that the tutors and teachers were most alike at the top and at the bottom of the rank order. In other words, they tended to select the same aims as of major or utmost importance and the same aims as of minor or no importance. Specifically, if the rank order of seventy-two aims is divided into four equal parts, 14 of the top eighteen aims and 14 of the bottom eighteen were common to the samples of both tutors and teachers. Only half of the second eighteen and 7 of the third eighteen were common.

Table 15.1   Rank order of 72 aims of primary education scored by the tutors' sample

Rank	Aim No.	Description	Mean	SD
		Major importance (upper)		
1	26	Read with understanding	4·45	0·76
2	58	Happy, cheerful and well balanced	4·35	0·92
3	13	Enjoyment in school work	4·34	0·79
4	24	Acquire moral values	4·19	0·86
5	66	Tolerance	4·10	0·86
6	12	Read fluently and accurately	4·06	0·92
7	21	Convey meaning clearly through speech	4·03	0·82
		Major importance (lower)		
9=	7	Individuality	3·99	0·97
9=	3	Acquire information other than by reading	3·99	0·84
9=	65	Questioning attitude	3·99	0·88
9=	40	Self-confident	3·99	0·93
12	9	Make reasoned judgements and choices	3·91	0·92
13	60	Inventiveness and creativity	3·90	0·92
14	11	Enjoyment in leisure interests	3·86	0·93
15	4	Everyday maths	3·82	0·88
16	27	Kind and considerate	3·75	0·91
17	47	Enthusiastic and eager	3·72	1·07
18	55	Wide vocabulary	3·71	0·88
19	15	Observe	3·68	0·89
20	1	Communicate feelings through some art forms	3·64	0·97
22=	38	Control behaviour and emotions	3·63	0·91
22=	51	General knowledge of local environment	3·63	0·89
22=	25	Careful and respectful of property	3·63	0·91
22=	57	Plan independent work	3·63	0·93
25=	28	Engage in discussion	3·62	0·90
25=	29	Arithmetic—4 rules	3·62	0·95
27	50	Listen with concentration and understanding	3·57	0·93
29=	31	Know moral values	3·55	0·95
29=	71	Modern maths	3·55	0·89
29=	22	Form a considered opinion	3·55	1·18
31	56	Acquire information from written material	3·54	0·90

Table 15.1—*cont.*

Rank	Aim No.	Description	Mean	SD
		Important (upper)		
32	30	Good social mixer	3·48	0·91
33	20	Behave appropriately	3·45	0·95
34	46	Personal appreciation of beauty	3·44	0·90
35	64	Community responsibility	3·43	0·95
36	45	Adaptable and flexible	3·41	1·02
37	43	Courtesy and good manners	3·38	1·01
38	8	Write legibly	3·37	0·85
39=	62	Simple science	3·34	0·93
39=	23	Principles of health, hygiene and safety	3·34	0·89
41=	39	Write interestingly	3·31	0·80
41=	59	Deal with emergencies	3·31	0·98
43	32	Speak in a clear and fluent manner	3·30	0·99
44=	14	General knowledge	3·28	0·87
44=	5	Correct spelling	3·28	0·86
46	54	Techniques of some arts and crafts	3·25	0·87
47	41	Sex education	3·24	1·00
48	37	Critical and discriminating	3·23	0·98
49	17	Industrious, persistent and conscientious	3·19	0·93
50	52	Understand own emotions	3·09	1·05
51	19	Behave in accordance with own religion	3·08	1·21
52	53	Swim	3·05	1·05
53=	48	Understand aesthetic experiences	3·04	0·94
53=	18	Obedient	3·04	0·92
55=	69	Play a part in own development	3·02	1·11
55=	34	Write clear and meaningful English	3·02	1·01
		Important (lower)		
57	44	Maintain lasting relationships	2·96	1·13
58	67	Behave in accordance with Christian religion	2·95	1·16
59	2	Understanding of how body works	2·91	0·84
60	33	Precise and economic body control	2·89	0·87
61	72	Movement and gymnastic skills	2·88	0·81
62	6	Knowledge of the Bible and Christian beliefs	2·83	1·07
63	16	Knowledge and skill for simple music-making	2·77	0·86
64	70	Listen to and enjoy a range of music	2·73	0·89
65	42	Basic grammar	2·66	0·95
66	63	Play a variety of games	2·65	0·85
67	36	Understanding of modern technology	2·60	0·84
		Minor importance (upper)		
68	10	Spiritual awareness	2·48	1·07
69	61	Knowledge of world religions	2·35	1·00
70	49	Play a musical instrument	2·30	0·80
71	35	Ordered subject knowledge	2·08	0·76
		Minor importance (lower)		
72	68	Second language	1·99	0·80

Both tutors and teachers stressed above all a small group of basic skills and certain personal and social qualities. Both clearly hoped to see children happy, self-confident and developing in their own individual way. Both were very concerned that children should have positive attitudes to school, enjoying their work, finding satisfaction in their achievements and showing enthusiasm and eagerness for all activities. Socially, both tutors and teachers seemed most concerned that children should be kind, considerate and tolerant. Additionally, they hoped to see children acquiring a set of moral values on which to base their own behaviour.

There was no doubt that reading fluently and with understanding was the pre-eminent basic skill for both tutors and teachers. Other aims in the top quarter of the order of importance for both samples were the capacity to convey meaning clearly and accurately through speech, being able to acquire information other than by reading and having a wide vocabulary. Of similar importance was everyday maths—the capacity to use mathematical techniques in ordinary life situations. There seems to be a shared emphasis here on the practical skills for everyday competence—reading, speaking and simple maths.

Aims in the second quarter of the order of importance for both tutors and teachers were competence in arithmetic, the capacity to think and solve problems mathematically, and the skills of acquiring information from written material. In this same sector came social qualities of a rather different order from those which were given most importance. Whereas most importance seemed to be accorded to aims relating to the child being happy, assured and positive, the aims in this second group were more concerned with the child knowing and abiding by the social rules. These included knowing moral values, knowing how to behave appropriately in social situations, being able to control behaviour and emotions, being able to make easy social contacts in work and play situations, and beginning to show community responsibility. Also included were aims concerned with the child's being able to plan independent work and organize his own time.

Still considered important but less so by both samples were writing interestingly and with sensitivity, having a wide general knowledge, speaking clearly and fluently, and knowing the appropriate techniques of some arts and crafts. Also in this third quarter of the order of importance came the child's beginning to understand his own emotions and behaving in accordance with his own religion.

Accorded little or no importance by both samples was the child's capacity to play a part in his own development by recognizing his strengths and limitations and setting his own goals accordingly. Neither was the capacity to maintain lasting relationships or spiritual awareness given much importance. All three of these may have been rejected on the grounds of difficulty of accomplishment or of being judged to lie outside the province of the primary school.

Most strikingly, the tutors accorded little or no importance to aims related to the very same group of curriculum areas as the teachers had done. With the exception of swimming, all the aims related to physical education came in this group. Music was wholly relegated to this position, as was a second language. So, too, were specific areas of knowledge—of major world religions, of modern technological developments, and of history and geography as subjects.

Overall, tutors and teachers alike considered the child's practical competence for living, especially the ability to read, and his happiness, self-confidence, and positive attitudes to work and to others as their most important aims for primary education. Clearly least important for both were specific areas of knowledge, physical development and music.

It remains to look at how tutors and teachers differed. A difference of ten places or more in the position of any aim in the two rankings was arbitrarily chosen as indicative of an appreciable difference in importance assigned. Three-quarters of the seventy-two aims fell within ten places of one another in the two rank orders. Twelve aims fell ten or more places higher in the tutors' rank order than in the teachers' and twelve fell lower. Table 15.2 (p. 112) shows these two lists of aims.

There appears to be a distinctive character to both of these lists. Neither is simply a collection of disparate aims. Although the procedure by which the lists were arrived at was a very simple one, the coherence of each list merits it being given careful consideration with a view to further exploration.

Seven of the twelve aims which tended to be scored higher by tutors than teachers related to various intellectual capacities. There is a strong flavour here of the child being able to use his mind independently, seeking information in various ways, reaching his own opinions and making his own judgements and choices. It must be remembered that the tutors apparently shared much of the teachers' concern with competence in the basic skills. But to this they appear to add rather higher aspirations for children's intellectual development. The remaining aims which they tended to stress more than the teachers are all suggestive of concern with a rather wider range of knowledge and experience. Particularly interesting is the relatively greater stress on science, indicative perhaps of more concern with social relevance as a criterion of curriculum content. This may also be relevant to the tutors' greater emphasis on sex education. Overall, the aims which the tutors tended to rate higher than the teachers did seem to be generally related to concern with a higher order, broader and more autonomous kind of intellectual development.

Aims which the teachers tended to rate higher have two components. One, in interesting contrast with the tutors' greater emphases, consists of relatively small areas of competence—spelling, grammar, legible writing and knowing the principles of health, hygiene and safety. The other consists of 'good', work-oriented behaviour. This particular group of aims virtually defines the conventional good pupil role. Together they describe a child who is generally obedient, courteous, well-mannered, careful and respectful of

Table 15.2 Aims falling ten or more places higher in the rank order of
(i) tutors than primary teachers and (ii) primary teachers
than tutors

Aim	Tutors' rank	Teachers' rank	Difference in placing
(i) Simple science	39	62	23
Form a considered opinion	30	50	20
Communicate feelings through some art forms	20	39	19
General knowledge of local environment	22	40	18
Observe	19	37	18
Inventiveness and creativity	13	30	17
Sex education	47	63	16
Questioning attitude	9	24	15
Engage in discussion	25	37	12
Make reasoned judgements and choices	12	23	11
Adaptable and flexible	36	47	11
Personal appreciation of beauty	34	44	10
(ii) Obedient	53	17	36
Courtesy and good manners	37	8	29
Careful and respectful of property	22	6	16
Basic grammar	65	51	14
Listen with concentration and understanding	27	13	14
Write legibly	38	25	13
Industrious, persistent and conscientious	49	36	13
Principles of health, hygiene and safety	39	27	12
Correct spelling	44	33	11
Write clear and meaningful English	55	44	11
Swim	52	42	10
Behave in accordance with Christian religion	58	48	10

property, industrious, persistent and conscientious. That teachers tend to
consider aiming for these attributes as more important than tutors do is
surely indicative of their different standpoint. It is only likely that teachers'
aims will reflect their consciousness of the practicalities of pursuing them,
and thus they will attach importance to the development of the kind of
personal qualities which may make easier the achievement of their other aims.
Tutors appear to be less aware of this possible area of difficulty.

The evidence presented here is no more than a basis for conjecture about
this important point. The area needs to be explored again and in more detail.

GROUPS OF AIMS

A factor analysis was performed upon the tutors' scoring of the seventy-two aims. Seven factors, or groups of aims, were shown up by this procedure. The factors and their constituent aims are listed in Table 15.3 and will be discussed and compared with the teachers' factors below.

On the whole, these seven factors bear marked similarity to the seven

Table 15.3   Seven factors identified from analysis of tutors' scores on 72 aims of primary education

Aim		Factor loading
No.	Description	
	Factor I Basic skills (variance 6·28%)	
29	Arithmetic—4 rules	−0·714
26	Read with understanding	−0·643
5	Correct spelling	−0·619
12	Read fluently and accurately	−0·580
4	Everyday maths	−0·549
8	Write legibly	−0·541
42	Basic grammar	−0·439
	Factor II Intellectual autonomy (variance 7·57%)	
9	Make reasoned judgements and choices	+0·718
22	Form a considered opinion	0·710
15	Observe	0·548
57	Plan independent work	0·539
45	Adaptable and flexible	0·531
3	Acquire information other than by reading	0·514
69	Play a part in own development	0·501
21	Convey meaning clearly through speech	0·442
37	Critical and discriminating	0·439
65	Questioning attitude	0·432
28	Engage in discussion	0·425
	Factor III Intellectual and personal competence (variance 6·99%)	
32	Speak in a clear and fluent manner	+0·682
35	Ordered subject knowledge	0·603
33	Precise and economic body control	0·597
34	Write clear and meaningful English	0·581
30	Good social mixer	0·546
36	Understanding of modern technology	0·540
39	Write interestingly	0·498
37	Critical and discriminating	0·448
38	Control behaviour and emotions	0·440
28	Engage in discussion	0·424
40	Self-confident	0·410

Table 15.3—*cont.*

Aim		Factor loading
No.	Description	
	Factor IV Contemporary knowledge (variance 4·52%)	
61	Knowledge of world religions	−0·581
41	Sex education	−0·536
62	Simple science	−0·443
2	Understanding of how body works	−0·438
36	Understanding of modern technology	−0·437
52	Understand own emotions	−0·407
	Factor V Child as a person (variance 6·90%)	
58	Happy, cheerful and well balanced	+0·582
64	Community responsibility	0·571
27	Kind and considerate	0·566
66	Tolerance	0·560
25	Careful and respectful of property	0·533
24	Acquire moral values	0·498
40	Self-confident	0·453
13	Enjoyment in school work	0·450
43	Courtesy and good manners	0·427
59	Deal with emergencies	0·427
47	Enthusiastic and eager	0·418
	Factor VI Spiritual/religious (variance 6·35%)	
6	Knowledge of the Bible and Christian beliefs	−0·793
10	Spiritual awareness	−0·774
67	Behave in accordance with Christian religion	−0·732
19	Behave in accordance with own religion	−0·687
18	Obedient	−0·563
43	Courtesy and good manners	−0·465
	Factor VII Cultural (variance 7·24%)	
16	Knowledge and skill for simple music-making	+0·632
54	Techniques of some arts and crafts	0·615
1	Communicate feelings through some art forms	0·589
72	Movement and gymnastic skills	0·586
70	Listen to and enjoy a range of music	0·548
53	Swim	0·546
49	Play a musical instrument	0·541
60	Inventiveness and creativity	0·507
51	General knowledge of local environment	0·442
55	Wide vocabulary	0·440
46	Personal appreciation of beauty	0·432
68	Second language	0·423
63	Play a variety of games	0·409

factors which arose from the teachers' data (Table 9.5). There are, however, three interesting and perhaps significant differences. The similarities will be considered first. The cultural factor was virtually identical; wide vocabulary was added in the tutors' sample and the simple science aim disappeared but came up in another factor. The omission of simple science from this factor may be quite important; apart from general knowledge of the local environment, all the items in this factor relate to physical education and the arts. It was argued that the teachers may see all of these as peripheral or enrichment subjects; the removal of science from this group to a knowledge factor in the tutors' sample may well reflect a rather more 'serious' evaluation of science on their part. It is interesting to see that, with this one exception, teachers and tutors alike responded to this quite varied group of aims in a similar way; these aims are perhaps non-academic and it is noteworthy that for both samples they appear together as a single group.

The spiritual/religious factor was very similar for both samples. The same four aims appeared in both and the tutors added two more. These were obedience and courtesy and good manners; these two aims are much concerned with 'good' behaviour, and much in the data which arose from the teachers' sample showed a close association between concern for religious development and concern for conformist behaviour.

The seven aims which constituted the tutors' basic skills factor also appeared in the teachers' basic skills factor. Eight other aims which the teachers included were dropped; five disappeared altogether and three made their appearance in other factors. Comparison of the constituent aims of this factor for both samples suggests that, while both discerned these kinds of aims as related, the teachers included rather more within their conception of the basic skills. The tutors' 'basic skills' aims were restricted to something much more redolent of the traditional 'three Rs' and consisted only of reading fluently and with understanding; writing legibly, grammatically and with correct spelling; and arithmetic and everyday maths.

The teachers' and tutors' intellectual autonomy factor had seven aims in common. These were knowing how to observe, having a questioning attitude, knowing how to acquire information from sources other than written material, making reasoned judgements and choices, forming a considered opinion, planning independent work, and the child playing a part in his own development. Certainly the core here is independent mental activity. The aims which the teachers included concerning individuality, general knowledge and understanding how the body works disappeared from the tutors' intellectual autonomy factor. In their place were four aims which seem to extend the essence of the factor in a coherent way. These were that the child should know how to convey his meaning clearly and accurately through speech for a variety of purposes, should be critical and discriminating towards his experiences, should know how to engage in discussion, and should be adaptable to changing circumstances and flexible in outlook. It seems that the same concept of intellectual autonomy was seen by the tutors to have more constituents.

Six aims were grouped to form the teachers' intellectual competence factor. With the exception of one item, basic grammar, the same aims were associated by the tutors, thus retaining the same element of intellectual competence. The tutors, however, again associated more aims with this same group and thus seemed to extend its meaning to include personal competence. Specifically, the additional aims were writing interestingly, knowing how to engage in discussion, having precise and economic body control, being able to control behaviour and emotions, being self-confident and a good social mixer. It was interesting that in this way the tutors seemed to blur the teachers' quite sharp distinction between this certain kind of intellectual development and personal development. The association of these two kinds of development in a way which characterizes the well-functioning, knowledgeable, thinking person almost foreshadows the complex of capabilities which are probably hoped for in a student of much greater than primary years.

The two remaining factors reflect the greatest differences from those arising from the analysis of the teachers' sample. The factor which has been called 'contemporary knowledge' had no counterpart among the teachers' data. This group of six aims has been given the label contemporary knowledge because it contains references both to knowledge of the modern world, specifically to science and technology, and to areas of knowledge which have only been thought to be appropriate for primary age children comparatively recently. These latter areas are those of other religions, sex education, simple physiology and the child's own emotions. Although these six areas of knowledge are disparate to some extent, they all share the characteristic of being functional for adequate coping with the modern world and it is interesting to see them associated in this way. Again it could be argued that this particular juxtaposition of these aims gives them a somewhat adult flavour.

The last of the tutors' factors has been named 'the child as a person'. This factor is largely an amalgam of the aims which the teachers distributed into two groupings, personal and social/moral. Whereas the teachers tended to distinguish the child's individual, personal development from his development in a social context, the tutors seem to have compounded these. Overall, their scoring of the aims gave rise to four groups or factors very largely to do with intellectual development; one concerned with the cultural, perhaps peripheral areas; one concerned with spiritual/religious development; and everything else to do with the child as a distinctive human social being is grouped together. It is of considerable interest that the tutors appear to have been rather less discriminating than the teachers about these personal aspects of children's development.

GROUPS OF AIMS AND BROAD PURPOSES

The data were examined for significant relationships between high scoring of the groups of aims and preference for each of the two broad purposes of education. The results are shown in Table 15.4. Only three significant

Table 15.4   Significant relationships between tutors' preference for one of 2 broad purposes of primary education and emphasis on 7 aims factors

Factor	Significance level	
	Societal purpose: equipping child with skills and attitudes appropriate to society	Individual purpose: development of child's individuality and independence
I Basic skills	0·01	—
II Intellectual autonomy	—	0·05
III Intellectual and personal competence	—	—
IV Contemporary knowledge	—	—
V Child as a person	—	—
VI Spiritual/religious	0·001	—
VII Cultural	—	—

relationships occurred between the stressing of particular groups of aims and preference for one or other broad purpose of primary education. The three relationships, however, paralleled those found in the teacher sample exactly. Both teachers (Table 9.7) and tutors who preferred the concept of education as a preparation for membership of society tended to stress aims related to competence in the basic skills and to spiritual/religious development. It will be remembered that the tutors had added obedience and courtesy and good manners to the latter group of aims. Both teachers and tutors who preferred the individual, independent development view of education tended significantly more often to stress the intellectual autonomy group of aims, which included such items as making reasoned judgements and choices, forming a considered opinion and planning independent work.

16 Summary and conclusions

Tutors in colleges of education completed the same questionnaire on the aims of primary education as had been earlier completed by teachers. Throughout this report the findings have been compared with those which arose from the teachers' sample. A total of 348 tutors in fourteen colleges, all involved in teaching primary students, have been compared with 1513 teachers in 201 primary schools. The balance of the teacher sample on biographical variables conformed very closely to the national proportions. The tutor sample tended to be older, in higher positions and biased towards members of education departments in comparison with the national proportions of these variables. These biases were attributed to self-selection on the part of the questionnaire respondents.

It was hypothesized at the outset that, in keeping with the most relevant recent evidence, the results of the questionnaire would indicate greater liberalism, child-centredness and general progressivism among tutors than among teachers. On the whole, this has not been borne out. The most striking feature of this evidence is the extensive similarity, as revealed by this particular instrument, between the opinions about primary education held by tutors and those held by teachers. There does, however, seem to be one important area of difference, further exploration of which could be regarded as a matter of urgency.

The areas of similarity will be considered first. Social, emotional/personal and intellectual development were most widely thought to be the most important aspects of development by both teachers and tutors. Aesthetics, physical and spiritual/religious development were most widely thought to be least important by both samples. For both, moral development occupied an intermediate position. Thus, in respect of opinions about the broad emphases to be observed in primary schools, the samples of tutors and teachers corresponded closely.

In respect of agreement with five descriptions of teachers' roles, tutors and teachers were similarly disposed. The largest single group of both samples agreed with the moderate role. Very similar proportions agreed or strongly agreed with the progressive role (teachers: 69·6%, tutors: 73·2%) and with the most progressive role (teachers: 45·2%, tutors: 49·1%). The two samples were most different in respect of the traditional roles, proportionately rather more teachers agreeing with these; 74·5% of teachers agreed or strongly agreed with the traditional role, as opposed to 51·8% of tutors, and 42·2% of teachers agreed with the most traditional role, as opposed to 19·6% of tutors.

The largest single group of both teachers and tutors chose the moderate role as nearest to their own approach to teaching. The remaining teachers split almost equally between traditional and progressive roles, but almost three times as many tutors opted for the progressive roles as for the traditional ones. There is obvious evidence here of more widespread progressivism among tutors than teachers but it is not nearly as marked as might have been expected. The largest single choice of both samples was clearly a middle-of-the-road one.

The most striking similarity between teachers and tutors was in regard to their scoring of the seventy-two aims for importance in primary education. The two samples were remarkably similar in their selection of aims to rate as of major or utmost importance and in their choice of aims of minor or no importance. The priorities for teachers and tutors alike seemed to be competence in the basic skills, especially reading, happiness and self-confidence, and positive attitudes towards school, work and other people. Generally of lesser importance for both teachers and tutors were the specific areas of knowledge, physical development and music. Aims related to aesthetic and spiritual/religious development, too, tended to appear in the lower half of both rank orders.

In regard to the two broad purposes of primary education, between which the respondents were asked to share five points, there was evidence of more widespread liberalism and child-centredness among the tutors than among the teachers, although again the difference was not dramatic. Specifically, two-thirds of the tutors put their greater emphasis on developing the child's individuality and independence as compared with equipping him with the skills and attitudes appropriate to society, while 42·1% of the teachers did so.

The evidence discussed so far in this summary does seem to point to a very substantial core of both teachers and tutors who would agree with one another about the broad purposes of primary education, the aspects of development they think should be stressed, the aims which they think should be given respectively greater and lesser importance and the role of the teacher. Certainly, where there is a disagreement, it is consistently in the direction of tutors being more progressive and child-centred and teachers being more traditional and teacher-directed. These differences should not be allowed to cloak the evidence both that many are in agreement and that the same varieties of opinion exist equally as much among teachers as among tutors.

Careful examination of the data, however, does suggest that there may be one crucial area of divergence. Discussion of this must be inevitably more speculative, since it rests on combining separate pieces of the evidence into an only possibly meaningful whole. There appears to be reason to suppose that in general tutors are appreciably more concerned with the higher order intellectual development of children and the teachers with the personal development of children, particularly in relation to their behaviour. There is a flavour to the tutors' opinions of a certain detachment from the business of teaching children which frees them to consider, perhaps more objectively, perhaps more idealistically, the possibilities for children's achievements in the primary school. The teachers' opinions, by contrast, so often reflect an acute consciousness of the actual job of teaching and working with children, of the real context within which aims are pursued. It is a fact, of course, that teachers are directly involved with children and tutors are not; to draw attention to the likelihood that this difference gives rise to a different perspective upon children is really a rather trite and common observation. What is important is not the fact, but the nature, of the difference in perspectives. The differences arising from this investigation seem not so much in the area of styles of teaching and learning—tutors being more child-centred and progressive and teachers more teacher-directed and traditional, as might have been expected—but in areas of emphasis. Tutors appeared to emphasize intellectual development much more, and teachers to emphasize personal development. It seems a reasonable hypothesis that, for teachers, the children's personal development is a crucial intervening variable between aims and their accomplishment. No matter what aims teachers have, certain kinds of behaviour on the part of children may be a necessary condition for achieving them. It would not be remarkable that tutors, or anyone not directly and currently involved in teaching children, should be rather less sensitive to this.

The evidence for the foregoing argument is as follows. First, at a simple level, 68·0% of tutors selected intellectual development as one of the two most important aspects, as opposed to 52·9% of teachers. Majorities of both samples also selected social and emotional/personal development as one of the two most important aspects but rather more teachers than tutors did so. Social development was selected by 53·6% of teachers and 46·1% of tutors. Emotional/personal development was selected by 53·6% of teachers and 43·6% of tutors. In short, there was a bias among the tutors towards intellectual development which was rather less marked among the teachers.

The scores assigned to the seventy-two aims by both tutors and teachers were very similar. However, a rather significant group of aims were stressed more by tutors than teachers and another group more by teachers than tutors. The aims which tutors tended to score more highly were largely related to areas of knowledge and to higher order intellectual capabilities such as forming a considered opinion, making reasoned judgements and choices, having a questioning attitude and engaging in discussion. By contrast, the teachers laid more stress than the tutors on basic grammar, correct spelling, writing clear and meaningful English and writing legibly but, more significantly, on obedience, listening with concentration and understanding, courtesy and good manners, industry, persistence and conscientiousness, and behaving in accordance with the Christian religion. It is not difficult to appreciate the usefulness of this latter group of attributes for the teacher working daily with thirty-five or more children.

The factor analysis performed on the scores assigned to the aims by both samples respectively showed up differences in some important particulars in the perceived groupings of aims. While analysis of both samples gave rise to very similar groupings of basic skills, intellectual autonomy, spiritual/ religious and cultural aims, the remaining aims were rather differently grouped. The tutors' sample revealed a contemporary knowledge grouping which did not exist among the teachers at all. The teachers' intellectual competence factor was extended to include personal competence, thus indicating again the perception of a particularly intellectual character to aims for the child's total development. It suggests that, for the tutors, controlling behaviour and emotions, being self-confident and a good mixer, are not so much of value in themselves but in their contribution to effective intellectual functioning.

The teachers, then, discriminated two clear groups of aims, one related to children's personal development and one to their social and moral development. Both were concerned with the child as a person rather than specifically as a learner in the formal sense, but the teachers discriminated between the child's development as an individual and as a social being. This discrimination suggests that the growing person of the child, as a child rather than a pupil, is of sufficient central importance for its two major facets to be identified and distinguished. This discrimination did not arise among the tutors; everything to do with the child which was not learning in the more formal sense simply appeared in a single factor.

Not forgetting the widespread similarities of opinion between tutors and teachers, the hypothesis which has been developed from this evidence is that more tutors more often perceive the aims of primary education as primarily related to children as learners, and teachers tend more often to see the aims as related to children who are both people and learners. It has been suggested that this difference may stem from the teachers' direct involvement with children and the tutors' lack of it. Direct involvement in working with children may give rise to a perception among teachers that achieving their educational aims for children depends upon certain kinds of personal and social behaviour on the part of the children. The apparently greater concern of the tutors with higher order intellectual development may spring from their different standpoint of experience and academic background.

It should be remembered that the aims which both teachers and tutors scored had been formulated by practising teachers. Thus the tutors' aspirations for children can hardly be called unrealistic when judged by the

A.P.E.—5*

criterion of what teachers consider possible. It is their perceptions of the relationships between aims and the emphases which they tend to give that are different from those of the teachers.

A careful re-examination of the propositions which have been spelled out above is clearly necessary. Should further evidence support the hypothesis, then the practical implications are obvious. Better feedback seems needed from teachers of two or three years' experience to tutors about the kinds of shifts of emphasis which seemed to them to be necessary once they had started teaching. Equally valuable would be further work through the medium of in-service courses, at the stage when teachers felt themselves to be established, on the achievement of the higher order intellectual type aims with which the tutors are no doubt rightly concerned.

Related exploratory studies

Opinions of secondary teachers

17 Introduction

The main task of the Aims of Primary Education Project was to discover the aims of primary teachers for the children in their schools. It was felt that there would be some value in a study of the views of secondary teachers about the aims of primary education. Such a study is of obvious interest. In the staff rooms of secondary schools, comments about primary education are sometimes unflattering. But it is not clear how far the aims of secondary teachers for primary education differ from those of colleagues in the primary schools. It may be that both secondary and primary teachers have similar aims for primary education and that the differences concern methods rather than aims. On the other hand, it is possible that secondary school teachers would prefer a more 'academically' oriented primary education.

This study makes some attempt to discover the views about the aims of primary education held by secondary teachers who are actively concerned with eleven- to twelve-year-old children. The resources of the project would not extend to a large-scale study of secondary teachers, and the results presented here should be viewed as an indication of likely trends rather than as definitive answers. Within this limitation, it is suggested that these results may have some value as an indication of the possible differences and similarities between primary and secondary teachers' aims for primary education.

THE QUESTIONNAIRE

The questionnaire was substantially the same as that used with primary school teachers. Section I (biographical) was appropriately altered to meet the different organizational setting of secondary school teachers. This section is reproduced in Appendix K. Sections II and III were identical with those used with the primary teachers (Appendix B). Section IV (teacher's role) was inapplicable and thus deleted.

THE SAMPLE

The population of secondary schools and middle schools from which the sample was drawn consisted of schools in two county councils and three county boroughs. A random sample of one school in seven was taken from the lists of these five areas.[1] Adjustments were made in order to maintain a balance of pupils between each region. Cognizance was taken of the different organization of secondary education and an attempt was made to balance the different types of secondary school. The detailed composition of the sample is given in Appendix L (schools and authorities in Table L.1).

Procedure

The head teacher of each school in the sample was asked for permission to approach those members of his staff who were concerned with the eleven- to twelve-year-old children in the school. At the same time the heads were asked to complete a questionnaire similar to that used for primary school heads, with details of school size, type, etc. A total of fifty-one schools was approached; the relevant teachers of thirty-five schools returned questionnaires. In terms of schools this is a response rate of 69%. Unfortunately, the final sample (Appendix L, Table L.2) does not accurately reflect the different types of school in the regions surveyed. Secondary modern schools are under-represented and comprehensives are over-represented. The differences in attitudes to aims of primary education between teachers in the different types of secondary school are not known, but it may be advisable to treat the results with some caution in view of this sample bias.

From the heads' questionnaire it was possible to ascertain the number of teachers actively concerned with the eleven to twelve year-olds in the schools sampled (Appendix L, Table L.3). From these figures can be calculated the percentage of such teachers who completed questionnaires. The total number of teachers in the schools who were actively concerned with the eleven to twelve year-olds was 761 (this includes an estimate for one of the schools). The total number of questionnaires returned was 459, which is a response rate of 60%. This is rather lower than the response rate from the primary school teachers (80%) and may be an indication of a more detached view of primary education among secondary teachers.

BIOGRAPHICAL DATA (see Appendix M, Tables M.1 to M.10)

This sample of secondary school teachers of eleven to twelve year-olds had an over-representation of young women teachers as compared with national proportions. Older teachers and those in middle rank positions were under-represented. It is not possible to say, however, if this is because it is the younger women assistant teachers who are most actively concerned with the eleven to twelve year-old child, or if it is this type of teacher who is more interested in primary education.

Only eighty teachers (18·1%) had taught in a primary school previous to their work in a secondary school. This proportion is not unexpected, and the fact that so few of the teachers had had previous primary experience may be due to the large proportion of young teachers.

Nearly all teachers in the sample were responsible for teaching more than one subject. Their interest in the eleven to twelve year-olds was largely through subject teaching or class/form responsibilities. Just over half taught the school's entire ability range, although one-quarter taught one ability group only.

Nearly one-quarter of the teachers taught English and about one-sixth taught mathematics. Art and music were taught by the smallest number of teachers in the sample; these subjects appear to be more specialized and teachers of art and music tended not to teach other subjects.

Reference

1   Taken from the *Education Committees Year Book, 1969–70*, Councils and Education Press, 1969. The middle schools were obtained from local education authority lists of primary schools.

18 Broad purposes of primary education and aspects of development

BROAD PURPOSES

Table 18.1 shows the distribution of the secondary teachers' scores for the societal and individual purposes (section II.A of the questionnaire).

Table 18.1 Distribution of scores between 2 broad purposes of primary education: secondary teachers' sample* compared with primary teachers' sample

Score	Societal purpose		Individual purpose	
	Secondary teachers (%)	Primary teachers (%)	Secondary teachers (%)	Primary teachers (%)
0	3·2	2·1	4·3	3·3
1	13·9	10·1	14·3	12·2
2	25·3	29·9	39·0	42·4
3	39·0	42·4	25·3	29·9
4	14·3	12·2	13·9	10·1
5	4·3	3·3	3·2	2·1
TOTALS	100·0	100·0	100·0	100·0

Mean scores: societal purpose 2·60 (primary teachers 2·62)
individual purpose 2·40 (primary teachers 2·38)

* From Appendix M, Table M.11.

As was the case with the primary school teachers the majority of secondary school teachers opted for a mixture of the two purposes. Sixty-four per cent of the secondary teachers' sample balanced the two purposes as closely as possible, assigning a two to one purpose and a three to the other. The secondary school teachers were less moderate, however, than the primary school teachers. Thirty-six per cent of the secondary teachers, as compared with 28% of the primary school teachers, gave a high score to one of the purposes of education. Nineteen per cent of the secondary teachers gave a high score to the societal purpose and 17% gave a high score to the individual purpose.

Among the primary school teachers 16% of the sample gave a high score to the societal purpose and 12% gave a high score to the individual purpose.

ASPECTS OF DEVELOPMENT

The secondary teachers were asked to choose from the seven aspects of development the two they considered most important and the two they considered least important (section II.B of the questionnaire). The results are shown in Table 18.2. The level of consensus was somewhat low. The highest

Table 18.2   Percentages of the secondary teachers' sample judging each of 7 aspects of development as one of the two most important, one of the two least important, or neither*

Aspect of development	Most important	Neither	Least important	TOTALS
Aesthetic	4·4	44·4	51·2	100·0
Emotional/personal	45·7	44·8	9·5	100·0
Intellectual	55·9	35·3	8·8	100·0
Moral	28·1	63·3	8·6	100·0
Physical	4·9	44·3	50·8	100·0
Social	55·0	38·5	6·5	100·0
Spiritual/religious	6·5	28·0	65·5	100·0

* From Appendix M, Table M.12.

agreement was on rating the spiritual/religious aspect as of least importance (65·5% of the sample). Just over half the sample agreed that the intellectual and social aspects of development were most important. The fact that nearly half the sample did not consider the intellectual aspect of development as one of the most important seems surprising.

It appears that the intellectual, social and emotional/personal aspects of development were seen as the three most important aspects and the aesthetic, physical and spiritual/religious aspects as the least important. The moral aspect of development is intermediate; over a quarter of the sample considered this one of the most important aspects of development, but nearly two-thirds (63·3%) considered it neither most nor least important.

Table 18.3 (p. 130) compares the secondary and primary teachers' rating of the importance of the different aspects of development. The largest difference between the two sets of teachers is in the consensus concerning the importance of the emotional/personal aspect of development. Whereas 54% of the primary teachers rated this as one of the most important aspects of development, only 46% of secondary teachers did so. This difference in the rating of the emotional/personal aspect of development may be due to the different ages taught in primary and secondary schools. Although both sets of teachers were considering aims in relation to the eleven-year-old child, they

Table 18.3 Percentages of the secondary teachers' sample and
the primary teachers' sample rating each of 7 aspects
of development as most important

Secondary teachers		Primary teachers	
Aspect	%	Aspect	%
Intellectual	55·9	Social	53·6
Social	55·0	Emotional/personal	53·6
Emotional/personal	45·7	Intellectual	52·9
Moral	28·1	Moral	22·7
Spiritual/religious	6·5	Spiritual/religious	7·5
Physical	4·9	Aesthetic	6·2
Aesthetic	4·4	Physical	3·6

appear to have viewed the eleven-year-old from somewhat different perspectives. The primary school teachers seem to have been influenced by their experience of the intense emotional/personal development which takes place between the ages of five and eleven. The secondary school teachers may have tended to consider the eleven-year-old rather in the context of the older age groups in the secondary school. Bearing in mind the small number of secondary teachers who had had previous primary experience, and the large proportion of young teachers in the secondary sample, it is likely that many of the secondary teachers had had little first-hand experience of young children and thus, when considering the aims of primary education, appeared to be more influenced by the needs of the child in the secondary school than by his needs in the primary school.

As far as the other aspects of development are concerned, the percentage of teachers rating them as most important was similar for both the primary and the secondary teachers' samples.

BIOGRAPHICAL VARIABLES AND CHOICE OF IMPORTANT ASPECTS OF DEVELOPMENT

It will be recalled that information was obtained from the teachers on nine biographical variables (see pp. 126–7 and Appendix M). These variables were sex, age, qualifications, position in school, primary experience, length of teaching experience, subject(s) taught, percentage of time spent teaching eleven to twelve year-olds and nature of interest in the eleven to twelve year-olds. (Unfortunately it was not possible for statistical reasons to study the relationship between this last variable and aspect choice.)

The secondary teachers choosing each aspect as most important were studied for significant biographical characteristics.* Table 18.4 shows which biographical sub-groups significantly preferred or rejected each of the seven

* The measure of relationship used in this analysis was standardized *G* (see Appendix F).

Table 18.4   Sub-groups of the secondary teachers' sample rating
each of 7 aspects of development as more/less
(=*negative*) important significantly more often

Aspect of development	Sub-group	Significance level
Aesthetic	Art and craft teachers	0·001
	Physical education teachers (*negative*)	0·001
Emotional/ personal	Art and craft teachers	0·01
	Lower positions	0·05
Intellectual	Graduates	0·01
	More experienced	0·05
Moral	English teachers (*negative*)	0·01
	Older	0·05
	More experienced	0·05
Physical	Physical education teachers	0·001
	Lower positions	0·01
	Music teachers (*negative*)	0·01
Social	Teachers spending greater time with 11–12 year-olds	0·01
	Women	0·05
	Lower positions	0·05
	English teachers	0·05
Spiritual/ religious	Older	0·001
	More experienced	0·001
	Higher positions	0·001
	Religious education teachers	0·001

aspects of development. There appears to be no significant relationship between previous experience in a primary school and the favouring of any
particular aspect of development. But all other variables studied did prove to
have some significant relationship with the choice of aspect of development
considered most important.

The relationships with the highest level of significance concerned the
subjects taught by the teacher. Some of these relationships were exactly
those that might be expected—art and craft teachers preferred aesthetic
development, religious education teachers preferred the spiritual/religious
aspect and physical education teachers preferred the physical aspect. Some
of the other relationships between subject taught and choice of important
aspect are, however, not so obvious. English teachers preferred the social
aspect and considered the moral aspect least important. Art and craft teachers
considered the emotional/personal aspect most important. Music teachers
considered the physical aspect of development to be one of the least important,

while the physical education teachers regarded the aesthetic aspect as one of the least important. It will be remarked that only some specialist teaching groups significantly favoured particular aspects of development. These were the art and craft, English and physical education teachers—who were all distinguished in two aspects—and the music and religious education teachers —who were distinguished in one aspect.

SIGNIFICANT RELATIONSHIPS BETWEEN RESPONSES ON BROAD PURPOSES AND ASPECTS OF DEVELOPMENT

The responses to the two purposes of education paragraphs were examined for relationships with preferences for particular aspects of development. The results are shown in Table 18.5. These results are comparable with those of

Table 18.5   Significant relationships between preference for each of 2 broad purposes of primary education and choice of most important of 7 aspects of development

Aspect	Broad purpose	Significance level
Aesthetic	—	—
Emotional/personal	Individual	0·001
Intellectual	Societal	0·001
Moral	Societal	0·001
Physical	—	—
Social	—	—
Spiritual/religious	Societal	0·001

the primary school teachers (Table 8.6). Societal teachers in the primary schools significantly favoured the intellectual, moral, spiritual/religious and physical aspects of development. Individualistic teachers in the primary schools significantly preferred the aesthetic and emotional/personal aspects of development.

19 Aims of primary education

THE RANK ORDER OF SEVENTY-TWO AIMS

The secondary school teachers were asked (section III of the questionnaire) to judge the seventy-two aims in the light of the average child in their school. This meant that teachers from the different types of secondary school were considering the aims in relation to children of different ability ranges. Only the comprehensive and the middle schools would approach the same range of ability as the primary schools. The teachers at the grammar and secondary modern schools would, of course, have considered the aims in relation to children from a more limited ability range.

The aims were scored on the five-point scale previously described (p. 57). (See Appendix M, Table M.13 for full data on the scores.) Table 19.1 (p. 134) shows the seventy-two aims in mean rank order; the standard deviations for each aim are also given. The means are grouped as in Table 9.1, the first group containing values of 4·0 and above.

In comparing the secondary teachers' rank order with the results for primary teachers (Table 9.1), caution should be exercised as explained on p. 107 in connection with the college tutors' results. The first noticeable feature is the marked similarity between the primary and secondary teachers' order of importance of aims. The rank order correlation is 0·97, which suggests a virtually identical ranking for both sets of teachers. The top group of eight aims is the same with one exception. The bottom eight aims are identical in both lists.

A difference of ten ranks was chosen as representing a meaningful difference of opinion about the importance of an aim. It will be seen from Table 19.2 (p. 136) that there were only six aims which had a ten-rank difference between the two samples.

The three aims which were given a higher mean score by the secondary teachers are all aims concerned with formal basic skills. The secondary teachers presumably regarded these skills as a necessary foundation for secondary school work and would apparently prefer the eleven-year-olds to arrive at the secondary school equipped with these basic techniques.

The three aims to which the secondary teachers gave a lower score are

Table 19.1   Rank order of 72 aims of primary education scored by secondary teachers' sample

Rank	Aim No.	Description	Mean	SD
		Major importance (upper)		
1	26	Read with understanding	4·35	0·79
2	24	Acquire moral values	4·33	0·81
3	58	Happy, cheerful and well balanced	4·27	0·89
4	13	Enjoyment in school work	4·26	0·83
5	12	Read fluently and accurately	4·22	0·92
6	25	Careful and respectful of property	4·05	0·89
7=	43	Courtesy and good manners	4·01	0·93
7=	47	Enthusiastic and eager	4·01	0·93
		Major importance (lower)		
9	18	Obedient	3·97	0·95
10	29	Arithmetic—4 rules	3·93	0·98
11	21	Convey meaning clearly through speech	3·92	0·89
12	3	Acquire information other than by reading	3·88	0·86
13	31	Know moral values	3·86	0·98
14	8	Write legibly	3·84	0·89
15=	66	Tolerance	3·83	0·97
15=	11	Enjoyment in leisure interests	3·83	0·96
17	5	Correct spelling	3·80	0·94
18	4	Everyday maths	3·76	0·90
19=	50	Listen with concentration and understanding	3·74	0·97
19=	38	Control behaviour and emotions	3·74	0·91
21	7	Individuality	3·70	1·07
22	23	Principles of health, hygiene and safety	3·69	0·99
23	27	Kind and considerate	3·68	0·96
24	55	Wide vocabulary	3·67	0·94
25	20	Behave appropriately	3·65	0·97
26	65	Questioning attitude	3·64	1·02
27	64	Community responsibility	3·63	0·96
28=	59	Deal with emergencies	3·61	1·03
28=	60	Inventiveness and creativity	3·61	0·97
30	40	Self-confident	3·60	0·94
31	17	Industrious, persistent and conscientious	3·59	0·98
32	9	Make reasoned judgements and choices	3·58	0·95
		Important (upper)		
33	30	Good social mixer	3·46	0·88
35=	28	Engage in discussion	3·43	0·94
35=	15	Observe	3·43	0·85
35=	56	Acquire information from written material	3·43	1·00
37	57	Plan independent work	3·37	0·98
38	71	Modern maths	3·32	1·02
39	51	General knowledge of local environment	3·30	0·93
40=	14	General knowledge	3·29	0·94
40=	34	Write clear and meaningful English	3·29	1·03

Table 19.1—*cont.*

Rank	Aim No.	Description	Mean	SD
42=	1	Communicate feelings through some art forms	3·27	1·09
42=	53	Swim	3·27	1·19
44	39	Write interestingly	3·24	0·88
45	45	Adaptable and flexible	3·21	0·98
46	42	Basic grammar	3·18	1·10
47=	19	Behave in accordance with own religion	3·16	1·20
47=	32	Speak in a clear and fluent manner	3·16	0·99
49	46	Personal appreciation of beauty	3·14	0·89
50	22	Form a considered opinion	3·11	1·10
51	54	Techniques of some arts and crafts	3·03	0·91
52	52	Understand own emotions	3·10	0·97
53	67	Behave in accordance with Christian religion	3·00	1·15
		Important (lower)		
54	44	Maintain lasting relationships	2·96	1·14
56=	69	Play a part in own development	2·94	1·04
56=	62	Simple science	2·94	0·98
56=	37	Critical and discriminating	2·94	1·01
58	41	Sex education	2·93	1·18
59	33	Precise and economic body control	2·90	0·90
60	63	Play a variety of games	2·89	1·02
61	6	Knowledge of the Bible and Christian beliefs	2·88	1·06
62	48	Understand aesthetic experiences	2·86	0·92
63	2	Understanding of how body works	2·81	0·92
64	72	Movement and gymnastic skills	2·74	0·89
65	70	Listen to and enjoy a range of music	2·72	0·94
66	16	Knowledge and skill for simple music-making	2·66	0·90
67	36	Understanding of modern technology	2·56	0·90
		Minor importance		
68	35	Ordered subject knowledge	2·46	0·94
69	10	Spiritual awareness	2·42	1·04
70	61	Knowledge of world religions	2·32	0·98
71	49	Play a musical instrument	2·15	0·78
72	68	Second language	2·06	0·89

all 'personal' aims, concerned to encourage the development of certain personal characteristics in the child. The differences in ranking of these three aims may be due to the difference in the child's position in school. It is likely that secondary teachers would not expect the eleven-year-old in his first year at school to be sufficiently mature and self-assured to show kindness or self-confidence.

Summary
The primary and secondary teachers agreed to a remarkable extent in their judging of the importance of the seventy-two aims of primary education.

Table 19.2 Aims falling ten or more places higher in the rank order of (i) primary than secondary teachers, (ii) secondary than primary teachers

	Aim	Primary teachers' rank	Secondary teachers' rank
(i)	Individuality	*6*	21
	Self-confident	*18*	30
	Kind and considerate	*13*	23
(ii)	Correct spelling	33	*17*
	Write legibly	25	*14*
	Arithmetic—4 rules	20	*10*

Large differences in opinion about the importance of aims were few. Only three very formal basic skills were regarded by the secondary teachers as rather more important than they were by the primary teachers. This difference appears to reflect the different perspective of the two groups of teachers, for, although both were considering the aims in relation to primary education, the secondary teachers are more concerned with the demands of secondary education than the primary teachers. The latter appear to be more influenced by the years preceding eleven and slightly to prefer aims which are of greater significance to the child during his primary schooling.

GROUPS OF AIMS

In this section the results of a factor analysis (Varimax solution), prepared on the teachers' scoring of the seventy-two aims, is presented and discussed. This analysis reveals the way in which the teachers grouped the aims, by showing which aims were constantly scored in a similar manner. Seven groups of aims, or factors, were chosen as this was the number of factors which showed the most interesting grouping of the primary teachers' aims. The seven factors account for 50·5% of the total variance of secondary teachers' scores.

These factors are presented in Table 19.3. They are given as far as possible in the same order as those of the primary teachers (Table 9.5) to facilitate comparison between the two samples. However, it should be borne in mind that the amount of variance accounted for by each factor is not the same for both sets of teachers.

In some cases the groupings of aims were similar for both the primary and the secondary teachers, in other instances the two samples of teachers combined aims rather differently. The basic skills factor (I) is essentially the same for both samples of teachers. Both primary and secondary teachers included the same group of personal aims in this factor: the child should be industrious, persistent and conscientious, and he should be obedient. It may be that the teachers feel these qualities are required for the successful acquisition of basic skills. The intellectual aims included are almost the same for both primary and secondary teachers. The latter omitted the aim of acquiring information from written material from the basic skills and grouped it with the cultural aims. Secondary teachers included writing interestingly and with sensitivity, which was not grouped in the basic skills factor by the primary teachers. These small differences merely give a slight change of emphasis; essentially, the basic skills factor was the same for both primary and secondary teachers.

Factor II is the intellectual autonomy group of aims and is similar for both

Table 19.3 Seven factors identified from analysis of 72 aims of primary education scored by secondary teachers

Aim No.	Description	Factor loading
	Factor I Basic skills (variance 9·15%)	
5	Correct spelling	−0·694
12	Read fluently and accurately	−0·694
8	Write legibly	−0·683
21	Convey meaning clearly through speech	−0·621
29	Arithmetic—4 rules	−0·582
17	Industrious, persistent and conscientious	−0·580
4	Everyday maths	−0·564
26	Read with understanding	−0·561
55	Wide vocabulary	−0·524
18	Obedient	−0·490
34	Write clear and meaningful English	−0·477
50	Listen with concentration and understanding	−0·477
32	Speak in a clear and fluent manner	−0·429
42	Basic grammar	−0·408
39	Write interestingly	−0·405
71	Modern maths	−0·404
	Factor II Intellectual autonomy (variance 6·06%)	
3	Acquire information other than by reading	+0·617
2	Understanding of how body works	0·600
7	Individuality	0·572
11	Enjoyment in leisure interests	0·544
9	Make reasoned judgements and choices	0·534
22	Form a considered opinion	0·512
15	Observe	0·468
13	Enjoyment in school work	0·446
1	Communicate feelings through some art forms	0·440
14	General knowledge	0·423

Table 19.3—*cont.*

Aim No.	Description	Factor loading
	Factor III Intellectual and personal competence (variance 8·67%)	
37	Critical and discriminating	+0·665
40	Self-confident	0·650
28	Engage in discussion	0·608
45	Adaptable and flexible	0·578
52	Understand own emotions	0·516
22	Form a considered opinion	0·477
30	Good social mixer	0·477
44	Maintain lasting relationships	0·464
39	Write interestingly	0·439
48	Understand aesthetic experiences	0·438
38	Control behaviour and emotions	0·435
32	Speak in a clear and fluent manner	0·432
66	Tolerance	0·425
36	Understanding of modern technology	0·424
	Factor IV Social/personal/moral (variance 8·72%)	
43	Courtesy and good manners	+0·687
24	Acquire moral values	0·621
25	Careful and respectful of property	0·602
31	Know moral values	0·598
64	Community responsibility	0·523
58	Happy, cheerful and well balanced	0·512
20	Behave appropriately	0·503
38	Control behaviour and emotions	0·496
18	Obedient	0·485
59	Deal with emergencies	0·449
47	Enthusiastic and eager	0·447
33	Precise and economic body control	0·412
30	Good social mixer	0·406
	Factor V Aesthetic enjoyment v. formal learning (variance 2·98%)	
35	Ordered subject knowledge	−0·459
13	Enjoyment in school work	0·440
1	Communicate feelings through some art forms	0·429
34	Write clear and meaningful English	−0·417
60	Inventiveness and creativity	0·403
	Factor VI Spiritual/religious (variance 4·56%)	
10	Spiritual awareness	+0·789
6	Knowledge of the Bible and Christian beliefs	0·782
19	Behave in accordance with own religion	0·692
67	Behave in accordance with Christian religion	0·670

Table 19.3—*cont.*

Aim		Factor loading
No.	Description	
	Factor VII Cultural (variance 10·38%)	
54	Techniques of some arts and crafts	−0·654
70	Listen to and enjoy a range of music	−0·647
72	Movement and gymnastic skills	−0·622
62	Simple science	−0·613
63	Play a variety of games	−0·592
60	Inventiveness and creativity	−0·591
71	Modern maths	−0·584
51	General knowledge of local environment	−0·546
46	Personal appreciation of beauty	−0·539
49	Play a musical instrument	−0·538
56	Acquire information from written material	−0·513
48	Understand aesthetic experiences	−0·500
61	Knowledge of world religions	−0·479
57	Plan independent work	−0·476
53	Swim	−0·409
36	Understanding of modern technology	−0·407
55	Wide vocabulary	−0·402

samples. The core of this factor, in both cases, is the child's independent intellectual functioning. Primary teachers included the ability to plan independent work in this factor, as well as the child having a questioning attitude and being able to play a part in his own development. The secondary teachers did not include these aims in this factor but rather emphasized enjoyment of school work and in leisure interests. The secondary teachers appeared to combine intellectual independence with art, enjoyment and leisure. The primary teachers saw intellectual autonomy in a somewhat more intellectual context.

In the cultural factor (VII) both samples of teachers grouped physical, musical and scientific aims. The secondary teachers added some aims to this factor which had been grouped with intellectual aims by the primary teachers. Secondary teachers included acquiring knowledge from written material, planning independent work, understanding modern maths and having a wide vocabulary. The inclusion of these last two 'basic skills' aims in the cultural factor gives it a somewhat tougher intellectual flavour and suggests a closer relationship between the cultural and intellectual aspects of the curriculum. On the other hand, the placing of the capacity to plan independent work in a cultural rather than an intellectual context may be an indication that the secondary teachers regarded academic or intellectual work as too important to be independently planned by the eleven-year-olds.

Factor IV, social/personal/moral, was largely the same for both secondary and primary teachers. In this factor is a group of aims which are concerned with the child behaving correctly in a variety of social situations. Unlike the primary teachers, however, the secondary teachers included a small number of personal aims which give their factor a slightly less passive flavour. These personal aims are that the child should be happy, cheerful and well balanced, and that he should be enthusiastic and eager. Interestingly, the secondary teachers included precise and economic body control in this group of social/personal aims, interpreting 'body control' in a social context, whereas the primary teachers tended to interpret this aim in a more personal, physical maturational context.

Factor III, intellectual and personal competence, is a mixture of two of the primary teachers' factors: 'intellectual competence' and 'personal'. In the intellectual and personal competence factor the secondary teachers included aims concerned with self-confidence and self-control as well as such aims as speaking in a clear and fluent manner and forming a considered opinion. The secondary teachers appeared to conceptualize a child who has ideas of his own and the skills to communicate them in a tolerant, controlled manner. A picture, in fact, of the ideal intellectual in our society, and one which looks ahead to the end of secondary education rather than back to primary education.

Lastly, the secondary teachers produced a group of aims for which there was found no equivalent among the primary teachers. This is factor V, 'aesthetic enjoyment v. formal learning', and it appears to express an antagonism between formal, structured learning (ordered subject knowledge, writing clear and meaningful English) and an aesthetic, creative approach (inventiveness and creativity, communication of feelings through some art forms), which is associated with enjoyment. This antagonism does not occur among the primary teachers' sample. Perhaps this is because the ideals of freer, modern methods of teaching have gained a wider acceptance in the primary schools than they have in the secondary schools.

Summary

While several factors of the secondary teachers were similar to those of the primary teachers, it is perhaps the differences that are more interesting. The most striking difference is the absence from the secondary teachers' set of aims groupings of a separate personal factor. The secondary teachers combined most of the aims included in the primary teachers' personal factor with intellectual competence. A few of these 'personal' aims were included by secondary teachers in the social/moral factor. It may be that the more specialized training and teaching activities of the secondary teachers lead them to view personal development as very closely integrated with higher order intellectual and social skills. The position of primary teachers as class teachers may lead them, on the other hand, to see a process of personal development taking place which is independent of intellectual or social activities. The different age ranges of the children with whom the two groups of teachers are concerned may influence their views of the 'independence' of the personal element.

GROUPS OF AIMS AND BIOGRAPHICAL VARIABLES

Table 19.4 shows the different biographical sub-groups who scored higher on each factor significantly more often. All seven factors were significantly preferred by sub-groups of the sample. Half the significant aims preferences

Table 19.4 Sub-groups of the secondary teachers' sample scoring higher on each of 7 aims factors significantly more often

	Factor	Sub-group favouring	Signif. level	Sub-group disfavouring	Signif. level
I	Basic skills	Graduates	0·01	PE teachers	0·001
		No prev. primary experience	0·05	Art teachers	0·05
II	Intellectual autonomy	Younger	0·01	Music teachers	0·001
		Less experienced	0·01	RE teachers	0·01
		Non-graduates	0·05		
		Art teachers	0·05		
III	Intellectual and personal competence	English teachers	0·01	PE teachers	0·001
IV	Social/ personal/ moral	Non-graduates	0·05	Art teachers	0·01
				English teachers	0·05
				History teachers	0·05
V	Aesthetic enjoyment v. formal learning	English teachers favour aesthetic	0·001		
		Art teachers favour aesthetic	0·05		
		Higher positions favour formal	0·05		
		Maths teachers favour formal	0·05		
VI	Spiritual/ religious	Older	0·001		
		More experienced	0·001		
		RE teachers	0·001		
		Previous primary experience	0·01		
		Higher positions	0·05		
VII	Cultural	Non-graduates	0·01	Science teachers	0·05
		PE teachers	0·05		
		Previous primary experience	0·05		

were related to specialized teaching activities. The basic skills were significantly emphasized by graduate teachers. This was the only factor significantly preferred by graduates, who also (Table 18.4) significantly favoured the intellectual aspect of development. It would appear that their understanding of 'intellectual' was seen rather narrowly in terms of the basic skills. It is possible that the graduates saw these skills as essential for further intellectual advances, and perhaps considered the more independent intellectual activities encouraged under the intellectual autonomy group of aims as beyond the intellectual capabilities of the primary school child. On the other hand, it may be that graduate teachers do not favour those independent intellectual activities described in the intellectual autonomy factor.

The non-graduate teachers favoured intellectual autonomy rather than basic skills. These teachers also significantly favoured the cultural factor. It will be recalled that the intellectual autonomy factor contained some 'aesthetic' aims and other aims associated with enjoyment of school and leisure pursuits. It would appear that non-graduates favour those aims encouraging the child's independent intellectual activity within an aesthetic context. The preference of the non-graduates for the social/personal/moral factor is curious as, by and large, this group of aims is not favoured by those teachers who emphasize aesthetic enjoyment or personal autonomy (see Tables 19.5 and 19.6 below). It would appear that the non-graduate teachers in the sample favoured a socially contented but somewhat conformist child whose independence is intellectual and aesthetic rather than social.

Intellectual autonomy was also significantly emphasized by younger, less experienced teachers. Older teachers with longer experience emphasized the spiritual/religious factor. These are the only factors which are associated significantly with age and experience. Teachers in higher positions emphasized spiritual/religious aims and the formal aims in 'aesthetic enjoyment v. formal learning'.

The other associations between biographical sub-groups and factor preferences concerned specialist teaching. English teachers significantly preferred intellectual and personal competence and rejected the social/personal/moral factor. Art teachers favoured the intellectual autonomy factor and the aesthetic aims in 'aesthetic enjoyment v. formal learning'. They scored lower the basic skills and the social/personal/moral groups of aims. Interestingly, the art teachers did not significantly favour the cultural factor, although it contained many aesthetic aims. Art teachers seemed to prefer grouping aesthetic aims with personal or intellectual aims rather than with the physical education and science aims, as occurred in the cultural factor. The physical education teachers rated basic skills and intellectual and personal competence low; they significantly favoured only the cultural factor, which contains all the physical aims. Why the physical education teachers rated the two intellectual factors lower than other teachers is unclear.

It is interesting that the science teachers significantly rated the cultural factor lower, as this factor contained several aims concerned with science, such as the child knowing some simple science and understanding modern technology. It is not easy to understand the science teachers' low rating of these aims and whether it is due to their disapproval of the way science is taught in the primary school or if it is because the science teachers consider that the primary child is too young to be taught science. Further investigation of their attitudes may prove of interest.

A less unexpected association is the significant preference of mathematics teachers for formal, ordered learning. The 'aesthetic enjoyment v. formal learning' factor reveals a polarization between the mathematics teachers and the art and English teachers, the latter favouring a freer, aesthetic set of aims concerned with creativity and enjoyment, while the former approve a more formal, ordered learning situation. No doubt the nature of their specialized subjects influenced the teachers' choice of aims. It is interesting to see, however, that the demands of their specialist subjects appeared to influence their wider view of educational aims.

GROUPS OF AIMS AND BROAD PURPOSES

High scoring on each of the factors was compared with the teachers' responses to the question about the two broad purposes of primary education, where respondents were asked to share five points between a societal and an individual purpose. The results are shown in Table 19.5. Preference for the cultural factor was significantly related to neither purpose. Apart from this

Table 19.5 Significant relationships between secondary teachers' preference for one of 2 broad purposes of primary education and emphasis on 7 aims factors

	Factor	Significance level	
		Societal purpose: equipping child with skills and attitudes appropriate to society	Individual purpose: development of child's individuality and independence
I	Basic skills	0·001	—
II	Intellectual autonomy	—	0·001
III	Intellectual and personal competence	—	0·001
IV	Social/personal/moral	0·01	—
V	Aesthetic enjoyment v. formal learning	0·001 (formal learning)	—
VI	Spiritual/religious	0·01	—
VII	Cultural	—	—

factor there was a marked division of emphasis between those teachers who gave a high score to either of the purposes.

It would appear that both primary and secondary teachers who gave high scores to the societal or to the individual purpose of primary education emphasized different groups of aims. Those teachers scoring high on the individual purpose favoured a more 'active' intellectual and personal set of aims, while the teachers who gave a high score to the societal purpose favoured basic skills, formal learning and the spiritual/religious aims.

GROUPS OF AIMS AND ASPECTS OF DEVELOPMENT

The data were examined for significant relationships between the rating of the seven aspects of development as most or least important and emphasis on the aims in each of the seven factors. Table 19.6 shows the significant relationships.

Table 19.6 Significant relationships between secondary teachers' emphasis on 7 aims factors and support for 7 aspects of development

Factor	Most important aspects	Signif. level	Least important aspects	Signif. level
I Basic skills	Intellectual	0·001	Emotional/ personal	0·001
II Intellectual autonomy	Emotional/ personal Aesthetic	0·001 0·01	Moral Spiritual/ religious	0·001 0·001
III Intellectual and personal competence	Emotional/ personal	0·001	Moral	0·01
IV Social/ personal/ moral	Moral Physical	0·001 0·01	Aesthetic	0·001
V Aesthetic enjoyment v. formal learning	Moral (*formal aims*)	0·05	Emotional/ personal (*formal aims*)	0·01
VI Spiritual/ religious	Spiritual/ religious Moral	0·001 0·05	Physical Aesthetic Emotional/ personal Social	0·001 0·01 0·01 0·05
VII Cultural	Aesthetic	0·05	—	

The social/personal/moral and the spiritual/religious factors were emphasized by teachers who regarded the moral aspect of development as one of the most important. These teachers also emphasized the formal, ordered learning expressed in the 'formal' aims in 'aesthetic enjoyment v. formal learning'. The teachers who emphasized these three factors regarded the emotional/personal aspect of development as one of the least important. At the same time, the intellectual autonomy and personal and intellectual competence factors were emphasized by teachers who considered the emotional/personal or the aesthetic aspect of development as one of the most important and the moral aspect as one of the least important.

The emphasizing of the intellectual autonomy and the intellectual and personal competence factors by those teachers who considered the emotional/personal aspect of development as one of the most important is interesting, as it could imply that the personal aims were dominant. It is also worth noticing that it is the teachers who considered the emotional/personal aspect of development as one of the most important who favoured the higher order intellectual skills. Teachers who regarded the intellectual aspect of development as one of the most important emphasized the basic skills factor, indicating that intellectual development was defined in rather narrow terms. Teachers emphasizing the basic skills factor also considered the emotional/personal factor as one of the least important.

An interesting feature of the relationship between emphasis on groups of aims and the choice of different aspects of development as important is the close association between the emotional/personal aspect of development and the aesthetic aspect. The emotional/personal and the aesthetic aspects of development were rated in the 'opposite' direction to moral development in connection with five out of the seven factors. It can be inferred that in 'aesthetic enjoyment v. formal learning' the aesthetic aims were emphasized by those teachers who considered the emotional/personal aspect of development as one of the most important and not by teachers who regarded the aesthetic aspect of development as one of the most important. This may suggest that the aesthetic aims are regarded as a method of fostering personal development rather than increasing aesthetic understanding in its own right.

20 Summary and conclusions

Secondary teachers who had an active interest in the eleven to twelve year-olds completed the questionnaire on the aims of primary education. The balance of the primary teacher sample on biological variables conformed closely to national proportions. The secondary teachers' sample tended to be over-representative of women and under-representative of older teachers as compared to national proportions. It is not possible to determine if this bias is due to self-selection by respondents or whether young women are given more than their proportional share of teaching eleven to twelve year-olds. The proportion of teachers from secondary modern schools responding to the questionnaire is much lower than national proportions and this should be borne in mind when considering the results of the secondary teachers' survey.

The major interest of this study is to provide evidence of differences or similarities of aims for primary education between primary and secondary teachers. Overall the results indicate remarkable similarities of view as to the relative importance of aims. Differences of stress and detail appear but the structure was the same for both sets of teachers.

The same groups of aims were ranked as of utmost importance and as of least importance by both the primary and the secondary teachers. The group of aims with the highest mean score included reading and a set of personal and social aims concerned with the well-behaved, teachable child. The aims with the lowest mean score were the same for both samples and were those aims concerned with physical education, music and science.

The three aims which the secondary teachers considered more important than the primary teachers had done concern three very formal basic skills—arithmetic, spelling and legible writing. This is consistent with the secondary teachers' view of primary education as a foundation for further academic work. The primary teachers attached more importance to aims concerning self-confidence, individuality and kindness. Differences between the sets of respondents in this case may well be due to the age ranges taught. On the whole, secondary teachers gave slightly greater emphasis to those basic skills which prepare the child for secondary 'academic' work, while the primary teachers slightly preferred those skills which enable the child to function adequately in his daily life. These differences, however, are to be seen within a context of fundamental agreement.

The intellectual, social and emotional/personal aspects of development were most commonly thought to be the most important by both primary and secondary teachers. The aesthetic, physical and the spiritual/religious aspects of development were most widely considered to be of least importance by both samples. Fifty-three per cent of the primary and 56% of the secondary sample agreed that the intellectual aspect of development was the most important. However, only 46% of the secondary sample considered the emotional/personal aspect of development as one of the most important, as compared with 54% of the primary teachers. The greater interest of the primary teachers in the child's personal development is noticeable throughout, and it has been suggested that this may be due to the ages of the children taught or to the different functions of the primary teachers—who are mainly class-teachers—and the specialist subject teachers in the secondary school.

Most of the teachers in both samples gave a nearly equal score to both the societal and the individual purpose of primary education. A larger proportion of secondary teachers than primary teachers gave a high mark to one of the purposes. Seventeen per cent of the secondary teachers and 12% of the primary teachers gave a high score to the individual purpose. Nineteen per cent of the secondary teachers and 16% of the primary teachers gave a high score to the societal purpose. In both samples the high societal and the high individual scorers were fairly evenly balanced. A similar close relationship between a high score for one of the purposes and choice of important aspects of development was found in both samples. High societal scorers favoured the intellectual and the spiritual/religious aspects of development. High individual scorers favoured the emotional/personal aspect of development.

The factor analysis performed on the scores given to the aims by both samples reveals interesting differences in the way aims were grouped together. Both samples produced very similar groups of basic skills, spiritual/religious, intellectual autonomy and cultural aims. The most striking difference was the absence from the secondary teachers' groupings of a separate personal factor. The secondary teachers showed a marked tendency to combine personal aims with intellectual competence and social/moral aims. This fusion of the personal with intellectual and moral aims may spring from the more intellectual training and interests of the secondary teachers, who appear to conceive of personal development in terms of intellectual and social development, rather than as an end in itself. There is less of an active independent flavour in the secondary teachers' aims groupings but a slightly greater stress on enjoyment and enthusiasm than appears among the primary teachers.

Biographical sub-groups of each sample did not emphasize the same groups of aims. Whereas most differences about aims among primary teachers are associated with age, experience and length of service, the most marked differences among secondary teachers are associated with specialist teaching activities. There appears to be a division between the physical education, religious education and music teachers, on the one hand, and the art and English teachers, on the other. The former teachers disfavoured the freer, aesthetic aims of the latter. Another subject-based division appears to be between English and art teachers, favouring the freer, aesthetic aims, and the maths teachers, emphasizing formal ordered learning. In both primary and secondary samples the older, more experienced teachers in high positions favoured the spiritual/religious aims.

Overall, it will be seen that primary and secondary teachers have similar views about the aims of primary education. Differences that arise appear to be the result of the divergent age groups taught. For the primary school teacher, the eleven-year-old is at the end of the process; for the secondary school teacher, he is only at the beginning. This difference of perspective may account in some measure for the few differences of opinion about aims.

Related exploratory studies

Aims and approaches of primary head teachers

21 Introduction

The Aims of Primary Education Project was primarily concerned with studying teachers' opinions about aims. Subsidiary studies were concerned with examining teaching methods and approaches. What was clearly necessary was a means of tying the two together and making an exploration of the relationship between preferred aims and chosen teaching approaches.

THE SAMPLE

In a random sample of 201 primary schools, 1513 teachers had completed a questionnaire about the aims of primary education. Of this number, 169 were head teachers (the remaining 32 omitted to return a teacher's questionnaire for themselves). Since so much information was available about the opinions of aims of this sample of teachers, it was economical to use the same sample for a follow-up questionnaire about methods. However, since the 'aims' questionnaire had been anonymous, it was impossible to associate a second questionnaire with the first from any one person. Head teachers, however, were identifiable from the question on position in the biographical section. Only 30% of the heads had full-time, or nearly full-time, responsibility for a class and were thus personally involved in using teaching methods. It was therefore decided to ask the head teachers about which approaches they *advocated*. A questionnaire was prepared and sent to the heads of all the sample schools.

THE QUESTIONNAIRE

By the time of preparation of this questionnaire, many discussions had been held with teachers about teaching methods and approaches. In particular, it had been attempted to discover what were the main areas of difference between (a) one teacher and another, and (b) work concerned with different aims. There are obviously so many components to teaching methods: type and nature of content, resources, the nature of children's activity, the style of teaching, the amount and nature of teacher–child contact, and so on. An attempt was therefore made to identify a small number of major 'keys' to these differences. Eventually, five were established as follows:

(a) the time allotted to each curriculum area;
(b) the degree to which each curriculum area is treated as a separate subject or is integrated with other areas of work;
(c) the flexibility of time allowed for different curriculum areas;
(d) the kinds of grouping of childern used;
(e) the teaching style: whether teacher-directed, child-centred or a combined approach.

One question was designed to cover each of these items. The first (section 1 of the questionnaire) was dealt with by asking the head teachers to fill in a 'pie' diagram divided into twenty segments. Alternative answers were supplied for each of the remaining items (section 2 of the questionnaire). A grid was prepared with ten columns, each headed with the name of a subject or curriculum area. The heads were asked to fill in the code letter of the alternative they chose for each question for each curriculum area. If the names given to the curriculum areas were not the ones they used themselves, they were asked to use the nearest equivalent. Thus if they used the name 'creative activities', they would insert the relevant answers under 'art/craft'. The full text of the questionnaire is given as Appendix N.

The questionnaire sample consisted of heads of infant, junior and primary (5–11) schools. It was explained to the head teachers in a covering letter that it was not known whether it was possible for them to give one set of answers for the whole age group within their schools. They were asked to do so if they could but, if not, to indicate the part of their age range for which they were supplying answers.

RESPONSE

A total of 123 completed questionnaires were returned by the head teachers. Of these, 16 referred to the 5–11 age group, 26 to the infant age group and 81 to the junior age range.

PRESENTATION OF FINDINGS

The findings will be presented in two parts. The first part will deal with the distribution of alternative responses to the five questions. The second part will deal with the exploration of relationships between those responses and preferred aims.

For the purposes of the first part, only the responses of the head teachers of junior schools are presented; infant and primary schools were underrepresented and their numbers are too small for meaningful comparison with the junior schools. Yet even the small numbers revealed probable differences from the junior schools, which precludes any value in combining the results for the three kinds of schools. Furthermore, results will be presented only for the six curriculum areas common to all eighty-one junior schools. The remaining four—second language, science, history and geography as separate subjects, and environmental studies—were not engaged in by substantial minorities of the schools. For the purposes of this exploration of the range of approaches in use, the six common curriculum areas were deemed to provide a sufficient basis. As a matter of interest, Table 21.1 shows the numbers and percentages of the junior schools engaged in each of the less common curriculum areas.

Table 21.1   Proportions of the sample of 81 junior schools engaging in second language, science, history and geography as separate subjects, and environmental studies

Subject	No.	%
Second language	27	33·3
Science	34	42·0
History and geography	17	21·0
Environmental studies	51	63·0

22 Analysis of responses (junior school head teachers)

TIME ALLOCATION

The data for this section are taken from the pie diagrams (section 1, questions 1–2) filled in by sixty-eight of the junior head teachers. The remaining thirteen omitted to complete this question. The diagrams were divided into twenty segments, each thus representing 5% of the total. In completing the diagrams the head teachers gave their own names to the curriculum areas. In order to make comparison possible, the names were translated into their nearest equivalents on the standard list prepared for the remainder of the questionnaire. Table 22.1 shows the results.

Table 22.1 Percentage range of time and percentage mean time given to six common curriculum areas by 68 junior school head teachers

Curriculum area	% range of time	% mean time	SD
Mathematics	15–30	20·3	4·4
Language	15–53	27·7	7·5
Religious education	5–15	6·7	3·3
Physical education	5–20	9·6	3·6
Art and craft	5–20	10·7	4·0
Music	5–15	5·4	3·0

It needs to be remembered that most of these percentages are based upon estimates. Probably few head teachers had actual timetables to work from and, as several of them pointed out, it was very difficult to estimate just how much time was spent upon different curriculum areas, particularly if they worked some kind of integrated day. Nevertheless, most of the head teachers who completed this question were faced with the same problem and all filled in the diagram, thus showing the space–time relationship of each area within the whole. There is therefore this common basis in the material.

The most striking feature of the table is the quite wide discrepancy in time allocation to different areas within various schools. Even allowing for the approximation, and for whether or not head teachers have included incidental time within the percentages or have restricted them to time spent exclusively in each area of work, the range of 15% to 53% of time spent on language, for example, is remarkable. It may be convenient to remember that, equating one week to 100% of time, 1% represents just about a quarter of an hour. Thus, in practical terms, the time spent on language in different schools varied from something like $3\frac{3}{4}$ hours per week to $13\frac{1}{4}$ hours per week. This was the largest difference but the remaining ranges all represented a time in excess of $2\frac{1}{2}$ hours per week. The standard deviations, or average differences from the mean, were of course much less. For example, on average, these schools varied by about two hours in the time given to language. Nevertheless, it is important to recognize that the range of time given to each curriculum area is so wide, even among this small sample of schools.

A minority of the head teachers had introduced the newest primary school subjects of second language and science. Table 22.2 shows the range of time and mean time given to each of them in the relevant schools.

Table 22.2   Percentage range of time and percentage mean time given to second language and science by junior school head teachers

Curriculum area	No. of schools	% range of time	% mean time
Second language	27	2–10	5·7
Science	34	3–10	5·7

It was thought interesting to look for an indication of where time tended to be taken from so that it could be given to these two curriculum areas. Table 22.3 shows the results of this calculation. It seems fairly clear that there is a tendency to take the time for these 'new' subjects from the language area.

Table 22.3   Percentage mean time given to six common curriculum areas in 68 junior schools engaging/not engaging in second language and science

Curriculum area	No second language, no science	Second language but no science	Science but no second language	Second language + science
Mathematics	19·5	18·8	19·3	19·8
Language	32·3	26·1	27·3	23·5
RE	7·2	7·3	7·3	6·5
PE	10·1	10·2	9·1	9·3
Art/craft	11·9	11·0	10·2	9·2
Music	4·5	5·2	6·0	8·0

The percentages in the other areas are remarkably consistent. The increase in time spent on music, which appears to go along with the introduction of new subjects, is a curious indication. There are certainly striking new developments in the approaches to, and equipment for, teaching music and it is an interesting speculation that the generally innovatory head, as evidenced by his introduction of a second language and/or science, may be particularly likely to take them up and give more time to music.

The evidence presented above is based on responses from only sixty-eight head teachers. However, that such wide discrepancies should occur within so small a sample is suggestive, and further exploration should be worth while.

SUBJECT INTEGRATION

Data for this and the remaining portions of this chapter are based upon the responses of eighty-one head teachers of junior schools. The head teachers were asked (section 2, question 3) to what extent they advocated the treatment of each curriculum area as a separate subject or to what extent they advocated its integration with other areas of work. They were given the following list of alternatives, from which they were asked to pick one for each curriculum area:

A   Treated entirely as a separate subject; few or no references made to it at any other time.

B   Treated as a separate subject but used frequently in the course of other work.

C   Treated about equally as much as a separate subject and as a part of other work.

D   Treated as a separate subject to a minor extent, most work being done in other areas.

E   Not treated as a separate subject at all.

Once again, results in Table 22.4 are given only for the six common curriculum areas.

Table 22.4   Proportions of the sample of 81 junior school head teachers advocating alternative approaches to six common curriculum areas

Curriculum area	Percentages supporting five approaches				
	Wholly subject	Mostly subject	Half and half	Mostly integrated	Wholly integrated
Mathematics	6·2	80·2	9·9	1·2	2·5
Language	0·0	21·2	42·5	23·8	12·5
RE	28·7	37·5	15·0	12·5	6·3
PE	72·8	23·5	2·5	0·0	1·2
Art/craft	3·7	24·6	39·5	26·0	6·2
Music	42·5	48·8	6·3	1·2	1·2

The only unanimity was in respect of language not being treated wholly as a separate subject and of physical education not being largely integrated. Otherwise, there was at least one head (1·2% of the sample) who advocated every approach. The highest agreement in favour of any particular approach was in the 'mostly subject' approach to mathematics and the 'wholly subject' approach to physical education. Few heads advocated a 'wholly integrated' approach to any of the curriculum areas. As might be expected, language and art/craft were most often given an integrated treatment at least half of the time. Overall, mathematics, religious education, physical education and music were largely recommended for a subject approach, and language and art/craft for a part-subject, part-integrated approach. Interestingly, there was a slightly more even distribution of approaches to religious education than to any other area. In every other case, the bulk of the sample tended to divide between two alternatives, or three in the case of language.

TIME FLEXIBILITY

The head teachers were asked to indicate what kind of time flexibility they advocated in relation to each curriculum area (section 2, question 4). The following alternatives were given:

A   A regular amount of time which should be adhered to fairly consistently.
B   A minimum regular amount of time which can be freely increased.
C   Considerable flexibility so long as a long-term proportion of time is maintained.
D   Complete flexibility with neither upper nor lower time limits.

The distribution of the responses of the eighty-one head teachers concerned with the junior age range is shown in Table 22.5.

Once again, a diversity of policy was apparent. The highest agreement,

Table 22.5   Proportions of the sample of 81 junior school head teachers advocating alternative degrees of time flexibility for six common curriculum areas

Curriculum area	Percentages supporting four degrees of flexibility			
	Regular time	Minimum time which can be increased	Flexible— long-term balance	Complete flexibility
Mathematics	22·5	31·3	38·7	7·5
Language	7·4	18·5	59·3	14·8
RE	40·5	30·4	16·4	12·7
PE	61·9	21·3	15·5	1·3
Art/craft	10·5	25·0	45·6	18·9
Music	39·5	40·7	13·6	6·2

around 60% of the heads, was that language should be given a very flexible time allocation so long as a long-term balance was maintained and that physical education should be given a regular and fixed amount of time. Otherwise, the heads were more evenly divided.

This question, like the others in the questionnaire, was formulated because extensive discussion with teachers gave rise to the suggestion that it covered a point of real and fundamental difference between teachers' approaches. This particular question was perhaps the most novel and surprising. After all, it is a matter of common observation that teachers have different opinions about the time that should be given to different curriculum areas, about the integration of subjects, about how children should be grouped, and about their own role as teachers. This question, though, covered a point which is perhaps not so commonly observable, and that teachers do indeed differ in this respect is certainly confirmed by the range of the head teachers' responses. Differences on this question seem to imply quite different valuations of the curriculum areas and views about the nature of learning within them. In relation to mathematics, for example, two out of ten of this (albeit small) sample of head teachers thought that there should be a regular, probably daily mathematics period, no more and no less. Three out of ten thought that there should be that regular period but that more time could be spent freely. Almost four out of ten did not advocate the regular time for mathematics but thought that the time spent could be very flexible so long as there was a long-term balance; this would probably mean that perhaps no mathematics would be done for a period of perhaps days, followed by an intensive session. Just fewer than one in ten would give no particular time allocation to mathematics at all but advocated as much, or as little, time being spent as circumstances directed. These differences were echoed in the other five curriculum areas. It would seem worth while for this question to be more extensively re-examined, in view of the probably crucial nature of differences between these opinions.

GROUPING

The head teachers indicated which of the following grouping alternatives they advocated for each curriculum area (section 2, question 5):

A   Groups larger than a class.
B   The whole class.
C   Groups.
D   Individuals.
E   Both the whole class and groups.
F   Both the whole class and individuals.
G   Both groups and individuals.
H   The whole class, groups and individuals.

The junior school heads' responses were distributed as shown in Table 22.6.

Table 22.6   Proportions of the sample of 81 junior school head teachers showing preference for alternative kinds of grouping in six common curriculum areas

Grouping	% preferring each grouping, by curriculum area					
	Maths	Language	RE	PE	Art/craft	Music
Class plus	0·0	0·0	4·4	5·9	0·0	4·9
Class	5·0	1·2	50·0	35·8	4·9	23·4
Groups	11·1	9·9	2·5	11·1	23·5	6·2
Individuals	9·9	7·4	0·0	0·2	7·4	1·2
Class and groups	11·1	4·9	22·8	27·2	9·9	38·3
Class and individuals	0·0	7·4	5·1	2·5	3·7	2·5
Groups and individuals	25·9	21·0	1·3	1·2	18·5	2·5
Class, groups and individuals	37·0	48·2	13·9	16·1	32·1	21·0

Generally, there was more agreement on this question. Only small minorities advocated a grouping larger than the class, wholly individual-based organization, or a mixture of class and individuals. Apart from the quarter, third and half respectively who advocated class work in music, physical education and religious education, and the quarter who preferred a wholly group organization for art and craft, the majority preferred mixed approaches involving the class and groups, groups and individuals, or all three. In these circumstances, the real difference is probably between those who did and those who did not advocate an element of class work. Table 22.7 shows the sample divided on the criterion of advocating an element of class work.

Table 22.7   Proportions of the sample of 81 junior school head teachers advocating/not advocating an element of class work in six common curriculum areas

Curriculum area	Element of class work (%)	No class work (%)
Religious education	91·8*	3·8
Music	85·2*	9·9
Physical education	81·6*	12·5
Language	61·7	38·3
Mathematics	53·1	46·9
Art and craft	50·6	49·4

* Omitting percentages of the sample who favoured a grouping larger than a class: 4·4% for religious education, 4·9% for music, 5·9% for physical education.

Bearing in mind that, in almost every case, the majority option was for a mixed approach involving at least two different kinds of grouping, it is interesting that there is such a lack of consensus about the use of the 'class group'. Given the range of alternative groupings and combinations of alternatives that the head teachers were asked to choose among, choice of the class group must imply class teaching. Working with the whole class group other than by teaching would be described as individual or group organization. It is interesting that head teachers who saw no place at all for class teaching were always in a minority. However, in regard to language, mathematics, and art and craft, the minority became substantial; in the latter two cases, it was almost half. Nevertheless, while the majority of heads clearly like to see flexibility and a variety of ways of organizing children, many advocate some class teaching element in all curriculum areas.

TEACHER'S ROLE

Three brief descriptions of alternative teacher's roles were given (section 2, question 6):

A   The teacher's task is to have full knowledge of what he wants his children to know, to be capable, by analysis and experience, of presenting it to them interestingly in as well-programmed a manner as possible, and to set the pace of learning.

B   The teacher's task is to present work as stimulatingly as possible so that each child, sometimes following his own direction and sometimes the teacher's, can learn as much as he is capable of.

C   The teacher's task is to create a psychological environment in which inquiry can arise and a physical environment rich and stimulating enough to enable it to be pursued successfully at the child's own pace.

These can be abbreviated respectively as a teacher-directed approach, a mixed approach and a child-centred approach. The head teachers were asked

Table 22.8   Proportions of the sample of 81 junior school head teachers showing preference for each of three teacher's roles in six common curriculum areas

Curriculum area	Teacher-directed %	Mixed %	Child-centred %
Mathematics	36·7	58·9	4·4
Language	12·0	64·8	23·2
Religious education	30·8	42·3	26·9
Physical education	12·8	61·6	25·6
Art and craft	1·3	41·0	57·7
Music	29·9	53·2	16·9

to indicate which approach they advocated in each curriculum area. Table 22.8 shows the results.

A mixed approach was the most frequent policy in all curriculum areas except art and craft, in which a majority advocated a child-centred approach. Relatively few head teachers advocated a teacher-directed approach in these areas; the exceptions were mathematics, religious education and music, where around a third of the heads thought a teacher-directed approach was appropriate. About a quarter of the heads recommended a child-centred approach to language, religious education and physical education, and rather less (16·9%) for music.

CONCLUSIONS

This was an exploratory study. The responses of only eighty-one head teachers of the junior age range have been presented. Nonetheless, the lack of consensus is striking. There was some overall preference for using a mixture of types of grouping and for a moderate teaching approach involving both teacher-direction and child-centredness. However, there was certainly not unanimity even in these respects, and there was a wide distribution of the heads' responses over the alternatives in respect of time allocation, integration and time flexibility.

23 Relationships between preferred approaches and aims stressed (entire sample)

For the purpose of this chapter, responses from all the head teachers—infant, junior and primary—were used. All of the heads had completed a questionnaire on the aims of primary education as part of the earlier, major study described in Part I of this book. A factor analysis was performed on the scores given by the total sample of 1513 teachers, including the heads, to each of the seventy-two aims. Seven factors emerged and these, together with their constituent aims, are listed in Table 9.5 (p. 66). The total sample was split into four parts for each factor according to whether their average score for aims within each factor occurred within the first, second, third or fourth quarter of the whole range (see p. 68). The scores of those in the first quarter were the highest given. The head teachers whose aims scores had placed them in the highest quarter for each factor were separated out. Their responses to each of the questions under discussion in the present study were then analysed for significant tendencies. These are discussed in turn below.

TIME ALLOCATION

There were seventy possible relationships here between high scoring on each of the seven factors, or groups of aims, and the total of ten curriculum areas (listed in Tables 21.1 and 22.1). As a time economy measure, the eight combinations thought most likely to show a relationship were tested first:

High scoring on	Time spent on
Basic skills aims	Language
Basic skills aims	Mathematics
Cultural aims	Physical education
Cultural aims	Art and craft
Cultural aims	Music
Cultural aims	Science
Spiritual/religious aims	Religious education
Social/moral aims	Religious education

Of these eight, only two showed a significant relationship. Stress on the cultural group of aims was related to spending more time on science; this relationship was significant beyond the 0·001 level. Stress on the spiritual/ religious group of aims was significantly related to spending more time on religious education, a relationship significant beyond the 0·01 level. Since these were the only two relationships of the eight found to be significant, no more were tested; it was assumed that there was little relationship between the stressing of particular groups of aims and the time spent on related curriculum areas.

SUBJECT INTEGRATION

The significant relationships between preferences on this question and high scoring on groups of aims are shown in Table 23.1. High scoring on the basic

Table 23.1   Significant relationships between high scoring by sample heads on 7 aims factors and preference for a subject-based or an integrated approach to curriculum areas

	Factor	Approach	Curriculum area	Signif. level
I	Basic skills	—	—	—
II	Intellectual autonomy	Integrated	Physical education	0·01
			Religious education	0·05
III	Intellectual competence	—	—	—
IV	Personal	Integrated	Religious education	0·01
			Physical education	0·01
			Music	0·01
			Second language	0·01
			Science	0·01
			Mathematics	0·05
V	Social/moral	—	—	—
VI	Spiritual/ religious	Subject-based	Second language	0·01
			Language	0·05
VII	Cultural	Integrated	Religious education	0·05

skills, intellectual competence and the social/moral group of aims bore no significant relationship with any preference for subject-based or integrated approaches in any curriculum area. High scoring of aims within the personal, cultural and intellectual autonomy groups was significantly related to preferences for an integrated approach to some areas of the curriculum. As might be expected, high scoring on the personal aims was related to the most wide-spread preference for integration. Indeed, the only curriculum areas common to all schools not to emerge in this connection were those of language and art/craft. It is interesting that religious education seems to be a key curriculum area. It is the one subject in which an integrated approach was advocated by all three groups of heads distinguished by their stress on personal, cultural and intellectual autonomy aims.

Head teachers who stressed the spiritual/religious group of aims tended to prefer a subject-based approach in two areas of the curriculum. Particularly interesting is their tendency to advocate a more subject-based approach to language, since the earlier evidence suggested a very widespread preference for the integration of language work. In this respect the heads who stressed spiritual/religious aims seem particularly at variance with the trend.

TIME FLEXIBILITY

This was thought to be a particularly important question, and it was seen (p. 157) that the junior head teachers were well distributed between the alternatives in their responses. Whatever underlies these differences of opinion, however, among the whole sample of infant, junior and primary heads there was only very limited relevance to aims. Not surprisingly, head teachers who scored highly on the basic skills group of aims tended more often (significant beyond the 0·01 level) to favour the spending of fixed and regular amounts of time on mathematics and language. Those who stressed the cultural group of aims tended (significant beyond the 0·05 level) to favour a more flexible allocation of time to mathematics and religious education.

GROUPING

Since the data for this were unordered, with overlapping categories, it was not possible statistically to relate this material to the aims data.

TEACHER'S ROLE

Table 23.2 shows the significant relationships between preferences for different teaching approaches and high scoring on different groups of aims. Once again, most significant relationships occurred between stress on the personal group of aims and preference for teaching approaches. All of these relationships were with a preference for a child-centred approach. A child-centred approach to art and craft was significantly more often preferred by those who stressed the intellectual autonomy group of aims; it was interesting that this was the one area in which this preference, on the part of the particular group of heads, showed up. The preference for a more traditional, teacher-directed approach on the part of those head teachers who stressed the spiritual/religious group of aims is entirely consistent with the data arising from the main study. It is of interest, however, that the preference emerged significantly only in the one area of mathematics.

Table 23.2   Significant relationships between sample heads' preference for a teacher-directed or a child-centred approach to curriculum areas and high scoring on 7 aims factors

	Factor	Approach	Curriculum area	Signif. level
I	Basic skills	—	—	—
II	Intellectual autonomy	Child-centred	Art/craft	0·01
III	Intellectual competence	—	—	—
IV	Personal	Child-centred	Science	0·001
			Music	0·01
			Second language	0·01
			Environmental studies	0·01
			Religious education	0·05
V	Social/moral	—	—	—
VI	Spiritual/ religious	Teacher-directed	Mathematics	0·001
VII	Cultural	—	—	—

CONCLUSIONS

It may be fairly concluded that while detailed examination of the junior heads' responses, at any rate, showed up the tendency of substantial numbers of heads to advocate most of the alternative approaches offered in most of the curriculum areas, these marked differences of opinion fail to show much relationship with preferred aims. It may be that, despite the careful initial discussion work with teachers, the wrong questions were asked. It might be, on the other hand, that these choices of approach are not related to aims by teachers, although it would intuitively be expected that at least some of them would be. If the latter is the case, then most choices of methods and approaches seem to be made on criteria other than those of following through from the aims to which teachers have chosen to subscribe.

Interestingly, the most pervasive group of aims, in so far as high scoring of them was most frequently and most extensively related to advocating particular methods, was the personal one. Quite widespread preference for the integration of curriculum areas and for a child-centred approach were related to high scoring on aims related to children's personal development. It is interesting to speculate whether indeed curriculum and method changes in primary schools tend to originate in regard for children's personal rather than intellectual development.

Appendices

The primary school study

Appendix A
Head teachers' questionnaire

Aims of Primary Education Project

A. DESCRIPTION OF THE SCHOOL

The name of a school does not always convey its type and denomination and therefore it would be appreciated if you would first answer the following three questions.

1. Of what type is your school? Please tick as appropriate.

   Infant ☐
   Junior ☐
   Primary or JMI ☐
   [junior mixed and infants]

2. Do you have a nursery class or classes?

   Yes ☐
   No ☐

3. What is the denomination of your school? Please tick as appropriate.

   C of E ☐
   RC ☐
   Other denomination ☐
   Non-denominational ☐

   If 'other denomination', please specify. ....

B. THE SCHOOL, ITS ENVIRONMENT AND ORGANIZATION

Please answer the following questions by putting a tick in the appropriate box. Please tick only ONE alternative unless requested to do otherwise.

1. In which of the following kinds of areas is your school situated?

   Inner urban area ☐
   Suburban area ☐
   Traditional rural area ☐
   Commuter rural area ☐

2. What is the socio-economic
   background of the children?
   The difficulty of making
   such an assessment is
   appreciated but an indication
   of background would be
   useful.

   Middle class ☐
   Mixed intake but
     mainly middle class ☐
   Mixed intake; about
     50% middle class,
     50% working class ☐
   Mixed intake but mainly
     working class ☐
   Working class ☐

3. Which of the following attitudes
   to school is closest to that of
   the majority of parents of
   children in your school?

   Highly interested ☐
   Interested ☐
   Indifferent ☐

4. Which of the following best
   describes your school building
   and facilities as an environment
   for primary education?

   Good ☐
   Adequate ☐
   Limited ☐

5. How many children have you
   on roll?

   Up to 25 ☐
   26–50 ☐
   51–100 ☐
   101–200 ☐
   201–300 ☐
   301–400 ☐
   401–600 ☐
   601 upwards ☐

6. How many teachers are there
   on your staff NOT including
   yourself? Please fill in the
   appropriate numbers.

   Full-time ....

   Part-time ....

7. Do you have full-, or nearly
   full-time responsibility for
   a class?

   Yes ☐
   No ☐

8. How many children are there
   in most of your classes?

   Under 20 ☐
   21–29 ☐
   30–39 ☐
   40–49 ☐
   Over 50 ☐

9. How are the children grouped in the school?

In year groups ☐
In 2-year vertical groups ☐
In 3-year vertical groups ☐
In 4-year vertical groups ☐
In both year and vertical groups ☐

10. If there are two or more parallel classes, how are the children assigned to them? Please indicate by ticking more than one alternative if you use more than one system.

By age ☐
By ability ☐
Other ☐

11. Do you use any form of team teaching, i.e. large groups of children in the joint charge of two or more teachers?

All the time for all children ☐
All the time for some children ☐
Part of the time for all or some of the children ☐
No team teaching, as defined above, at all ☐

12. How far are you responsible for the planning of work for most individual classes?

To a very large extent ☐
To some extent ☐
To a very limited extent ☐
Not at all ☐

13. What form does most of your consultation with the staff take?

Regular formal meetings ☐
Occasional formal meetings ☐
Frequent informal contact ☐
Occasional informal contact ☐
Contact only when special issues arise ☐

14. Has your school any special characteristics; for example, a large, more than 20%, proportion of immigrant children, Welsh language teaching, involvement in a curriculum development project,

designation as an EPA [educational priority area] school etc?
If it has any special characteristics of this kind, please give
brief details below.

....

....

If there are any comments you would like to make, please do so below.
[Page left for comments]

Appendix B
Teachers' questionnaire

Aims of Primary Education Project

The questionnaire consists of four sections. Please read the instructions for each section carefully before completing it.

The three main sections ask you to give a rating of issues of importance in primary education. Please try to ensure that your answers accurately reflect your personal views.

Teachers have participated extensively in the construction of the questionnaire and have found it possible to complete it satisfactorily.

SECTION I

Please answer the following questions by putting a tick in the appropriate box.

1. Sex   Male   ☐

                                             Female   ☐

2. Age   21–29   ☐

                                             30–39   ☐

                                             40–49   ☐

                                             50–59   ☐

                                             60 or over   ☐

3. Marital status   Married   ☐

                                             Single   ☐

4. Have you ever spent at least two years, or more, in continuous paid employment other than teaching?   Yes   ☐

                                             No   ☐

5. What are your qualifications?
Please tick more than one if
appropriate

Teacher's Certificate ☐
Trained graduate ☐
Untrained graduate ☐
Higher degree, advanced
   diploma, etc. in education ☐

6. How long have you been
teaching?

Under 1 year ☐
1–5 years ☐
6–10 years ☐
11–20 years ☐
Over 20 years ☐

7. How long have you been in
your present school?

Under 1 year ☐
1–3 years ☐
4–10 years ☐
Over 10 years ☐

8. Are you a full- or part-time
teacher?

Full-time ☐
Part-time ☐

9. What is your present
position?

Head teacher ☐
Deputy head ☐
Head of dept ☐
Post of responsibility ☐
Class teacher ☐

10. Do you have particular
responsibility for teaching
any of the following to
more than one class of
children? Please tick
more than one if appropriate.

Physical education/games/
   dance ☐
Music ☐
Mathematics ☐
Art/craft ☐
Religious education ☐
Second language ☐
Other ☐

If other, please specify. . . . .

11. Please answer EITHER question (a) OR (b).

   (a) If your class comprises a
   ONE YEAR AGE RANGE,
   please indicate which one.

Nursery 3–4 year-olds ☐
Nursery 4–5 year-olds ☐
Reception ☐

Middle infants ☐
Top infants ☐
1st year juniors ☐
2nd year juniors ☐
3rd year juniors ☐
4th year juniors ☐

(b) If your class is VERTICALLY GROUPED, please indicate the age range.

Nursery ☐
5–6+ ☐
5–7 ☐
7–9 ☐
9–11 ☐
7–11 ☐

12. Which of the following age groups have you taught in the past? Please tick more than one if appropriate.

Nursery ☐
Infant ☐
Lower junior ☐
Upper junior ☐
Secondary ☐
Adult ☐

SECTION II

A. Below are two fundamental purposes of primary education. Would you please indicate the relative weight you would give to each by sharing 5 points between the two statements. If you wish you can give 5 to one and 0 to the other.

Please put the number you give to each statement in the appropriate box. Please use only whole numbers to make up the total of 5.

1. The purpose of primary education is to begin to equip the child with skills and attitudes which will enable him to take his place effectively and competently in society, fitting him to make a choice of an occupational role and to live harmoniously in his community. ☐

2. The purpose of primary education is to foster the development of the child's individuality and independence enabling him to discover his own talents and interests, find a full enjoyment of life in his own way and arrive at his own attitudes towards society. ☐

PLEASE ENSURE THAT THE TOTAL ADDS UP TO 5.

B.   Primary education is concerned with various aspects of the child's development.

Please indicate which you consider are:

(a) the two *most important* of these aspects by putting an M in each of the 2 appropriate boxes;

(b) the two *least important* of these aspects by putting an L in each of the 2 appropriate boxes.

aesthetic   ☐
emotional/physical   ☐
intellectual   ☐
moral   ☐
physical   ☐
social   ☐
spiritual/religious   ☐

PLEASE ENSURE THAT YOU HAVE GIVEN TWO MS AND TWO LS.

SECTION III

The aims and objectives on the following pages define the knowledge, the skills and the qualities which many teachers think that in general children in the MIDDLE RANGE OF ABILITY should have AT THE END OF THEIR PRIMARY EDUCATION.

Please consider these aims and objectives in relation to such children IN YOUR SCHOOL deciding what you would hope FOR THEM by the time they leave primary school at the age of eleven.

Each statement is concerned with an important aspect of primary education; to help to judge each one on its own merits, the statements have been mixed so that adjacent ones are not about the same aspects of primary education.

There are a large number of statements to rate and you might find it helpful to take a break now and again.

Please indicate your opinion of the importance of these aims and objectives of primary education for children in your school by using the scale 5, 4, 3, 2, 1, 0 as set out [below] and putting a circle round the number you choose for each statement.

5   I think that this aim is of the *utmost importance* in primary education.

4   I think that this aim is of *major importance* in primary education.

3   I think that this aim is *important* in primary education.

2   I think that this aim is of *minor importance* in primary education.

1   I think that this aim is of *no importance* in primary education.

0   I think that this *should not be* an aim of primary education.

Points to remember when rating these statements
  (i) To have in mind children IN YOUR SCHOOL.
 (ii) To have in mind the children IN THE MIDDLE RANGE OF ABILITY.
(iii) To have in mind the children AT THE END OF THEIR PRIMARY
       EDUCATION.

1. The child should be able to communicate his
    feelings through some art forms; for example,
    painting, music, drama, movement.   5 4 3 2 1 0

2. The child should have an understanding of how
    his body works.   5 4 3 2 1 0

3. The child should know how to acquire
    information other than by reading; for example,
    by asking questions, by experimenting, from
    watching television.   5 4 3 2 1 0

4. The child should know how to use mathematical
    techniques in his everyday life; for instance,
    estimating distances, classifying objects, using
    money.   5 4 3 2 1 0

5. The child should know the correct spelling of
    a basic general vocabulary.   5 4 3 2 1 0

6. The child should have some knowledge of the
    Bible and Christian beliefs.   5 4 3 2 1 0

7. The child should be an individual, developing
    in his own way.   5 4 3 2 1 0

8. The child should be able to write legibly and
    know how to present his work attractively.   5 4 3 2 1 0

9. The child should be developing the ability to
    make reasoned judgements and choices, based
    on the interpretation and evaluation of
    relevant information.   5 4 3 2 1 0

10. The child should be developing awareness of
    the spiritual aspects of prayer and worship.   5 4 3 2 1 0

11. The child should find enjoyment in some
    purposeful leisure time interests and activities
    both on his own and with others.   5 4 3 2 1 0

A.P.E.—7

12. The child should be able to read fluently and
    accurately at a minimum reading age of eleven.   5 4 3 2 1 0

13. The child should find enjoyment in a variety
    of aspects of school work and gain satisfaction
    from his own achievements.   5 4 3 2 1 0

14. The child should have a wide general (not
    subject-based) knowledge of times and places
    beyond his immediate experience.   5 4 3 2 1 0

15. The child should know how to observe
    carefully, accurately and with sensitivity.   5 4 3 2 1 0

16. The child should have sufficient knowledge
    and skill to be able to engage in simple
    music-making; for example, singing, percussion,
    home-made instruments.   5 4 3 2 1 0

17. The child should be industrious, persistent
    and conscientious.   5 4 3 2 1 0

18. The child should be generally obedient to
    parents, teachers and all reasonable authority.   5 4 3 2 1 0

19. The child should try to behave in accordance
    with the ideals of his own religion whether or
    not this is Christian.   5 4 3 2 1 0

20. The child should know how to behave
    appropriately in a variety of situations; for
    example, talking to visitors, going on outings,
    answering the telephone.   5 4 3 2 1 0

21. The child should know how to convey his
    meaning clearly and accurately through speech
    for a variety of purposes; for example,
    description, explanation, narration.   5 4 3 2 1 0

22. The child should be developing the capacity
    to form a considered opinion and to act upon it
    even if this means rejecting conventional
    thought and behaviour.   5 4 3 2 1 0

23. The child should know how to apply the basic
    principles of health, hygiene and safety.   5 4 3 2 1 0

24. The child should be beginning to acquire a set of moral values on which to base his own behaviour; for example, honesty, sincerity, personal responsibility.   5 4 3 2 1 0

25. The child should be careful with and respectful of both his own and other people's property.   5 4 3 2 1 0

26. The child should be able to read with understanding material appropriate to his age group and interests.   5 4 3 2 1 0

27. The child should be kind and considerate; he should, for example, be willing to give personal help to younger or new children, to consider the elderly, the disabled.   5 4 3 2 1 0

28. The child should know how to engage in discussion; for example, he should be able to talk about his own and others' opinions in a reasonable way.   5 4 3 2 1 0

29. The child should know how to compute in the four arithmetic rules using his knowledge of, for instance, number, multiplication tables and different units of measurement.   5 4 3 2 1 0

30. The child should be a good mixer; he should be able to make easy social contacts with other children and adults in work and play situations.   5 4 3 2 1 0

31. The child should know those moral values, relating to people and property, which are shared by the majority of members of the society.   5 4 3 2 1 0

32. The child should know how to speak in a clear and fluent manner appropriate to different situations; for example, informal occasions with children and adults, formal occasions.   5 4 3 2 1 0

33. The child should have precise and economic body control for all ordinary physical activities including the handling of tools and equipment.   5 4 3 2 1 0

34. The child should know how to write clear and meaningful English appropriate to different formal purposes; for example, factual reports, letters, descriptive accounts.   5 4 3 2 1 0

35. The child should have ordered subject
     knowledge in, for example, history, geography.   5 4 3 2 1 0

36. The child should have some understanding of
     modern technological developments; for
     example, space travel, telecommunications,
     automation.   5 4 3 2 1 0

37. The child should be developing a critical and
     discriminating attitude towards his experiences;
     for example, of the mass media.   5 4 3 2 1 0

38. The child should be developing the ability to
     control his behaviour and his emotions.   5 4 3 2 1 0

39. The child should know how to write
     interestingly and with sensitivity.   5 4 3 2 1 0

40. The child should be self-confident; he should
     have a sense of personal adequacy and be able
     to cope with his environment at an appropriate
     level.   5 4 3 2 1 0

41. The child should know the basic facts of sex
     and reproduction.   5 4 3 2 1 0

42. The child should know the basic grammatical
     rules of written English.   5 4 3 2 1 0

43. The child should know how to behave with
     courtesy and good manners both in and out of
     school.   5 4 3 2 1 0

44. The child should be able to maintain lasting
     relationships with a few close friends.   5 4 3 2 1 0

45. The child should be adaptable to changing
     circumstances and flexible in outlook.   5 4 3 2 1 0

46. The child should be developing a personal
     appreciation of beauty in some of its forms,
     both natural and artistic.   5 4 3 2 1 0

47. The child should be enthusiastic and eager to
     put his best into all activities.   5 4 3 2 1 0

48. The child should be beginning to understand
     aesthetic experiences and should be able to
     talk about them; for example, looking at

      pictures and sculpture, listening to poetry and
plays.   5 4 3 2 1 0

49. The child should be able to play a musical
instrument such as a recorder, violin, guitar.   5 4 3 2 1 0

50. The child should be able to listen with
concentration and understanding.   5 4 3 2 1 0

51. The child should have a general knowledge of
his local environment in some of the following
aspects: historical, geographical, natural,
economic, social.   5 4 3 2 1 0

52. The child should be beginning to understand
his own emotions.   5 4 3 2 1 0

53. The child should be able to swim.   5 4 3 2 1 0

54. The child should know the appropriate
techniques of some arts and crafts; for example,
how to use paint, clay.   5 4 3 2 1 0

55. The child should have a wide vocabulary.   5 4 3 2 1 0

56. The child should be developing the skills of
acquiring knowledge and information from
written material; for example, summarizing,
taking notes accurately, the use of libraries.   5 4 3 2 1 0

57. The child should be developing the ability to
plan independent work and organize his own
time.   5 4 3 2 1 0

58. The child should be happy, cheerful and well
balanced.   5 4 3 2 1 0

59. The child should know what to do in
emergencies; for example, fire, sickness,
accident.   5 4 3 2 1 0

60. The child should be developing his
inventiveness and creativity in some fields;
for example, painting, music, mechanical
things, poetry, movement.   5 4 3 2 1 0

61. The child should have some knowledge of the
beliefs of the major world religions other than
Christianity.   5 4 3 2 1 0

62. The child should know some simple scientific
    experimental procedures and some basic
    scientific concepts; for example, properties
    of materials, the nature and significance of
    changes in living things.   5 4 3 2 1 0

63. The child should know how to play a variety
    of games; for example, football, skittle-ball,
    rounders.   5 4 3 2 1 0

64. The child should be beginning to feel
    community responsibility; for example, he
    should be loyal to groups such as class and
    school of which he is a member and, where
    possible, the wider community, and willing to
    accept the responsibilities which membership
    implies.   5 4 3 2 1 0

65. The child should have a questioning attitude
    towards his environment.   5 4 3 2 1 0

66. The child should be developing tolerance:
    respecting and appreciating others, their
    feelings, views and capabilities.   5 4 3 2 1 0

67. The child should try to behave in accordance
    with the ideals of the Christian religion.   5 4 3 2 1 0

68. The child should be able to conduct a simple
    conversation in a foreign language.   5 4 3 2 1 0

69. The child should be beginning to realize that
    he can play an important part in his own
    development by, for example, recognizing his
    strengths and limitations and setting his own
    goals accordingly.   5 4 3 2 1 0

70. The child should be able to listen to and
    enjoy a range of music; for example, pop, folk,
    classical.   5 4 3 2 1 0

71. The child should know how to think and solve
    problems mathematically using the appropriate
    basic concepts of, for example, the number
    system and place value, shape, spatial
    relationships, sets, symmetry and the
    appropriate language.   5 4 3 2 1 0

72. The child should have a range of movement
     and gymnastic skills.   5   4   3   2   1   0

SECTION IV

Below are five descriptions, each of a different approach to primary education.
(i) Please read through all five and then indicate your opinion of each one
     by using the following scale:

strongly agree	A
agree	B
neither agree nor disagree	C
disagree	D
strongly disagree	E

Please circle the appropriate letter for each statement.

1. There are certain basic language and number skills that should be
    learned through structured teaching. The remainder of the children's
    learning can best be guided by a mixture of children's and teacher's
    choice. The teacher's task is to teach the basic skills as individually as
    possible and to encourage and stimulate children to use them effectively
    and imaginatively in all other work.

    A   B   C   D   E

2. Children learn better when involved in individual work that absorbs
    them and this is fostered by giving children as much freedom of choice
    as possible in what they learn, when and how. To enable effective
    choices to be made, certain skills have to be mastered. The teacher's
    task is to provide stimulating opportunities to learn and practise the
    basic language and number skills in order to have the tools to use in
    their self-chosen inquiries.

    A   B   C   D   E

3. There is an ordered body of knowledge and skills that should be taught
    in the primary school. This is best taught in logical progression, and
    most economically to groups of children of roughly equal ability in a
    quiet, orderly atmosphere. The teacher's task is to have full knowledge
    of what he wants his children to know, to be capable, by analysis and
    experience, of presenting it to them interestingly in as well-programmed
    a manner as possible, and to set the pace of learning.

    A   B   C   D   E

4. Children only really learn what they want to learn—when not knowing
    becomes an obstacle to doing what they want to do. Learning, therefore,

takes place most effectively when children are involved in individual inquiries of their own choice; thus, the children's interests and needs as they arise constitute the curriculum. The teacher's task is to create a psychological environment in which inquiry can arise and a physical environment rich and stimulating enough to enable it to be pursued successfully at the child's own pace.

A   B   C   D   E

5.   There are certain basic language and number skills that should be taught in the primary school. As well as these there are certain other areas of knowledge that should form part of the curriculum. The teacher's task is to present work in each area of knowledge as stimulatingly as possible so that each child can learn as much as he is capable of.

A   B   C   D   E

(ii)   Will you please now put in the box [right] the number of the one description which is closest to your personal approach to primary education.   ☐

THANK YOU FOR YOUR CO-OPERATION

If there are any comments you would like to make, please do so below. [Page left for comments]

Appendix C
Sample data and findings from the heads' questionnaire

Sample data

Table C.1 Regional distribution of sample schools

Region	No.	%
1 North	20	*10·0*
2 Northeast (Yorkshire and Humberside)	22	*11·0*
3 East Midlands	20	*10·0*
4 East Anglia	8	*4·0*
5 London	20	*10·0*
6 Southeast	32	*15·5*
7 Southwest	21	*10·5*
8 West Midlands	20	*10·0*
9 Northwest	22	*11·0*
10 Wales	16	*8·0*
TOTALS	201	*100·0*
Nil response	0	

Table C.2 Sample schools by local authority area

Local authority*	No.	%
(a) Counties	139	*69·2*
(b) County boroughs—large (population over 250,000)	35	*17·4*
(c) County boroughs—medium (population 100,000–250,000)	23	*11·4*
(d) County boroughs—small (population under 100,000)	4	*2·0*
TOTALS	201	*100·0*
Nil response	0	

* Data on the local authorities derived from the
Education Committees Year Book, 1969–70 (Councils and
Education Press, 1969).

A.P.E.—7*

Findings from the heads' questionnaire

DESCRIPTION OF SCHOOL

Table C.3   Sample schools by type
(question A.1)

Type	No.	%
Infant	52	25·9
Junior	47	23·4
Primary/JMI	102	50·7
TOTALS	201	100·0
Nil response	0	

Table C.4   Schools in the sample with/without
nursery class (question A.2)

Nursery class	No.	%
Yes	16	8·1
No	182	91·9
TOTALS	198	100·0
Nil response	3	

Table C.5   Denomination of sample schools
(question A.3)

Denomination	No.	%
C of E	43	21·4
RC	12	6·0
Other denomination	2	1·0
Non-denominational	144	71·6
TOTALS	201	100·0
Nil response	0	

THE SCHOOL, ITS ENVIRONMENT AND ORGANIZATION

Table C.6 Sample schools by rural/urban area (question B.1) related to distribution by local authority area (Table C.2)

| Rural/urban | Schools by LEA area | | | | | | | | TOTALS | |
| | (a) | | (b) | | (c) | | (d) | | | |
	No.	%	No.	%	No.	%	No.	%	No.	%
Inner urban	21	10·6	19	9·6	8	4·0	0	0·0	48	24·2
Suburban	47	23·7	16	8·1	15	7·6	4	2·0	82	41·4
Traditional rural	37	18·7	0	0·0	0	0·0	0	0·0	37	18·7
Commuter rural	31	15·7	0	0·0	0	0·0	0	0·0	31	15·7
TOTALS									198	100·0
Nil response									3	

Key: (a) counties; (b) large county boroughs; (c) medium county boroughs; (d) small county boroughs.

Table C.7 Socio-economic background of pupils in sample schools (question B.2)

Background	No. of schools	%
Middle class	8	4·0
Mixed/middle class	17	8·6
Middle class/working class	46	23·1
Mixed/working class	80	40·2
Working class	48	24·1
TOTALS	199	100·0
Nil response	2	

Table C.8 Attitude of parents of children in sample schools (question B.3)

Attitude	No. of schools	%
Highly interested	52	25·9
Interested	122	60·7
Indifferent	27	13·4
TOTALS	201	100·0
Nil response	0	

Table C.9   Facilities for primary education in
sample schools (question B.4)

Facilities	No.	%
Good	68	34·2
Adequate	58	29·1
Limited	73	36·7
TOTALS	199	100·0
Nil response	2	

Table C.10   Number of children on roll in
sample schools (question B.5)

No. of children	No. of schools	%
Up to 25	3	1·5
26–50	15	7·5
51–100	21	10·4
101–200	41	20·4
201–300	62	30·9
301–400	34	16·9
401–600	21	10·4
601 upwards	4	2·0
TOTALS	201	100·0
Nil response	0	

Table C.11   Number of part-time teachers in
sample schools (question B.6)

No. of part-time teachers	No. of schools	%
0	75	37·3
1	70	34·8
2	42	20·9
3	9	4·5
4	5	2·5
TOTALS	201	100·0
Nil response	0	

Table C.12   Number of full-time teachers apart from the head in sample schools (question B.6)

No. of full-time teachers	No. of schools	%
1	21	10·6
2	13	6·5
3	12	6·0
4	12	6·0
5	14	7·1
6	18	9·1
7	24	12·1
8	24	12·1
9	11	5·5
10	11	5·5
11	7	3·5
12	10	5·0
13	5	2·5
14	7	3·5
15	2	1·0
16	3	1·5
17	0	—
18	1	0·5
19	0	—
20	1	0·5
21	0	—
22	0	—
23	1	0·5
24	0	—
25	0	—
26	0	—
27	1	0·5
28	0	—
29	0	—
30	0	—
31	0	—
32	1	0·5
TOTALS	199	100·0
Nil response	2	

Table C.13 Heads of sample schools with/without responsibility for a class (question B.7)

Responsibility for class	No.	%
Yes	60	29·9
No	141	70·1
TOTALS	201	100·0
Nil response	0	

Table C.14 Majority class size in sample schools (question B.8)

Class size	No. of schools	%
Under 20	14	7·1
21–29	42	21·1
30–39	137	68·8
40–49	6	3·0
Over 50	0	0·0
TOTALS	199	100·0
Nil response	2	

Table C.15 Types of child grouping in sample schools (question B.9)

Grouping	No. of schools	%
Year groups	97	49·0
2-year vertical groups	23	11·6
3-year vertical groups	17	8·6
4-year vertical groups	3	1·5
Year and vertical groups	58	29·3
TOTALS	198	100·0
Nil response	3	

Table C.16   Basis of assignment to parallel year classes in sample schools (question B.10)

Basis of assignment	No. of schools	% of respondents
Age	81	52·3
Ability	32	20·6
Other	53	34·2
	166	
TOTAL of respondents*	155	100·0
Nil response	46	

* Eleven heads gave more than one reply.

Table C.17   Sample schools using team teaching (question B.11)

Type of team teaching	No.	%
All time for all children	1	0·5
All time for some children	9	4·5
Part-time for all or some children	74	37·2
None at all	115	57·8
TOTALS	199	100·0
Nil response	2	

Table C.18   Sample heads' involvement in planning work for individual classes (question B.12)

Degree of involvement in planning work	No.	%
Very large extent	38	19·0
Some extent	108	54·0
Limited extent	49	24·5
Not at all	5	2·5
TOTALS	200	100·0
Nil response	1	

Table C.19   Heads' consultation with staff in
sample schools (question B.13)

Type of consultation	No.	%
Regular formal meetings	6	*3·3*
Occasional formal meetings	2	*1·1*
Frequent informal contact	135	*73·4*
Occasional informal contact	1	*0·5*
Contact for special issues only	0	*0·0*
Occasional formal meetings and		
frequent informal contact	40	*21·7*
TOTALS	184	*100·0*
Nil response	17	

Appendix D
Findings from the teachers' questionnaire

Table D.1   Sex of sample teachers
(question I.1)

Sex	No.	%
Male	360	23·8
Female	1152	76·2
TOTALS	1512	100·0
Nil response	1	

Table D.2   Ages of sample teachers
(question I.2)

Age group	No.	%
21–29	498	33·0
30–39	366	24·2
40–49	349	23·1
50–59	235	15·6
60 or over	62	4·1
TOTALS	1510	100·0
Nil response	3	

Table D.3   Marital status of sample teachers
(question I.3)

Status	No.	%
Married	1083	71·7
Single	428	28·3
TOTALS	1511	100·0
Nil response	2	

Table D.4   Sample teachers' employment other than teaching (question I.4)

Other employment	No.	%
Yes	433	28·7
No	1075	71·3
TOTALS	1508	100·0
Nil response	5	

Table D.5   First qualifications of sample teachers (question I.5)

Qualification	No.	%
Teacher's Certificate	1393	93·2
Trained graduate	83	5·6
Untrained graduate	18	1·2
TOTALS	1494	100·0
Nil response	19	

Table D.6   Sample teachers with higher qualifications (question I.5)

With/without higher qualification	No.	%
With higher qualification	54	3·6
No higher qualification	1440	96·4
TOTALS	1494	100·0
Nil response	19	

Table D.7   Teaching experience of sample teachers (question I.6)

Experience	No.	%
Under 1 year	142	9·4
1–5 years	418	27·7
6–10 years	248	16·5
11–20 years	336	22·3
Over 20 years	363	24·1
TOTALS	1507	100·0
Nil response	6	

Table D.8 Time spent in present school by sample teachers (question I.7)

Time	No.	%
Under 1 year	390	25·9
1–3 years	488	32·4
4–10 years	397	26·3
Over 10 years	232	15·4
TOTALS	1507	100·0
Nil response	6	

Table D.9 Full-time and part-time teachers in the sample (question I.8)

Full-time/part-time	No.	%
Full-time	1391	92·6
Part-time	112	7·4
TOTALS	1503	100·0
Nil response	10	

Table D.10 Present positions of sample teachers (question I.9)

Position	No.	%
Head teacher	169	11·5
Deputy head	139	9·4
Head of department	60	4·1
Post of responsibility	202	13·7
Class teacher	905	61·3
TOTALS	1475	100·0
Nil response	38	

Table D.11 Sample teachers with special responsibilities (question I.10)

Responsibility for	No.	%
Physical education/games/dance	274	*18·1*
Music	211	*14·0*
Mathematics	66	*4·4*
Art/craft	146	*9·7*
Religious education	53	*3·5*
Second language	51	*3·4*
Other*	200	*13·2*
TOTALS	1001	*66·3*
No special responsibilities	512	*33·7*
	1513	*100·0*

* Other responsibilities specified:

science/astronomy/biology	audio-visual aids
needlework	group work
literature (poetry/story)	history
reading	library
swimming	miscellaneous
English	writing
remedial work/reading	humanities
drama	sex education
nature study	commercial subjects
geography/environmental studies	immigrants

Table D.12 Year and vertical groups taught by sample teachers (question I.11)

Group	No. of teachers	%
Age 3–4	0	*0·0*
Age 4–5	4	*0·3*
Reception	111	*8·3*
Middle infants	97	*7·2*
Top infants	137	*10·2*
First year juniors	162	*12·1*
Second year juniors	136	*10·1*
Third year juniors	127	*9·5*
Fourth year juniors	147	*10·9*
5–6+ years	86	*6·4*
5–7 years	138	*10·3*
7–9 years	68	*5·0*
9–11 years	87	*6·5*
7–11 years	43	*3·2*
TOTALS	1343	*100·0*
Nil response	170	

Table D.13 Age ranges previously taught by sample teachers (question I.12)

Age group	No.	%
Nursery	121	8·0
Infant	791	52·3
Lower junior	987	65·2
Upper junior	809	53·5
Secondary	427	28·2
Adult	164	10·8
TOTAL in sample	1513	100·0

Table D.14 Rating by sample teachers of 2 broad purposes of primary education (section II.A)

Rating	Purpose 1 (societal)		Purpose 2 (individual)	
	No.	%	No.	%
0	31	2·1	49	3·3
1	149	10·1	180	12·2
2	440	29·9	625	42·4
3	625	42·4	440	29·9
4	180	12·2	149	10·1
5	49	3·3	31	2·1
TOTALS	1474	100·0	1474	100·0
Nil response	39		39	

Table D.15 Rating by 1432 sample teachers* of 7 aspects of development as one of the two most important, one of the two least important, or neither (section II.B)

Aspect	Rating	No.	%
Aesthetic	Least important	724	50·6
	Neither	618	43·2
	Most important	89	6·2
	TOTALS	1431	100·0
	Nil response	1	

* Eighty-one teachers omitted this question entirely.

Table D.15—*cont.*

Aspect	Rating	No.	%
Emotional/personal	Least important	112	*7·8*
	Neither	551	*38·6*
	Most important	768	*53·6*
	TOTALS	1431	*100·0*
	Nil response	1	
Intellectual	Least important	181	*12·7*
	Neither	493	*34·4*
	Most important	758	*52·9*
	TOTALS	1432	*100·0*
	Nil response	0	
Moral	Least important	147	*10·3*
	Neither	959	*67·0*
	Most important	325	*22·7*
	TOTALS	1431	*100·0*
	Nil response	1	
Physical	Least important	731	*51·0*
	Neither	650	*45·4*
	Most important	51	*3·6*
	TOTALS	1432	*100·0*
	Nil response	0	
Social	Least important	83	*5·8*
	Neither	581	*40·6*
	Most important	768	*53·6*
	TOTALS	1432	*100·0*
	Nil response	0	
Spiritual/religious	Least important	887	*61·9*
	Neither	438	*30·6*
	Most important	107	*7·5*
	TOTALS	1432	*100·0*
	Nil response	0	

Table D.16   Sample teachers' rating of 72 aims of primary education (section III)

Aim no.	Rating						Nil response	Mean
	1	2	3	4	5	0		
1	18	162	698	376	243	1	15	3·444
2	51	429	749	189	69	16	10	2·863
3	2	33	472	558	436	0	12	3·928
4	5	59	460	544	433	1	11	3·893
5	6	108	656	452	275	3	13	3·589
6	53	344	665	238	165	38	10	3·081
7	13	53	367	418	642	9	11	4·087
8	2	55	642	493	314	0	7	3·705
9	10	81	570	477	353	11	11	3·726
10	153	527	478	120	89	137	9	2·609
11	8	75	479	517	421	5	8	3·845
12	1	23	246	422	809	3	9	4·342
13	0	9	240	513	745	0	6	4·323
14	13	210	764	397	113	7	9	3·259
15	7	110	698	506	176	3	13	3·490
16	56	491	744	168	39	7	8	2·762
17	13	126	695	381	270	15	13	3·518
18	4	48	547	433	461	13	7	3·870
19	85	294	563	230	212	107	22	3·137
20	12	115	583	458	330	5	10	3·654
21	2	28	442	590	441	0	10	3·958
22	57	287	591	311	159	89	19	3·162
23	6	75	669	400	347	5	11	3·673
24	1	12	234	462	794	2	8	4·355
25	0	20	420	472	591	1	9	4·087
26	1	6	171	445	882	0	8	4·463
27	2	49	500	485	465	4	8	3·907
28	9	112	695	488	188	10	11	3·492
29	3	58	546	494	402	1	9	3·821
30	5	100	606	497	291	6	8	3·646
31	8	72	532	445	435	9	12	3·822
32	31	281	699	344	130	18	10	3·176
33	31	325	867	211	48	17	14	2·946
34	29	220	687	373	179	13	12	3·304
35	123	676	500	90	21	89	14	2·440
36	41	533	726	159	28	16	10	2·731
37	64	366	634	291	123	24	11	3·029
38	6	51	505	601	339	1	10	3·810
39	4	122	759	464	155	1	8	3·428
40	3	73	505	480	436	7	9	3·850
41	75	425	599	190	117	98	9	2·893
42	34	297	718	281	146	27	10	3·141
43	2	28	476	462	538	1	6	4·000

Table D.16—*cont.*

Aim no.	Rating						Nil res-ponse	Mean
	1	2	3	4	5	0		
44	64	355	603	252	133	96	10	3·025
45	34	233	713	335	166	20	12	3·247
46	12	179	811	350	148	4	9	3·295
47	6	64	420	494	509	7	13	3·962
48	25	326	759	298	84	13	8	3·060
49	180	850	358	46	5	65	9	2·198
50	6	48	482	503	463	3	8	3·912
51	13	143	740	393	213	0	11	3·433
52	52	308	701	263	126	40	23	3·071
53	37	269	612	293	273	23	6	3·334
54	15	175	805	351	161	1	5	3·311
55	1	48	473	574	405	0	12	3·889
56	12	88	615	495	291	8	4	3·643
57	13	128	557	501	298	8	8	3·630
58	2	16	210	320	957	3	5	4·471
59	13	155	647	365	321	8	4	3·550
60	9	96	618	489	297	1	3	3·642
61	202	632	405	84	34	154	2	2·349
62	53	345	828	215	52	13	7	2·912
63	38	377	808	210	68	6	6	2·929
64	10	94	557	514	325	7	6	3·700
65	15	105	504	528	344	10	7	3·723
66	8	47	413	545	491	0	9	3·973
67	78	266	599	221	244	89	16	3·204
68	336	702	193	33	13	229	7	1·970
69	75	307	647	284	132	52	16	3·063
70	49	428	775	191	44	19	7	2·834
71	13	123	619	486	256	6	10	3·567
72	28	366	840	224	42	6	7	2·924

Table D.17 Sample teachers expressing five degrees of agreement/ disagreement with 5 descriptions of the teacher's role (section IV)

Degree of agreement/ disagreement	Role 1		Role 2		Role 3		Role 4		Role 5	
	No.	%	No.	%	No.	%	No.	%	No.	%
Strongly agree	722	48·2	367	24·5	234	15·7	215	14·4	460	30·8
Agree	632	42·2	676	45·1	396	26·5	458	30·8	653	43·7
Neither	120	8·0	225	15·0	352	23·6	370	24·8	230	15·4
Disagree	22	1·5	202	13·5	393	26·3	387	26·0	127	8·5
Strongly disagree	1	0·1	29	1·9	118	7·9	60	4·0	23	1·6
TOTALS	1497	100·0	1499	100·0	1493	100·0	1490	100·0	1493	100·0
Nil response	16		14		20		23		20	

Table D.18 Sample teachers selecting each of 5 role descriptions as closest to their own approach (section IV)

Role no.	'Traditional–progressive'	No.	%
1	Moderate	672	45·6
2	Progressive	253	17·1
3	Most traditional	131	8·9
4	Most progressive	119	8·1
5	Traditional	299	20·3
	TOTALS	1474	100·0
	Nil response	39	

Appendix E
Factor analysis of aims:
Varimax loadings

Aim	Factor I	II	III	IV	V	VI	VII
1	0·0931	−0·3574	0·0559	0·1257	0·0382	0·0272	**0·4977**
2	0·0512	**−0·4213**	−0·1515	−0·0633	0·1889	0·0291	0·3804
3	−0·1859	**−0·4966**	0·0352	0·0268	0·2337	0·0337	0·1776
4	**−0·4662**	−0·3626	0·1168	−0·0595	0·1231	0·0432	0·2467
5	**−0·6014**	−0·0496	−0·0721	−0·1227	0·1757	0·2299	0·1403
6	−0·1498	−0·0362	−0·0118	−0·0224	0.1438	**0·7818**	0·1488
7	0·0545	**−0·5045**	0·1423	0·1828	0·0452	0·0597	0·0755
8	**−0·5512**	−0·0418	−0·0487	−0·0505	0·2544	0·1773	0·1055
9	−0·1707	**−0·6155**	−0·1466	0·1240	0·0699	0·0018	−0·0527
10	−0·0742	−0·1026	−0·1004	0·0237	0·1113	**0·7914**	0·0912
11	−0·0516	−0·3944	0·0864	0·2119	0·3313	0·1199	0·1594
12	**−0·5614**	−0·0873	−0·0503	0·0217	0·1364	0·0292	−0·0386
13	−0·2642	−0·3535	0·2295	0·3018	0·1692	0;0422	0·0488
14	−0·2211	**−0·4147**	−0·2038	−0·0122	0·0497	0·1431	0·1021
15	−0·3008	**−0·4780**	−0·1229	0·2004	0·1304	0·0984	0·0935
16	−0·1063	−0·1413	−0·0064	0·1295	0·0661	0·1646	**0·5021**
17	**−0·4526**	−0·0014	−0·1215	0·2199	0·2376	0·2900	−0·0760
18	**−0·4269**	0·1665	0·0293	0·0602	**0·4413**	0·3473	−0·0019
19	−0·0355	−0·1095	−0·1266	0·0631	0·2709	**0·6382**	0·0437
20	−0·2259	−0·1711	−0·1382	0·0299	**0·5927**	0·0900	0·1356
21	**−0·4166**	−0·3781	−0·1279	0·0987	0·2884	−0·0722	0·0334
22	0·0915	**−0·5281**	−0·3559	0·0750	0·1419	−0·1088	−0·0318
23	−0·1336	−0·2050	−0·0617	−0·0427	**0·6190**	0·1073	0·1774
24	−0·1221	−0·2578	−0·0438	0·1661	**0·5304**	0·1967	−0·0000
25	−0·1769	0·0480	−0·0143	0·1090	**0·6606**	0·1500	0·0670
26	**−0·5581**	−0·0592	−0·0265	0·1746	0·1876	−0·0353	−0·0174
27	−0·0985	−0·0914	−0·0453	0·3089	**0·5867**	0·1174	0·0513
28	−0·1160	−0·3069	−0·3505	0·2477	0·2814	−0·1327	0·0880
29	**−0·6798**	0·0614	−0·1075	−0·1064	0·1713	−0·0026	0·0924
30	−0·0841	−0·0996	−0·0517	0·3958	**0·4319**	−0·0492	0·0589
31	−0·1110	−0·0490	−0·2037	0·2325	**0·5858**	0·1465	0·0221
32	−0·2247	−0·1365	**−0·4599**	0·1702	0·3405	0·0176	0·0469
33	−0·2111	−0·1290	−0·3438	0·2123	0·3113	−0·0172	0·1346
34	**−0·4210**	−0·0411	**−0·5035**	0·0701	0·1209	0·0772	0·0801

Aim	Factor I	II	III	IV	V	VI	VII
35	−0·2782	0·1093	**−0·5802**	0·0259	0·0749	0·1897	0·1204
36	−0·1423	−0·1420	**−0·5169**	0·1147	0·0887	0·0357	0·2720
37	0·0475	−0·3984	**−0·4976**	0·3180	0·0441	−0·0381	0·0537
38	−0·0554	−0·1152	−0·2347	**0·4738**	0·2991	0·1318	−0·0274
39	−0·3867	−0·0997	−0·3819	0·3259	−0·0020	0·0067	0·2400
40	−0·0654	−0·2688	−0·1427	**0·5714**	0·1281	−0·0097	0·0584
41	0·0803	−0·2652	−0·2661	0·0416	0·1480	−0·1275	0·2964
42	**−0·4650**	0·1295	**−0·4045**	−0·0132	0·1094	0·1933	0·1067
43	−0·2806	0·1500	−0·0750	0·2619	**0·5017**	0·2181	0·1417
44	0·0110	−0·0830	−0·3417	**0·4054**	0·2210	0·0434	0·1052
45	0·0347	−0·2944	−0·2846	**0·5091**	0·1488	−0·0983	0·1193
46	0·0895	−0·1726	−0·1897	**0·4900**	0·0802	0·0212	**0·4089**
47	−0·2443	0·0734	0·0251	**0·5337**	0·1544	0·1410	0·1785
48	−0·0088	−0·2130	−0·3142	0·3775	−0·0247	−0·0322	0·3842
49	−0·0120	0·0900	−0·2122	0·1485	−0·0374	0·1226	**0·5303**
50	**−0·4285**	−0·0130	−0·0278	0·3690	0·0628	0·0510	0·1573
51	−0·1909	−0·0494	−0·0995	0·1199	0·0913	−0·0682	**0·4809**
52	0·0934	−0·3105	−0·2296	0·3641	0·1019	0·0531	0·1510
53	−0·1044	0·0838	0·0170	−0·0252	0·2926	−0·0383	**0·4552**
54	−0·1187	−0·0460	0·0455	0·2046	0·1349	−0·0608	**0·6179**
55	**−0·4537**	−0·1568	−0·0571	0·2747	−0·0320	−0·0670	0·2164
56	**−0·4247**	−0·3717	−0·1202	0·1450	−0·0643	0·0009	0·1710
57	−0·2175	**−0·4904**	−0·1264	0·2779	−0·0528	−0·0569	0·1532
58	−0·0693	−0·1626	0·1802	**0·4600**	0·2052	0·0187	0·1141
59	−0·0564	−0·1500	−0·0933	0·0780	**0·4629**	0·0574	0·2651
60	−0·0102	−0·3489	0·1012	0·3288	−0·0068	−0·0019	**0·4786**
61	0·0665	−0·3117	−0·3606	−0·0518	0·0124	0·1783	0·3106
62	−0·1400	−0·3323	−0·2189	0·0059	−0·0323	0·0569	**0·4685**
63	−0·1782	0·0632	−0·0513	0·0279	0·1764	0·1216	**0·5769**
64	−0·1083	−0·1937	−0·0424	0·3206	0·2866	0·1870	0·2220
65	0·0319	**−0·4743**	0·0073	0·3471	0·0403	−0·0037	0·2523
66	0·0131	−0·3653	−0·0363	**0·4432**	0·2251	0·1260	0·1478
67	−0·1080	−0·0064	0·0308	0·1346	0·1895	**0·7555**	0·0979
68	−0·0205	−0·1375	−0·2709	−0·0310	−0·0794	0·1370	**0·4244**
69	−0·0298	**−0·4147**	−0·1795	0·2898	−0·0108	0·1804	0·1301
70	−0·0819	−0·1904	−0·1332	0·1889	0·0989	0·0617	**0·5761**
71	**−0·5105**	−0·2864	−0·0241	−0·0121	−0·0962	0·0305	0·3164
72	−0·1863	−0·1158	−0·0573	0·0432	0·1583	0·1119	**0·5259**

Variance

Factor	
I	6·9534
II	6·9336
III	4·5447
IV	5·8770
V	6·5315
VI	4·3737
VII	6·7686

Appendix F
G and standardized G

The following explanation of this statistic, by Professor P. H. Taylor, has also appeared in the report of the associated Schools Council Aims of Nursery Education project.*

This statistic was employed to estimate differences. Gamma is a directional measure of association for ordinal or metric data (see L. A. Goodman and W. H. Kruskal, 'Measures of association for cross-classification', *Journal of the American Statistical Association*, **49**, December 1954, 732–64; 'Further discussion and references', *JASA*, **54**, March 1959, 123–63; 'Approximate sampling theory', *JASA*, **58**, June 1963, 310–64). Provided that the dimensions on which it is used can be measured on an interval scale, or at least ranks can be assigned according to some criterion of magnitude, calculation of value for gamma will reveal not only the extent to which one phenomenon occurs in association with another, but also whether that association represents a situation of positive or negative correlation. Like r, gamma may assume any value between $+1 \cdot 0$ or $-1 \cdot 0$. G is the approximation to the gamma coefficient which can be calculated from available data. Confidence intervals can be set up (Goodman and Kruskal, *JASA*, June 1963) to determine the likelihood that the true value of gamma lies between certain limits and G can also be converted to a standard score from which it is possible to determine the likelihood that a particular value of G might have occurred by chance.

* Schools Council. *A Study of Nursery Education* (Working Paper 41). Evans/Methuen Educational, 1972, Appendix E.

Appendices

Opinions of tutors in colleges of education

Appendix G
College tutors' questionnaire

Aims of Primary Education Project

The questionnaire consists of four sections. Please read the instructions for each section carefully before completing it.

The three main sections ask you to give a rating of issues of importance in primary education. Please try to ensure that your answers accurately reflect your personal views.

Teachers have participated extensively in the construction of the questionnaire and have found it possible to complete it satisfactorily.

SECTION I

1.	Sex	Male	☐
		Female	☐
2.	Age	29 and under	☐
		30–39	☐
		40–49	☐
		50–59	☐
		60 or over	☐
3.	What are your qualifications? Please tick more than one if appropriate.	Teacher's Certificate	☐
		Trained graduate	☐
		Untrained graduate	☐
		Higher degree, advanced diploma, etc. in education	☐
		Higher degree, diploma, etc. in a subject other than education	☐
4.	How long have you taught in primary schools?	Not at all	☐
		Under 2 years	☐
		2–5 years	☐
		Over 5 years	☐

5. How long have you taught students concerned with the 5–11 age range in colleges of education?

- Under 1 year ☐
- 1–3 years ☐
- 4–10 years ☐
- Over 10 years ☐

6. What is your present position?

- Head of department ☐
- Principal lecturer ☐
- Senior lecturer ☐
- Lecturer ☐

7. Of which department are you a member?

- Art/craft ☐
- Biology ☐
- Education ☐
- French ☐
- Mathematics ☐
- Music ☐
- Religious education ☐
- Rural science ☐
- Other ☐

If other, please specify.   ....

8. Which age range are you concerned with?

- Infant ☐
- Infant/junior ☐
- Junior ☐
- Junior/secondary ☐

[For section II see the parallel section in the primary teachers' questionnaire (Appendix B, pp. 175–6).]

SECTION III

The aims and objectives on the following pages define the knowledge, the skills and the qualities which many teachers think that in general children in the MIDDLE RANGE OF ABILITY should have AT THE END OF THEIR PRIMARY EDUCATION.

Please consider these aims and objectives and decide how important you think they should be.

Each statement is concerned with an important aspect of primary education; to help you judge each one on its own merits, the statements have been mixed so that adjacent ones are not about the same aspects of primary education.

There are a large number of statements to rate and you might find it helpful to take a break now and again.

Please indicate your opinion of the importance of these aims and objectives of primary education by using the scale 5, 4, 3, 2, 1, 0 as set out [below] and putting a circle round the number you choose for each statement.

5   I think that this aim is of the *utmost importance* in primary education.
4   I think that this aim is of *major importance* in primary education.
3   I think that this aim is *important* in primary education.
2   I think that this aim is of *minor importance* in primary education.
1   I think that this aim is of *no importance* in primary education.
0   I think that this *should not be* an aim of primary education.

Points to remember when rating these statements
 (i) To have in mind the children IN THE MIDDLE RANGE OF ABILITY.
(ii) To have in mind the children AT THE END OF THEIR PRIMARY EDUCATION.

[For the rest of section III (the detailed list of aims) see the parallel section in the primary teachers' questionnaire (Appendix B, pp. 177–83). For section IV again see the primary teachers' questionnaire (Appendix B, pp. 183–4).]

Appendix H
Composition of the college sample

Table H.1 Size, sex composition and denomination of the fourteen
sample colleges (national proportions shown)

	Sample		Population*	
	No.	%	No.	%
Size				
0–400 students	2	14	23	17
401–800 students	8	57	71	51
801 students and over	4	29	45	32
Sex composition				
Women students	1	7	21	15
Men and women students	13	93	118	85
Maintaining body/denomination				
Church of England	1	7	20	14
Roman Catholic	1	7	13	9
Other denomination	0	0	8	6
Local education authority	12	86	97	70

* Data from the *Education Committees Year Book, 1969–70* (Councils and Education Press, 1969).

Appendix J
Findings from the tutors' questionnaire

Table J.1 Sex of sample tutors (question I.1)

Sex	No.	%
Male	236	68·0
Female	111	32·0
TOTALS	347	100·0
Nil response	1	

Table J.2 Ages of sample tutors (question I.2)

Age group	No.	%
29 and under	8	2·3
30–39	115	33·1
40–49	144	41·5
50–59	71	20·5
60 and over	9	2·6
TOTALS	347	100·0
Nil response	1	

Table J.3 First qualifications of sample tutors (question I.3)

Qualification	No.	%
Teacher's Certificate	121	36·2
Trained graduate	187	56·0
Untrained graduate	26	7·8
TOTALS	334	100·0
Nil response	14	

Table J.4   Sample tutors with higher qualifications in education or in other subjects* (question I.3)

	No.	%
With higher qualification in education	139	39·9
With higher qualification in another subject	107	30·7

* The numbers are shown as percentages of the entire sample (348 tutors).

Table J.5   Sample tutors' length of primary experience (question I.4)

Time	No.	%
None	111	32·2
Under 2 years	88	25·5
2–5 years	48	13·9
Over 5 years	98	28·4
TOTALS	345	100·0
Nil response	3	

Table J.6   Length of time sample tutors had taught students of the primary (5–11) age range in college (question I.5)

Time	No.	%
Under 1 year	19	5·5
1–3 years	67	19·5
4–10 years	206	59·9
Over 10 years	52	15·1
TOTALS	344	100·0
Nil response	4	

Table J.7   Present positions of sample tutors (question I.6)

Position	No.	%
Head of department	71	20·8
Principal lecturer	24	7·0
Senior lecturer	149	43·7
Lecturer	97	28·5
TOTALS	341	100·0
Nil response	7	

Table J.8   Departmental membership of sample tutors (question I.7)

Department	No.	%
Art/craft	21	6·1
Biology	10	2·9
Education	127	36·7
French*	6	
Mathematics	22	6·4
Music	11	3·2
Religious education	17	4·9
Rural science*	2	
Physics*	4	
Geography	30	8·7
English	33	9·5
Physical education	17	4·9
Sociology*	1	
History	16	4·6
Science	14	4·0
Design and technology*	2	
Social/contemporary studies*	3	
Geography/history*	1	
Drama*	3	
Home economics*	1	
Other*	5	
	346	91·9
Combined % for departments marked *		8·1
TOTALS	346	100·0
Nil response	2	

Table J.9   Primary age ranges of students taught by sample tutors (question I.8)

Age range	No. of tutors	%
Infant	14	*4·1*
Infant/junior	220	*63·9*
Junior	14	*4·1*
Junior/secondary	96	*27·9*
TOTALS	344	*100·0*
Nil response	4	

Table J.10   Rating by sample tutors of 2 broad purposes of primary education (section II.A)

Rating	Purpose 1 (societal)		Purpose 2 (individual)	
	No.	%	No.	%
0	19	*5·6*	2	*0·6*
1	65	*19·1*	20	*5·9*
2	145	*42·6*	89	*26·2*
3	89	*26·2*	145	*42·6*
4	20	*5·9*	65	*19·1*
5	2	*0·6*	19	*5·6*
TOTALS	340	*100·0*	340	*100·0*
Nil response	8		8	

Table J.11   Rating by sample tutors of 7 aspects of development as one of the two most important, one of the two least important, or neither (section II.B)

Aspect	Rating	No.	%
Aesthetic	Least important	135	*41·2*
	Neither	155	*47·2*
	Most important	38	*11·6*
	TOTALS	328	*100·0*
	Nil response	20	

Table J.11—*cont.*

Aspect	Rating	No.	%
Emotional/ personal	Least important	38	*11·6*
	Neither	147	*44·8*
	Most important	143	*43·6*
	TOTALS	328	*100·0*
	Nil response	20	
Intellectual	Least important	20	*6·1*
	Neither	85	*25·9*
	Most important	223	*68·0*
	TOTALS	328	*100·0*
	Nil response	20	
Moral	Least important	34	*10·4*
	Neither	226	*68·9*
	Most important	68	*20·7*
	TOTALS	328	*100·0*
	Nil response	20	
Physical	Least important	192	*58·5*
	Neither	124	*37·8*
	Most important	12	*3·7*
	TOTALS	328	*100·0*
	Nil response	20	
Social	Least important	27	*8·2*
	Neither	150	*45·7*
	Most important	151	*46·1*
	TOTALS	328	*100·0*
	Nil response	20	
Spiritual/ religious	Least important	209	*63·7*
	Neither	98	*29·9*
	Most important	21	*6·4*
	TOTALS	328	*100·0*
	Nil response	20	

Table J.12 Sample tutors' rating of 72 aims of primary education (section III)

Aim no.	Rating						Nil res-ponse	Mean
	1	2	3	4	5	0		
1	4	30	127	100	77	1	9	3·64
2	8	94	167	51	15	3	10	2·91
3	0	12	86	136	106	0	8	3·99
4	1	16	114	120	89	0	8	3·82
5	3	46	180	73	36	2	8	3·28
6	31	87	125	39	28	29	9	2·83
7	1	25	78	104	128	1	11	3·99
8	2	41	164	98	36	0	7	3·37
9	2	15	102	112	106	5	6	3·91
10	47	90	78	25	14	85	9	2·48
11	4	18	94	125	96	3	8	3·86
12	2	16	72	114	130	5	9	4·06
13	0	5	53	106	178	0	6	4·34
14	7	47	152	108	24	4	6	3·28
15	2	28	106	134	63	3	12	3·68
16	18	107	161	42	12	2	6	2·77
17	9	56	159	72	33	4	15	3·19
18	17	58	164	63	21	15	10	3·04
19	30	64	92	55	46	49	12	3·08
20	6	46	123	118	47	1	7	3·45
21	1	8	80	142	109	1	7	4·03
22	11	44	99	98	73	15	8	3·55
23	4	44	162	88	39	2	9	3·34
24	0	7	78	100	156	0	7	4·19
25	2	23	143	100	70	3	7	3·63
26	3	3	28	111	195	1	7	4·45
27	2	21	121	116	82	0	6	3·75
28	3	27	123	121	60	7	7	3·62
29	3	30	136	99	74	0	6	3.62
30	5	30	151	100	51	2	9	3·48
31	4	37	124	112	60	4	7	3·55
32	12	49	133	90	40	15	9	3·30
33	16	90	152	66	9	5	10	2·89
34	20	73	140	62	28	15	10	3·02
35	61	150	65	8	1	54	9	2·08
36	27	123	146	29	7	8	8	2·60
37	9	67	135	88	37	6	6	3·23
38	3	28	124	122	64	2	5	3·63
39	3	37	173	98	24	7	6	3·31
40	3	14	89	116	121	1	4	3·99
41	11	63	139	83	41	8	3	3·24
42	32	102	126	37	12	33	6	2·66
43	10	49	136	94	53	0	6	3·38

Table J.12—*cont.*

Aim no.	Rating						Nil res- ponse	Mean
	1	2	3	4	5	0		
44	31	74	104	60	32	38	9	2·96
45	8	54	122	96	56	7	5	3·41
46	7	30	152	104	45	1	9	3·44
47	7	32	109	78	101	10	11	3·72
48	13	77	145	71	23	7	12	3·04
49	45	164	106	11	5	10	7	2·30
50	3	34	129	107	61	2	12	3·57
51	1	31	121	127	61	0	7	3·63
52	21	70	122	77	32	14	12	3·09
53	20	85	125	55	43	11	9	3·05
54	7	50	162	96	26	1	6	3·25
55	4	14	129	121	72	0	8	3·71
56	7	20	146	111	52	3	9	3·54
57	3	28	129	110	68	4	6	3·63
58	2	2	58	78	182	2	24	4·35
59	8	54	146	78	47	5	10	3·31
60	0	22	97	116	106	1	6	3·90
61	57	117	89	18	12	46	9	2·35
62	11	35	160	94	40	1	7	3·34
63	24	121	145	38	7	6	7	2·65
64	7	42	135	107	47	3	7	3·43
65	2	9	93	123	113	2	6	3·99
66	1	7	84	117	134	1	4	4·10
67	30	60	100	40	34	73	11	2·95
68	74	141	53	5	3	66	6	1·99
69	29	73	117	69	35	18	7	3·02
70	28	95	160	39	11	9	6	2·73
71	4	31	125	128	48	2	10	3·55
72	13	86	173	55	8	4	9	2·88

Table J.13 Sample tutors expressing five degrees of agreement/
disagreement with 5 descriptions of the primary teacher's role
(section IV)

Degree of agreement/ disagreement	Role									
	Most traditional (3)		Traditional (5)		Moderate (1)		Progressive (2)		Most progressive (4)	
	No.	%	No.	%	No.	%	No.	%	No.	%
Strongly agree	15	4·5	53	15·9	124	36·9	110	32·7	54	16·2
Agree	50	15·1	120	35·9	156	46·4	136	40·5	110	32·9
Neither	74	22·3	91	27·2	49	14·6	61	18·2	76	22·8
Disagree	133	40·0	64	19·2	7	2·1	26	7·7	79	23·6
Strongly disagree	60	18·1	6	1·8	0	0·0	3	0·9	15	4·5
TOTALS	332	100·0	334	100·0	336	100·0	336	100·0	334	100·0
Nil response	16		14		12		12		14	

Table J.14 Sample tutors selecting each of 5 role
descriptions as closest to their own
approach to primary teaching
(section IV)

Role	No.	%
Most traditional (3)	5	1·6
Traditional (5)	46	14·2
Moderate (1)	132	40·9
Progressive (2)	96	29·7
Most progressive (4)	44	13·6
TOTALS	323	100·0
Nil response	25	

Appendices

Opinions of secondary teachers

Appendix K
Secondary teachers' questionnaire

Aims of Primary Education Project

The questionnaire consists of three sections. Please read the instructions for each section carefully before completing it.

The three main sections ask you to give a rating of issues of importance in primary education. Please try to ensure that your answers accurately reflect your personal views.

Primary school teachers have participated extensively in the construction of the questionnaire and have found it possible to complete it satisfactorily.

SECTION I

1. Sex

Male ☐
Female ☐

2. Age

21–29 ☐
30–39 ☐
40–49 ☐
50+ ☐

3. What are your qualifications? Please tick those appropriate.

Teacher's Certificate ☐
Graduate (trained or untrained) ☐
Higher degree (subject) ☐
Advanced qualifications in education: advanced diploma, M.Ed., etc. ☐

4. How long have you been teaching?

Under 1 year ☐
1–5 years ☐
6–10 years ☐
10+ ☐

5. Please state your present
    position in the school.   . . . .

6. What subject(s) do you   English   ☐
    specialize in teaching?   Mathematics   ☐
    Please tick more than one   Modern languages   ☐
    if appropriate.   Art   ☐
                                    Practical subjects: metal/
                                        wood/needlework/
                                        pottery/ crafts, etc.   ☐
                                    Physical education: games/
                                        dance/gymnastics, etc.   ☐
                                    History   ☐
                                    Geography   ☐
                                    Religious education   ☐
                                    Music   ☐
                                    Science: physics/chemistry/
                                        biology, etc.   ☐
                                    Other   ☐

        If other, please specify.   . . . .

7. Have you ever taught   Yes   ☐
    for a full year or more   No   ☐
    in a primary school?

8. What interest do you have   Form/class teacher   ☐
    in 11–12 year-old children?   Subject teacher   ☐
    Please tick more than one   House tutor   ☐
    if appropriate.   Other   ☐
        If other, please specify.   . . . .

9. What percentage of your time is   Under 10%   ☐
    concerned with the 11–12 year-   10–50%   ☐
    olds?   50%+   ☐

10. What ability range do you   Children high in my school's
    mainly teach? Tick   ability range   ☐
    more than one if appropriate.   Children in the middle of my
                                        school's ability range   ☐
                                    Children low in my school's
                                        ability range   ☐

[For sections II and III see the parallel sections in the primary teachers'
questionnaire (Appendix B, pp. 175–83).]

Appendix L
Composition of the secondary school sample

Table L.1 The five selected areas and the number of target schools in the secondary sample

School type	Area and number of schools			
	County council*	No.	County borough	No.
Selective				
Grammar	I	6	I	7
Sec. modern	I	11	I	13
Comprehensive	I	2	I	2
Non-selective				
Comprehensive	II	2	II	2
Non-selective				
Middle	I	3	III	3
TOTAL schools		24		27

* Certain divisions of these county councils had a selective system of secondary education: others had a middle school system.

Table L.2   Number and type of secondary schools returning
questionnaires

School type	No. of schools responding	Distribution of pupils by school type	
		Responding schools	Regional average*
Grammar	11	24%	26%
Sec. modern	12	27%	38%
Comprehensive	6	40%	25%
Middle	6	9%	11%
TOTALS	35	100%	100%

* Data derived from *Education Committees Year Book, 1969–70* (Councils and
Education Press, 1969).

Table L.3   Number of teachers in responding schools actively involved
with 11–12 year-olds compared with number of such teachers
completing questionnaires: by school type

School type	Teachers actively involved with 11–12 year-olds	Teachers responding to questionnaire	Respondents as % of those involved with 11–12 year-olds
Grammar	271*	135	50
Sec. modern	172	136	79
Comprehensive	287	160	56
Middle	31	28	90
OVERALL	761	459	60

* One school estimated, as head did not provide figures.

Appendix M
Findings from the secondary teachers' questionnaire

Table M.1 Sex of sample secondary teachers (question I.1)

Sex	No.	%*
Male	249	*56·0*
Female	196	*44·0*
TOTALS	445	*100·0*
Nil response	14	

* National proportions gave 40·5% women (DES, *Statistics of Education, 1968*, vol. 4, Table 13, estimate for February 1970).

Table M.2 Ages of sample secondary teachers (question I.2)*

Age group	No.	%
21–29	217	*48·9*
30–39	101	*22·7*
40–49	71	*16·0*
50+	55	*12·4*
TOTALS	444	*100·0*
Nil response	15	

* For national proportions see Table 5.1, p. 32.

Table M.3   Sample secondary teachers' length of
teaching experience (question I.4)

Time	No.	%
Under 1 year	55	*12·4*
1–5 years	146	*32·9*
6–10 years	84	*19·0*
10+	158	*35·7*
TOTALS	443	*100·0*
Nil response	16	

Table M.4   Positions and grades of sample
secondary teachers (question I.5)*

Position/grade	No.	%	
Head	16	*3.6*	
Deputy head	16	*3·6*	
Head of school or department	107	*24·3*	
Responsibility for subject (graded			
post, scale 1, 2, 3)	56	*12·7* ⎫	*67·8*
Assistant	243	*55·1* ⎬	
Student	3	*0·7* ⎭	
TOTALS	441		
Nil response	18		

* For national proportions see Table 5.3, p. 34.

Table M.5   Qualifications (first and higher) of
sample secondary teachers
(question I.3)

Qualification	No.	%
Teacher's Certificate	236	*53·4*
Graduate (trained or untrained)	122	*27·6*
Graduate with Teacher's Certificate	41	*9·3*
Higher subject degree:		
graduates	13	*2·9*
certificated teachers	2	*0·5*
Graduate with advanced		
qualification in education	9	*2·0*
Certificated teacher with advanced		
qualification in education	19	*4·3*
TOTALS	442	*100·0*
Nil response	17	

Subjects taught

The numbers and percentages of responding teachers who taught the various subjects of the curriculum are given in Table M.6. It should be borne in mind that many of the teachers in the sample taught more than one subject. The range was from one to five subjects, but some teachers appeared to be class teachers who taught the entire curriculum apart from the specialized subjects like music or physical education.

Table M.6   Subjects taught by teachers in the secondary sample (question I.6)

Subject	No.	%
English	101	*22·0*
Mathematics	78	*17·0*
Science: physics/chemistry/ biology, etc.	72	*15·7*
Practical subjects: metal/wood/ needlework/pottery/crafts, etc.	66	*14·4*
Physical education: games/dance/ gymnastics, etc.	63	*13·7*
History	61	*13·3*
Geography	61	*13·3*
Modern languages	53	*11·5*
Religious education	44	*9·6*
Art	41	*8·9*
Music	26	*5·7*
Other*	72	*15·7*
TOTAL in sample	459	*100·0*

* The 'other' category included such subjects as remedial reading, horticulture, current affairs.

Table M.7   Sample secondary teachers with primary experience (question I.7)

	No.	%
With primary experience	80	*18·1*
Without primary experience	363	*81·9*
TOTALS	443	*100·0*
Nil response	16	

Table M.8 Nature of sample secondary teachers' interest in 11–12 year-old children (question I.8)

Nature of interest	No.	%
Subject teacher only	245	55·3
Class/form and subject teacher	113	25·5
Class/form teacher only	23	5·2
Heads, deputy heads, etc.*	23	5·2
House tutors†	39	8·8
TOTALS	443	100·0
Nil response	16	

* Includes remedial teachers, 'co-ordinators of lower and upper school', and teachers in similar positions.

† Includes teachers who were both house tutors and subject or class/form teachers.

Table M.9 Percentage of time spent by sample secondary teachers with 11–12 year-olds (question I.9)

Proportion of time spent	No.	%
Under 10%	86	19·7
10–50%	280	64·2
50%+	70	16·1*
TOTALS	436	100·0
Nil response	23	

* This is a larger proportion of the sample than the proportion who were class/form teachers only (5·2%) and would suggest that some subject specialists or subject/form teachers spent over 50% of their time with the 11–12 year-olds. These were most likely those teachers who spent a high proportion of their time with the one form of 11–12 year-olds but who also taught their specialist subject to other forms—either 11–12 year-olds or older children

Table M.10   Ability range of 11–12 year-olds
taught by sample secondary teachers
(question I.10)

Ability of pupils	No.	%
High in school's ability range only	31	7·0
Middle of school's ability range only	58	13·2
Low in school's ability range only	28	6·3
Entire ability range of school	249	56·5
High+middle of school's ability range	47	10·7
Low+middle of school's ability range	19	4·3
High+low in school's ability range	9	2·0
TOTALS	441	100·0
Nil response	18	

Table M.11   Rating by sample secondary teachers
of 2 broad purposes of primary
education (section II.A)

Rating	Purpose 1 (societal)		Purpose 2 (individual)	
	No.	%	No.	%
0	14	3·2	19	4·3
1	61	13·9	63	14·3
2	111	25·3	171	39·0
3	171	39·0	111	25·3
4	63	14·3	61	13·9
5	19	4·3	14	3·2
TOTALS	439	100·0	439	100·0
Nil response	20		20	

Table M.12　Rating by sample secondary teachers
of 7 aspects of development as
one of the two most important, one
of the two least important, or neither
(section II.B)

Aspect	Rating	No.	%
Aesthetic	Least important	219	*51·2*
	Neither	190	*44·4*
	Most important	19	*4·4*
	TOTALS	428	*100·0*
	Nil response	31	
Emotional/ personal	Least important	41	*9·5*
	Neither	193	*44·8*
	Most important	197	*45·7*
	TOTALS	431	*100·0*
	Nil response	28	
Intellectual	Least important	38	*8·8*
	Neither	152	*35·3*
	Most important	241	*55·9*
	TOTALS	431	*100·0*
	Nil response	28	
Moral	Least important	37	*8·6*
	Neither	273	*63·3*
	Most important	121	*28·1*
	TOTALS	431	*100·0*
	Nil response	28	
Physical	Least important	218	*50·8*
	Neither	190	*44·3*
	Most important	21	*4·9*
	TOTALS	429	*100·0*
	Nil response	30	
Social	Least important	28	*6·5*
	Neither	165	*38·5*
	Most important	236	*55·0*
	TOTALS	429	*100·0*
	Nil response	30	

Table M.12—*cont.*

Aspect	Rating	No.	%
Spiritual/ religious	Least important	281	*65·5*
	Neither	120	*28·0*
	Most important	28	*6·5*
	TOTALS	429	*100·0*
	Nil response	30	

Table M.13 Sample secondary teachers' rating of 72 aims of primary education (section III)

Aim no.	Rating						Nil res- ponse	Mean
	1	2	3	4	5	0		
1	14	71	198	98	61	8	9	3·27
2	20	141	199	57	20	6	16	2·81
3						6	7	3·88
4		Not available				6	7	3·76
5						6	8	3·80
6						5	39	2·88
7	5	57	139	101	138	6	13	3·70
8	1	14	171	128	129	4	12	3·84
9	8	35	180	136	86	6	8	3·58
10	59	153	94	24	21	6	102	2·42
11	6	31	120	161	123	6	12	3·83
12	3	16	83	117	223	5	12	4·22
13	3	6	74	151	212	5	8	4·26
14	10	64	196	130	41	5	13	3·29
15	6	33	209	131	50	20	10	3·43
16	35	150	185	45	15	7	22	2·66
17	7	43	165	127	94	8	15	3·59
18	1	25	121	127	160	7	18	3·97
19	36	84	137	76	73	9	44	3·16
20	6	38	156	138	98	6	17	3·65
21	4	16	122	166	132	6	13	3·92
22	25	99	142	94	51	7	41	3·11
23	9	27	167	123	112	15	6	3·69
24	0	6	76	118	231	16	12	4·33
25	1	15	116	138	171	16	2	4·05
26	0	5	72	125	237	15	5	4·35
27	6	35	158	139	103	15	3	3·68
28	5	63	167	143	60	15	6	3·43
29	4	31	112	141	155	15	1	3·93

Aim no.	Rating						Nil res-ponse	Mean
	1	2	3	4	5	0		
30	5	44	188	142	56	16	8	3·46
31	7	21	140	129	140	16	6	3·86
32	23	73	189	104	42	15	13	3·16
33	17	121	211	61	26	13	10	2·90
34	12	83	166	105	63	12	18	3·29
35	55	181	133	36	14	12	28	2·46
36	45	165	165	41	12	12	19	2·56
37	28	112	184	68	37	14	16	2·94
38	5	20	163	146	103	14	8	3·74
39	9	66	215	114	38	13	4	3·24
40	3	44	167	135	88	15	7	3·60
41	29	117	165	57	45	14	32	2·93
42	23	91	161	86	64	13	21	3·18
43	3	16	119	131	166	14	10	4·01
44	37	114	142	69	52	14	31	2·96
45	14	79	189	99	50	14	14	3·21
46	9	84	218	91	37	13	7	3·14
47	2	22	108	138	161	15	13	4·01
48	31	109	203	75	18	14	9	2·86
49	74	215	98	12	4	13	43	2·15
50	6	32	150	140	117	13	1	3·74
51	6	77	189	120	50	12	5	3·30
52	21	98	196	76	35	15	18	3·01
53	25	94	144	72	93	12	19	3·27
54	14	102	217	80	32	12	2	3·03
55	4	34	163	141	97	14	6	3·67
56	11	59	171	125	71	15	7	3·43
57	11	67	168	128	60	14	11	3·37
58	0	15	85	105	232	14	8	4·27
59	8	47	156	114	107	16	11	3·61
60	7	39	168	132	96	15	2	3·61
61	79	161	113	26	13	15	52	2·32
62	25	118	177	84	29	13	13	2·94
63	29	131	177	65	37	11	9	2·89
64	9	37	151	156	88	12	6	3·63
65	8	48	147	132	107	14	3	3·64
66	7	22	142	140	133	13	2	3·83
67	31	103	130	60	52	18	65	3·00
68	92	165	62	18	5	15	102	2·06
69	33	108	166	81	34	14	23	2·94
70	34	149	169	62	17	13	15	2·72
71	15	68	183	103	68	12	10	3·32
72	27	145	210	37	23	11	6	2·74

Appendices

Aims and approaches of
primary head teachers

Appendix N
Follow-up questionnaire for
primary head teachers

Aims of Primary Education Project

SECTION 1

Please show your answers to these two questions on *Sheet 1* [included on p. 237].

1. What curriculum areas do you work with in your school?
2. What is the approximate time balance between them?

Please use the 'pie' diagram on Sheet 1 to show what areas you use and the approximate time balance between them.

SECTION 2

Please insert the answers to Questions 3, 4, 5, 6 on *Sheet 2* [included on p. 238]. Please note carefully the instructions on that sheet before completing it.

3. Each curriculum area can be taken as a separate entity and treated as a subject on its own or it can be integrated with other areas. Different approaches are probably appropriate to different parts of the curriculum. What degree of separateness or integration do you advocate for each curriculum area?
For *each* area please select *one* of the following alternatives and insert the appropriate letter in each column.

A   Treated entirely as a separate subject; few or no references made to it at any other time.

B   Treated as a separate subject but used frequently in the course of other work.

C   Treated about equally as much as a separate subject and as a part of other work.

D   Treated as a separate subject to a minor extent, most work being done in other areas.

E   Not treated as a separate subject at all.

4. What degree of flexibility in the use of time do you advocate for each curriculum area?

For *each* area please select *one* of the following alternatives and insert the appropriate letter in each column.

A   A regular amount of time which should be adhered to fairly consistently.

B   A minimum regular amount of time which can be freely increased.

C   Considerable flexibility so long as a long-term proportion of time is maintained.

D   Complete flexibility with neither upper nor lower time limits.

In relation to the last two questions you probably advocate a variety of approaches depending upon circumstances. However, bearing this in mind, would you please, in both cases, select for each curriculum area the *one* alternative which you would *most often* consider suitable.

---

5. What kind of grouping(s) do you advocate as most suitable for work in each curriculum area?

For *each* area please select *one* of the following alternatives and insert the appropriate letter in each column.

A   Groups larger than a class.
B   The whole class.
C   Groups.
D   Individuals.
E   Both the whole class and groups.
F   Both the whole class and individuals.
G   Both groups and individuals.
H   The whole class, groups and individuals.

6. What do you advocate as being the task most generally appropriate for the teacher in each curriculum area?

For *each* area please select *one* of the following alternatives and insert the appropriate letter in each column.

A   The teacher's task is to have full knowledge of what he wants his children to know, to be capable, by analysis and experience, of presenting it to them interestingly in as well-programmed a manner as possible, and to set the pace of learning.

B   The teacher's task is to present work as stimulatingly as possible so that each child, sometimes following his own direction and sometimes the teacher's, can learn as much as he is capable of.

c   The teacher's task is to create a psychological environment in which inquiry can arise and a physical environment rich and stimulating enough to enable it to be pursued successfully at the child's own pace.

If there are any comments you would like to make, please do so on the following page [a page then left for comments].

Sheet 1   Curriculum diagram

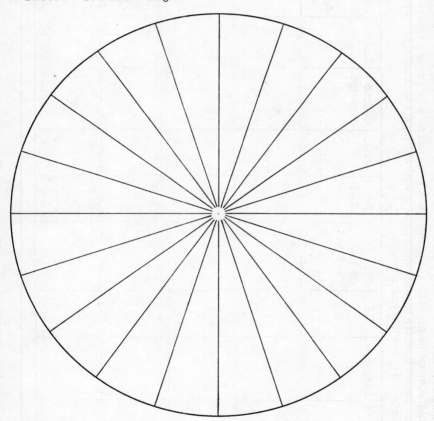

Age range ....

Sheet 2 Curriculum areas
These are the most common names of the curriculum areas. If you use different names please relate your answers to the nearest equivalent in each case. If there is a heading which refers to work which you do not cover, e.g. second language, please put a line through the column and ignore it in your answers.

	Maths	Language	RE	PE, games, movement	Art/craft	Music	Second language	Science	History, geography, nature study, etc.	
									As separate subjects	As environmental studies, etc.
Question 3										
Question 4										
Question 5										
Question 6										

Age range ....

Final set of aims from the teacher discussion groups

Aims related to intellectual development

KNOWLEDGE

1. The child should have a wide vocabulary.

2. The child should know the correct spelling of a basic general vocabulary.

3. The child should know the basic grammatical rules of written English

4. The child should have a general knowledge of his local environment in some of the following aspects: historical, geographical, natural, economic, social.

5. The child should have a wide general (not subject-based) knowledge of times and places beyond his immediate experience.

6. The child should have ordered subject knowledge in, for example, history, geography.

(column cont. on p. 240)

SKILLS

9. The child should know how to convey his meaning clearly and accurately through speech for a variety of purposes; for example, description, explanation, narration.

10. The child should be able to listen with concentration and understanding.

11. The child should be able to read fluently and accurately at a minimum reading age of eleven.

12. The child should be able to read with understanding material appropriate to his age group and interests.

13. The child should know how to write clear and meaningful English appropriate to different formal purposes; for example, factual reports, letters, descriptive accounts.

14. The child should know how to write interestingly and with sensitivity.

15. The child should know how to observe carefully, accurately and with sensitivity

(column cont. on p. 240)

QUALITIES

22. The child should be developing the ability to make reasoned judgements and choices, based on the interpretation and evaluation of relevant information.

23. The child should be developing a critical and discriminating attitude towards his experiences; for example, of the mass media.

Aims related to intellectual development—cont.

KNOWLEDGE

7. The child should know some simple scientific experimental procedures and some basic scientific concepts; for example, properties of materials, the nature and significance of changes in living things.

8. The child should have some understanding of modern technological developments; for example, space travel, telecommunications, automation.

SKILLS

16. The child should be developing the skills of acquiring knowledge and information from written material; for example, summarizing, taking notes accurately, the use of libraries.

17. The child should know how to acquire information other than by reading; for example, by asking questions, by experimenting, from watching television.

18. The child should know how to compute in the four arithmetic rules using his knowledge of, for instance, number, multiplication tables and different units of measurement.

19. The child should know how to think and solve problems mathematically using the appropriate basic concepts of, for example, the number system and place value, shape, spatial relationships, sets, symmetry and the appropriate language.

20. The child should know how to use mathematical techniques in his everyday life; for instance, estimating distances, classifying objects, using money.

21. The child should be able to conduct a simple conversation in a foreign language.

Aims related to physical development

KNOWLEDGE

24. The child should have an understanding of how his body works.

25. The child should know the basic facts of sex and reproduction.

SKILLS

26. The child should have a range of movement and gymnastic skills.

27. The child should know how to play a variety of games; for example, football, skittle-ball, rounders.

28. The child should be able to swim.

29. The child should know how to apply the basic principles of health, hygiene and safety.

QUALITIES

30. The child should have precise and economic body control for all ordinary physical activities including the handling of tools and equipment.

Aims related to aesthetic development

SKILLS

31. The child should know the appropriate techniques of some arts and crafts; for example, how to use paint, clay.

32. The child should have sufficient knowledge and skill to be able to engage in simple music-making; for example, singing, percussion, home-made instruments.

33. The child should be able to play a musical instrument such as a recorder, violin, guitar.

34. The child should be able to write legibly and know how to present his work attractively.

QUALITIES

35. The child should be developing a personal appreciation of beauty in some of its forms, both natural and artistic.

36. The child should be able to communicate his feelings through some art forms; for example, painting, music, drama, movement.

37. The child should be able to listen to and enjoy a range of music; for example, pop, folk, classical.

38. The child should be beginning to understand aesthetic experiences and should be able to talk about them; for example, looking at pictures and sculpture, listening to poetry and plays.

Aims related to spiritual/religious development

KNOWLEDGE

39. The child should have some knowledge of the Bible and Christian beliefs.

40. The child should have some knowledge of the beliefs of the major world religions other than Christianity.

QUALITIES

41. The child should try to behave in accordance with the ideals of the Christian religion.

42. The child should try to behave in accordance with the ideals of his own religion whether or not this is Christian.

43. The child should be developing an awareness of the spiritual aspects of prayer and worship.

Aims related to emotional/personal development

KNOWLEDGE

44. The child should be beginning to understand his own emotions

45. The child should be beginning to realize that he can play an important part in his own development by, for example, recognizing his strengths and limitations and setting his goals accordingly

SKILLS

46. The child should be developing the ability to control his behaviour and emotions.

47. The child should be developing the ability to plan independent work and organize his own time.

QUALITIES

48. The child should be an individual, developing in his own way.

49. The child should be developing the capacity to form a considered opinion and to act upon it even if this means rejecting conventional thought and behaviour.

50. The child should be self-confident; he should have a sense of personal adequacy and be able to cope with his environment at an appropriate level.

51. The child should be happy, cheerful and well balanced.

52. The child should be enthusiastic and eager to put his best into all activities.

53. The child should find enjoyment in a variety of aspects of school work and gain satisfaction from his own achievements.

54. The child should be developing his inventiveness and creativity in some fields; for example, painting, music, mechanical things, poetry, movement.

55. The child should be adaptable to changing circumstances and flexible in outlook.

56. The child should have a questioning attitude towards his environment.

57. The child should find enjoyment in some purposeful leisure time interests and activities both on his own and with others.

Aims related to social/moral development

KNOWLEDGE

58. The child should know those moral values, relating to people and property, which are shared by the majority of members of the society.

SKILLS

59. The child should know how to behave appropriately in a variety of situations; for example, talking to visitors, going on outings, answering the telephone.

60. The child should know how to behave with courtesy and good manners both in and out of school.

(column cont. on p. 244)

QUALITIES

65. The child should be kind and considerate; he should, for example, be willing to give personal help to younger or new children, to consider the elderly, the disabled.

66. The child should be developing tolerance: respecting and appreciating others, their feelings, views and capabilities.

(column cont. on p. 244)

Aims related to social/moral development—cont.

SKILLS

61. The child should be a good mixer; he should be able to make easy social contacts with other children and adults in work and play situations.

62. The child should know how to speak in a clear and fluent manner appropriate to different situations; for example, informal occasions with children and adults, formal occasions.

63. The child should know how to engage in discussion; for example, he should be able to talk about his own and others' opinions in a reasonable way.

64. The child should know what to do in emergencies; for example, fire, sickness, accident.

QUALITIES

67. The child should be beginning to feel community responsibility; for example, he should be loyal to groups such as class and school of which he is a member and, where possible, the wider community, and willing to accept the responsibilities which membership implies.

68. The child should be able to maintain lasting relationships with a few close friends.

69. The child should be careful with and respectful of both his own and other people's property.

70. The child should be beginning to acquire a set of moral values on which to base his own behaviour; for example, honesty, sincerity, personal responsibility.

71. The child should be industrious, persistent and conscientious.

72. The child should be generally obedient to parents, teachers and all reasonable authority.

Teachers and lecturers participating in the project

Miss M. I. Abbott, Deputy Head, Catchgate Infant School, County Durham

B. W. Abell, Head of Mathematics Department, Billesley Junior School, Birmingham

J. E. Addy, Assistant Master, Honiton County Primary School, Devon

G. Allen, Meadow Green Primary School, Wythall

A. T. Alvis, Head Teacher, Hopton Wafers CE Primary School, Kidderminster

K. Arnold, Headmaster, Ley Hill Junior and Infant School, Birmingham

Mrs Y. T. Aspinall, Ham Dingle Primary School, Stourbridge

*R. J. Bailey, Head Teacher, Dorchester County Primary School, Dorset

A. G. Baker, Head Teacher, Broadhempston County Primary School, Devon

*O. Barrass, Head Teacher, South Moor Greenland Junior School, County Durham

M. A. Bastian, Assistant Master, Sherwell Valley Junior School, Devon

B. G. Bayliss, Deputy Head, Axminster County Primary School, Devon

Miss J. Bayliss, Head Teacher, Countess Weir Infant School, Exeter

*H. O. Beaven, Head Teacher, Newton Poppleford County Primary School, Devon

G. Beckham, Head Teacher, Burnopfield County Junior and Infant School, Newcastle upon Tyne

Mrs D. M. Bell, Langley Moor County Primary School, Durham

J. Bell, Head Teacher, Sedgefield Secondary School, Teesside

Miss A. Bennett, St John's RC Junior and Infant School, Birmingham

Miss M. E. Bennett, Head Teacher, Chapel House County Infant School, Newcastle upon Tyne

Mrs J. Blanch, Bellfield Junior School, Birmingham

A. J. Blatchford, Head Teacher, Clawton County Primary School, Devon

Mrs E. Bowen, Crown Meadow Infant School, Alvechurch

W. T. Boyd, Assistant Master, South Moor Greenland Junior School, County Durham

Mrs M. Brabban, Assistant Mistress, Catchgate County Infant School, County Durham

* Group leader.

Miss M. R. Bradley, Durham St Joseph's RC Junior and Infant School, Durham

A. Brennan, Head Teacher, St George's CE Junior and Infant School, Devon

J. W. Brimer, Head Teacher, South Wellfield Junior School, Northumberland

L. Brown, Head Teacher, Holy Trinity CE Junior School, Teesside

Mrs A. Bull, Assistant Mistress, St Leonard's Junior School, Shropshire

P. Byrne, Remedial Teacher, Bovington County Primary School, Devon

D. C. Buckingham, Broadclyst County Primary School, Exeter

H. Burton, Head Teacher, Pallister Park Junior School, Teesside

D. G. Button, Assistant Master, Honiton County Primary School, Devon

Miss V. Callister, Head Teacher, Turves Green Infant School, Birmingham

*V. Carr, Head Teacher, Montgomery Junior and Infant School, Exeter

T. Carr, Head Teacher, Crofton Junior School, Northumberland

Miss J. Carter, Head Teacher, Uplowman V Primary School, Devon

E. F. Champion, Head Teacher, Elmore County Junior School, Devon

Mrs E. E. Charlton, Deputy Head, East Stanley County Junior and Infant School, County Durham

Miss R. Cheeseman, Meadow Green Primary School, Wythall

Miss V. Chennels, West Stanley Junior School, County Durham

*S. Childs, Senior Lecturer, Dudley College of Education, Worcestershire

D. J. Clay, Deputy Head, Henwick Grove Junior School, Worcester

Miss J. A. Clough, Gilesgate Junior School, Durham

Mrs J. E. Cobbold, Headless Cross CE JMI School, Redditch

Rev. A. A. Collins, Head Teacher, Church of the Ascension CE Junior School, Staffordshire

E. A. Copeman, Head Teacher, Warndon Junior School, Worcester

Miss M. Cox, Coventry College of Education, Coventry

C. C. Coxon, Senior Remedial Teacher, Oldway Remedial Centre, Devon

G. J. Creed, Broadmayne County Primary School, Dorset

Miss P. D. Crewe, St Peter's CE Primary School, Worcestershire

F. Cross, Shenstone New College, Bromsgrove

D. Cull, Dorchester Junior School, Dorset

G. Culverhouse, Head Teacher, Foxhole Junior School, Devon

*J. H. Dalton, Head Teacher, Honiton County Primary School, Devon

Miss A. E. Dart, Assistant Mistress, Catchgate County Infant School, County Durham

*Miss D. G. Davies, Senior Lecturer, Shenstone New College, Bromsgrove

*D. W. Davies, Deputy Head, St Paul's V Primary School, Hereford

*J. W. Davies, Head Teacher, Bovington County Primary School, Dorset

Mrs M. Davies, Crown Meadow Infant School, Alvechurch

Mrs S. M. Davies, Head Teacher, Alvechurch Crown Meadow County Primary School, Worcestershire

H. E. Day, Assistant Master, Sherwell Valley Primary School, Devon

P. S. Day, Head Teacher, Burlescombe CE Primary School, Devon

Mrs I. Dennison, Cestria County Junior School, Durham

Miss J. Downing, Head Teacher, Thornaby Village Infant School, Middlesbrough

D. L. Downton, Head Teacher, Hazelbury Bryan County Primary School, Dorset

K. W. Drayton, Head Teacher, Bradley Rowe Junior School, Exeter

S. J. Drew, Woodfield Primary School, Devon

F. Duerden, Head Teacher, Eden Park Junior School, Devon

R. F. Edwards, Deputy Head, Percy Shurmer Junior School, Birmingham

*Mrs N. Elliott, Head Teacher, South Moor Greenland Junior School, County Durham

*D. Evans, Head Teacher, Sherwell Valley Junior School, Devon

M. T. Ferris, Deputy Head Teacher, Dorchester County Primary School, Dorset

Mrs M. Ferry, Chester le Street CE Junior School, County Durham

D. P. Fielding, Head Teacher, Bromford Junior School, Birmingham

Mrs B. E. Finney, Ham Dingle Primary School, Stourbridge

Miss J. E. Fletcher, Head Teacher, Rounds Green Infant School, Worcestershire

A. J. C. Forde, Neville's Cross College, Durham

Mrs M. Forde, Esh Winning County Junior and Infant School, Durham

Mrs J. V. Forsey, Deputy Head, Puddletown RC County Primary School, Dorset

Mrs M. Fryer, Durham St Joseph's RC Junior and Infant School, Durham

*M. Garland, Head of Mathematics Department, Heathcoat County Junior School, Devon

A. G. Garner, Head Teacher, Silverton CE Primary School, Exeter

Mrs J. Gaunt, Shenstone New College, Bromsgrove

S. W. Gibson, Head Teacher, Ide County Primary School, Exeter

D. Gilliland, Head Teacher, Esh Winning County Junior and Infant School, Durham

Miss M. A. Golding, Assistant Mistress, Bovey Tracey County Primary School, Devon

E. J. Goodenough, Deputy Head Teacher, Henderson Avenue Primary School, Lincolnshire

T. Goss, Head of Mathematics Department, Sherwell Valley Junior School, Devon

A. R. Gowland, Head Teacher, Bramford County Primary School, Dudley

K. Graham, Head Teacher, Guide Post County Junior School, Northumberland

R. Graham, Head Teacher, Summervey Junior and Infant School, Exeter

*D. A. Grant, Head Teacher, Newham Bridge Primary School, Middlesbrough

Mrs G. M. Gray, Head Teacher, Ashington Wansbeck Primary School, Northumberland

Mrs B. Greaves, Deputy Head, Short Street Infant School, Staffordshire

D. Green, Shenstone New College, Bromsgrove

H. W. J. Green, Head Teacher, Bellfield Junior School, Birmingham

Mrs I. Greenacre, Deputy Head, Alvechurch CE Junior School, Worcestershire

Mrs I. Greenacre, Headless Cross CE JMI School, Redditch

L. V. Griffiths, Head Teacher, Trescott Junior School, Birmingham

Mrs P. Guest, Meadow Green Primary School, Wythall

A. C. Gurkin, Assistant Master, South Moor Greenland Junior School, Durham

Mrs J. Gurkin, Assistant Mistress, South Moor Greenland Infant School, Durham

*N. Haile, Head Teacher, Bishop Middleham CE Primary School, County Durham

*Mrs E. M. Haggitt, Bordesley College of Education, Birmingham

I. Hallatt, Head Teacher, Feniton CE Primary School, Devon

R. Haly, Ellacombe Primary School, Devon

Miss E. Handy, Deputy Head, South Moor Greenland Junior School, County Durham

E. A. Harle, King Street Infant School, County Durham

A. L. Harris, Middleton St George College of Education, Durham

R. Harris, Deputy Head, Broadmeadow Junior School, Birmingham

Miss J. Harrison, West Stanley Junior School, County Durham

R. Harrison, Head Teacher, Bolam Street Junior School, Newcastle upon Tyne

Miss S. L. Harrison, Deputy Head, Cromwell Road Infant School, Middlesbrough

W. N. Hedley, Head Teacher, North Road Junior School, County Durham

Miss M. E. Hayes, Assistant Mistress, Honiton County Primary School, Devon

Mrs M. D. Herniman, Head of Infant Department, Wilcombe County Primary School, Devon

*D. S. Herron, Head Teacher, Park Junior School, Northumberland

*J. R. Heslop, Head Teacher, St Matthew's CE Primary School, Worcestershire

W. Hetherington, Chief County Inspector of Schools, Durham

C. E. Hickman, Head Teacher, Clyst Hydon County Primary School, Devon

A. R. Hill, Chawson CP School, Droitwich

Miss M. Hill, Coventry College of Education, Coventry

S. Hill, Senior Adviser for Education, Warley, Worcestershire

Mrs R. Hind, Assistant Mistress, Tanfield Lee County Junior and Infant School, Newcastle upon Tyne

*C. R. Hodkinson, Head Teacher, Parkfield Primary School, Wolverhampton

Mrs M. E. Hodgson, Head Teacher, Trimdon Village County Infant School, County Durham

Miss E. Hogg, Head Teacher, Choppington Infant School, Northumberland

Mrs A. Hollingworth, Deputy Head, Gig Mill County Primary School, Worcestershire

W. I. Holmes, Head Teacher, Bishopsteighton County Primary School, Devon

L. G. Horne, Head Teacher, Highweek County Primary School, Devon

J. F. Horton, Joseph Clarke Primary School, Staffordshire

Mrs L. M. Horner, Remedial Teacher, Child Guidance Centre, West Bromwich

Miss B. M. A. Hull, Pitmaston Primary School, Worcester

R. Hunt, Dorchester County Primary School, Dorset

F. L. Hunt, St Thomas Junior and Infant School, Exeter

R. Hunter, Head Teacher, Bailey Green County Primary School, Newcastle upon Tyne

*P. G. Hytch, Principal Lecturer and Head of Primary Education, Worcester College of Education, Worcester

Miss M. A. Inglefield, Head Teacher, Awliscombe V Primary School, Devon

Miss K. V. F. Insleay, Chawson CP School, Droitwich

E. Jackson, Headless Cross CE JMI School, Redditch

Mrs J. Jackson, Head Teacher, West Harton CE Infant School, County Durham

Mrs L. A. Jackson, Assistant Mistress, Leighswood Infant School, Staffordshire

Miss M. E. Jackson, Head Teacher, Chapel House County Primary School, Newcastle upon Tyne

Mrs A. Jaques, Inkberrow CP School, Worcestershire

Mrs M. Jessop, Tipton CE Primary School, Devon

Mrs N. Jessop, Head Teacher, The Avenue Infant School, Teesside

T. J. Johnston, Annfield Plain County Junior School, County Durham

W. W. Jolly, Dorrington County Primary School, Birmingham

W. H. L. Jopling, Sedgefield Primary School, Teesside

Miss E. Kay, Head Teacher, Catchgate County Infant School, County Durham

Miss N. Kelsey, Head Teacher, Garthorpe CE Primary School, County Durham

T. H. Kerslake, Deputy Head, St Andrew's County Primary School, Devon

J. H. Knowles, Head Teacher, Tamerton Vale Primary School, Devon

S. Knowles, Head Teacher, Heavitree Junior and Infant School, Exeter

C. S. Lamb, Deputy Head, Blakenhale Junior School, Birmingham

Mrs J. B. Lambert, Head Teacher, Simonside County Infant School, Northumberland

E. G. Lane, Head Teacher, Stoodleigh County Primary School, Devon

G. Lane, Head Teacher, Hatchford Brook County Junior School, Warwickshire

R. G. Leach, Remedial Teacher, Child Guidance Centre, West Bromwich

*M. Lear, Head Teacher, County Primary School, Highampton, Devon

Mrs M. Lee, Deputy Head, Warndon Junior School, Worcester

M. E. Lee, Head Teacher, Atherstone South County Junior School, Warwickshire

A. Lever, Head Teacher, Walmley County Junior School, Warwickshire

G. E. Lewis, Hodge Hill Primary School, Birmingham

Miss M. Lewis, Head Teacher, Halwill County Primary School, Devon

Miss V. M. Little, Coventry College of Education, Coventry

A. T. Lloyd, Colley Lane CP School, Halesowen

*G. K. Lloyd-Williams, Overseal Manor School, Staffordshire

Miss J. E. Lock, Head Teacher, Sidmouth County Infant School, Devon

W. A. Longstaff, North Road Junior and Infant School, Durham

*W. R. Luke, Northumberland College of Education, Newcastle upon Tyne

Mrs M. Lynn, Marton Grove Junior School, Middlesbrough

Mrs M. McKennan, Plaistow Hill Infant School, Devon

Mrs J. McSkinning, Head Teacher, County Infant School, Devon

R. J. Maddocks, Deputy Head, Pitmaston Primary School, Worcester

Mrs B. March, Head Teacher, Brandon County Infant School, County Durham

*C. A. A. Marsh, Senior Lecturer in Primary Education, Dudley College of Education, Worcestershire

Miss J. Marsh, Bellfield Junior School, Birmingham

R. Marshall, Deputy Head, Kader Junior School, Middlesbrough

G. S. Marshment, Assistant Master, St Modwen's RC Junior and Infant School, Staffordshire

B. Martin, New Brancepeth Junior and Infant School, Durham

J. R. Mather, Head Teacher, Red Row Junior School, Northumberland

*J. M. Milburn, Head Teacher, County Junior and Infant School, County Durham

G. B. Miller, Head Teacher, St Oswald's RC Primary School, Newcastle upon Tyne

Miss J. Moss, Deputy Head, Abbey Park County Primary School, Pershore

Mrs M. Muir, Coventry College of Education, Coventry

K. Munro, Shenstone New College, Bromsgrove

Mrs M. Murray, South Moor Greenland Infant School, County Durham

Mrs H. M. Mylward, Broadmayne County Primary School, Dorset
Miss D. Nash, Fordington Infant School, Dorchester
*R. Naylor, Head Teacher, The Secondary School, Pelton, County Durham
R. P. Neal, Head Teacher, Henderson Avenue Primary School, Lincolnshire
Mrs G. Neville Jones, Head Teacher, North Prospect Infant School, Devon
J. Norrish, Head Teacher, Payhembury Primary School, Devon
Miss J. North, Assistant Mistress, Sherwell Valley Junior School, Devon
*F. Nutbrown, St Augustine Webster Primary School, Lincolnshire
Mrs S. M. Nutbrown, Parkwood Junior School, Lincolnshire
Mrs A. E. Nutman, Head Teacher, Gosforth East County Infant School, Northumberland
L. E. J. Oke, Head Teacher, Ottery St Mary Junior School, Devon
G. W. Oliver, Northumberland College of Education, Northumberland
*R. Pallister, Senior Lecturer in Education, Neville's Cross College, Durham
Miss P. F. Palmer, Langley Moor County Junior and Infant School, County Durham
J. Parfitt, Shenstone New College, Bromsgrove
Mrs S. Partridge, Head Teacher, Inkberrow County Primary School, Worcestershire
Mrs S. Partridge, Meadow Green Primary School, Wythall
Miss M. F. Paske, Clawton County Primary School, Devon
D. O. Pattison, Head Teacher, John Emmerson Batty County Primary School, Teesside
J. Pearce, Head Teacher, Stockland V Primary School, Devon
Miss P. Pearson, Assistant Mistress, Catchgate County Infant School, County Durham
P. H. Perks, Head Teacher, Rowington Primary School, Warwick
J. Perris, Head Teacher, Lynemouth County Primary School, Northumberland
J. Phillips, Worcester College of Education, Worcester
W. F. Pickup, Neville's Cross College, Durham
Mrs M. A. Pole, Head Teacher, Delves Infant School, Walsall
T. C. Powell, Head Teacher, Gig Mill County Junior School, Dudley
Mrs P. Pratt, King Street Infant School, County Durham
Mrs E. Price, Assistant Mistress, South Moor Greenland Junior School, County Durham
Mrs G. J. Priddle, Head of Department, Dorchester County Primary School, Dorset
L. Pringle, Head Teacher, Bloemfontein County Junior School, County Durham
D. H. Pryke, Deputy Head, St Leonard's Junior School, Shropshire
*R. Pullen, Middleton St George College of Education, Darlington
*A. R. Puttock, Senior Lecturer in Education, Worcester College of Education, Worcester

Miss D. M. Rawnsley, Remedial Teacher, St Matthew's CE Primary School, Birmingham

T. P. Reid, Deputy Head, St Joseph's Primary School, Durham

D. Rees, Worcester College of Education, Worcester

C. M. Richards, Deputy Head, Bishop Wilson CE Primary School, Warwickshire

Miss K. Richardson, Cassop Junior and Infant School, County Durham

D. Rigby, Head Teacher, Roxby CE Primary School, Lincolnshire

W. F. Risler, Head Teacher, Sedgefield Primary School, Teesside

Mrs M. M. Robertson, Deputy Head, Ouston Infant School, County Durham

Miss N. E. Rogers, Deputy Head, Moat Farm Infant School, Worcestershire

Mrs E. Ross, Tiverton County Primary School, Birmingham

Mrs M. M. Rosser, Head Teacher, Henry Parkes Infant School, Coventry

J. R. Ruddick, Head Teacher, Kelloe Junior and Infant School, Durham

Mrs E. Rush, Cornforth Lane Junior and Infant School, County Durham

Miss N. Sambells, Head Teacher, West Fordington V County Infant School, Dorset

Mrs A. E. Sanderson, Head Teacher, Sandyford Road Infant School, County Durham

P. Sanderson, Head Teacher, Mitford CE Primary School, Northumberland

W. H. Saunders, Deputy Head, Wilcombe County Primary School, Devon

Miss K. M. Saville, Assistant Mistress, Sherwell Valley Junior School, Devon

D. Sedgwick, Newcastle upon Tyne College, Newcastle upon Tyne

C. Seth, Shenstone New College, Bromsgrove

Miss L. I. Severs, Head Teacher, Hillsview Infant School, Northumberland

G. A. Scott, Deputy Head, Esh Winning Junior and Infant School, County Durham

G. C. Sharratt, Head Teacher, Kempsey County Primary School, Worcestershire

*Miss J. A. Sharratt, Senior Lecturer, Shenstone New College, Bromsgrove

J. E. C. Shepherd, Deputy Head, Coleshill Heath Junior School, Birmingham

A. W. M. Sherriff, Head Teacher, Christ Church CE Primary School, Newcastle upon Tyne

Miss B. Sherwood, St Osmund's CE Junior School, Dorset

J. Simpson, Head Teacher, Abbeyfields County Junior School, Northumberland

K. Skellern, Dorchester County Primary School, Dorset

Miss A. Smith, New Brancepeth Primary School, Durham

A. Smith, Deputy Head, Bovington County Primary School, Dorset

D. Smith, Colley Lane CP School, Halesowen

D. C. Smith, Assistant Master, Caslon County Primary School, Worcestershire

G. Smith, Head Teacher, Ilsington CE Primary School, Devon

R. E. Smith, Teacher in Charge, Coxlodge Teachers' Centre, Newcastle upon Tyne

J. Sowerby, Head Teacher, Brandon County Junior School, Durham

Mrs J. Sparey, Head Teacher, North Prospect Infant School, Devon

Mrs M. Speakman, Hodge Hill Junior School, Birmingham

Mrs D. Starmer, Chawson CP School, Droitwich

W. Staveley, Wolviston Primary School, Durham

Mrs D. Steele, Head of Department, Tanfield Lea Junior and Infant School, Newcastle upon Tyne

Miss A. J. Stephens, Headless Cross CE JMI School, Redditch

*J. A. Sullivan, Head Teacher, Hennock County Primary School, Devon

R. E. Taggesell, Head Teacher, Tudhoe Colliery Junior and Infant School, County Durham

Miss C. M. Taylor, Durham St Joseph's RC Junior and Infant School, Durham

D. Taylor, Deputy Head, St Matthew's CE Junior and Infant School, Worcestershire

Miss J. Taylor, Deputy Head, Dorchester Junior School, Dorset

Miss V. Taylor, Head Teacher, Sacriston County Infant School, County Durham

Mrs E. Thirlaway, Chester le Street County Infant School, County Durham

Miss S. Thistle, Shenstone New College, Bromsgrove

Mrs J. M. Thomas, Westcliffe Infant School, Lincolnshire

Mrs D. Thompson, Crown Meadow Infant School, Alvechurch

L. R. Tillson, Head Teacher, Hodge Hill Junior and Infant School, Birmingham

Miss D. Tingle, Head Teacher, Dipton Collierley Junior and Infant School, Newcastle upon Tyne

T. C. Tobin, Head Teacher, Durham St Joseph's RC School, Durham

Mrs G. J. Towns, Langley Moor RC Junior and Infant School, County Durham

Mrs Y. Trotter, St Nicholas Junior and Infant School, Exeter

Mrs E. Uren, Deputy Head, South Moor Greenland Infant School, County Durham

H. J. Van Zutphen, Sherwell Valley County Junior School, Devon

Miss J. Vernon, Head Teacher, Hill View Nursery School, Worcestershire

D. J. W. Vickery, Head Teacher, Sampford Peverell CE School, Devon

*N. P. N. Wake, Head Teacher, Broadmayne Primary School, Dorchester

Mrs E. M. Walker, Wollescote County Primary School, Worcestershire

Mrs S. A. Wallbank, Head of Remedial Department, Wren's Nest Junior School, Worcestershire

*Miss D. M. Walton, Head Teacher, Percy Shurmer Infant School, Birmingham

P. Ward, Shenstone New College, Bromsgrove

G. O. J. Warner, Deputy Head, Ashmore Park Primary School, Wolverhampton

P. J. Warner, Bovington County Primary School, Dorset

E. D. Watson, Assistant Master, St Philip's RC Primary School, Worcestershire

Mrs F. Watson, Head Teacher, Guide Post County Primary School, Northumberland

*J. West, Senior Inspector of Schools, Dudley Education Offices, Worcestershire

Mrs M. F. West, Inspector of Schools, Wolverhampton Education Offices, Wolverhampton

H. R. Weston, Head Teacher, Dawley Brook County Primary School, Worcestershire

Mrs I. M. Whale-Lomas, Head Teacher, Mount Nod Infant School, Coventry

J. Wharrier, Head Teacher, Morpeth Road Junior School, Northumberland

P. H. Whetter, Head Teacher, St Thomas Primary School, Exeter

Miss B. White, Worcester College of Education, Worcester

P. C. White, Head Teacher, Ashwater County Primary School, Devon

Miss I. P. Whitelaw, Head Teacher, Hirst South County Primary School, Northumberland

M. J. Whitewood, Deputy Head, Hillwest Junior School, Warwickshire

*P. D. Wicksteed, Senior Lecturer in Education, Worcester College of Education, Worcester

T. J. Wightman, Head Teacher, St Marychurch CE Primary School, Devon

A. J. Wilkins, Head Teacher, Chardstock St Andrew's V Primary School, Devon

Miss R. Wilkinson, Deputy Head, New Brancepeth Junior and Infant School, County Durham

D. B. Willetts, Head Teacher, Ham Dingle Primary School, Stourbridge

W. L. L. Williams, Bellfield Junior School, Birmingham

G. J. Wiseman, Deputy Head, Honiton County Primary School, Devon

Mrs J. Wood, Head Teacher, Broadstone First School, Dorset

*Mrs M. Wood, Inspector of Schools, Newcastle upon Tyne

J. M. Wrench, Deputy Head, Holsworthy V Primary School, Devon

Mrs V. Wyatt, Deputy Head, Bovey Tracey County Primary School, Devon

Mrs A. Yelland, Shenstone New College, Bromsgrove

Miss J. Yule, North Ormsby Infant School, Middlesbrough

The project team and consultative committee

PROJECT TEAM

Dr P. M. E. Ashton   *Director*
Mrs Frances Davies   *Research Associate*
Mrs Pat Kneen   *Research Associate*
Miss Ann Atherton   *Secretary*
Mrs Rosalind Cooke   *Secretary*

CONSULTATIVE COMMITTEE

Miss M. E. Aspinall, Headmistress, St Hilde's Demonstration School, Durham
Dr J. M. Carnie, Deputy Principal, Charlotte Mason College, Ambleside
D. Clay, Headmaster, Ashchurch Primary School, Tewkesbury
D. G. Gilbert, Headmaster, Underhill School, Wolverhampton
H. W. J. Green
Miss G. J. Harvey
Miss E. McDougall, HMI
Miss M. H. McGrath, Inspector of Schools, Birmingham
J. E. C. Shepherd
M. Stanton, Lecturer and Tutor to Diploma in Education Course, University of Birmingham School of Education
Professor P. H. Taylor, Head of Curriculum and Method Division, University of Birmingham School of Education